T0383840

# Starting Lean from Scratch

A Senior Leader's Guide to Beginning
and Steering an Organizational Culture
Change for Continuous Improvement

# Starting Lean from Scratch

## A Senior Leader's Guide to Beginning and Steering an Organizational Culture Change for Continuous Improvement

By
Brent D. Timmerman

Routledge
Taylor & Francis Group

A PRODUCTIVITY PRESS BOOK

First edition published in 2019

by Routledge/Productivity Press
711 Third Avenue New York, NY 10017, USA
2 Park Square, Milton Park, Abingdon, Oxon OX14 4RN, UK

© 2019 by Brent D. Timmerman
Routledge/Productivity Press is an imprint of Taylor & Francis Group, an Informa business

No claim to original U.S. Government works

Printed on acid-free paper

International Standard Book Number-13: 978-0-367-18569-5 (Hardback)

| Library of Congress Cataloging-in-Publication Data |
| --- |
| Names: Timmerman, Brent D., author. |
| Title: Starting lean from scratch : a senior leader's guide to beginning and steering an organizational culture change for continuous improvement / Brent D. Timmerman. |
| Description: New York, NY : Routledge, 2019. |
| Identifiers: LCCN 2018060426 (print) \| LCCN 2019001776 (ebook) \| ISBN 9780429196867 (e-Book) \| ISBN 9780367185695 (hardback : alk. paper) |
| Subjects: LCSH: Organizational change--Management. \| Organizational effectiveness--Management. \| Leadership. \| Corporate culture. |
| Classification: LCC HD58.8 (ebook) \| LCC HD58.8 .T56 2019 (print) \| DDC 658.4/013--dc23 |
| LC record available at https://lccn.loc.gov/2018060426 |

Visit the Taylor & Francis Web site at
http://www.taylorandfrancis.com

*To the countless private-sector employees and public servants*

*who diligently show up to work every day wanting to do a*

*good job to serve the customer, client, or their fellow citizens,*

*despite being forced to use systems which sometimes seem*

*to be designed to make it difficult to get things done.*

*"Personal leadership is...the ongoing process of keeping your vision and values before you and aligning your life to be congruent with these most important things"*

Stephen Covey[1]

# Contents

# PART II    Understanding the Space of Trust

## PART V   Understanding the New Way

# Foreword

For anyone that is paying attention, we hear and read lots these days about Lean. It's all good, but many times it's conceptual, or about a particular situation. It's hard to imagine anyone not believing that streamlining and optimizing processes so peoples' jobs are easier and more engaging would be a bad thing.

Brent takes a grass-roots approach to Lean and writes through the eyes of a senior leader, a practitioner, and a believer. He's written this book with extensive experience learning about, researching, and implementing Lean from inside the game—from the Gemba. Or, using a sports analogy, from the playing surface, not as an observer or from the sidelines or press box. It's a 'guide book' and it comes from relevant experience in both for-profit and not-for-profit businesses.

I'm impressed with the depth of thought and the realistic examples and learnings. It's a perspective from the leaders who manage and make decisions about the Gemba. Not executives like me that talk about it from 60,000 feet above, or from the front-line workers that can be passive but crave someone to help them work with simplicity and efficiency. It's all about the leader.

Brent's engineering training and background combined with his logical and thoughtful approach provides an easy-to-relate-to context. Even more important is Brent's commitment to life-long learning and deployment of simplicity. Brent learned in a very fast-paced industrial environment that business doesn't stop and allow you time to fix things. The reality is that the answer lies in learning how to diagnose and fix the bike while you ride. Oh, and it can't be done by one person. It takes a team all the way through the organization to believe, buy in, and make an effort to pursue world-best in everything they do.

I think the approach of Trust Principles, Change Principles and Continuous Improvement Principles is a perfect framework for Lean leaders. I hope this book provides you with a practical reference manual to refer to time and time again. I'm honoured to have been part of Brent's Lean development while we worked and learned together at StandardAero.

In fact, after I read the book, I found myself taking Brent's approach and assessing my own business today to determine where we are on track, and where we can improve in our own Lean journey.

**Paul Soubry**
President & CEO
NFI Group Inc.

# Preface

## WHY I WROTE THIS BOOK

*"Leadership is a choice, not a position."*

**Stephen R. Covey**[1]
*author*

Would you believe me if I told you that your people are not the problem? If you are a senior leader, you likely have several constructs that you believe to be so true that you might have trouble imagining a world without them.

You may believe that your knowledge and experience are tremendously valuable to those that you lead. You may also believe that this knowledge and experience is what makes you the leader that you are. You may believe that you can't make substantial improvements in team performance with the people that you have. You may believe that some of your people will never buy into a concept like Lean management. I understand. I once thought as you do. But it's wrong—all of it. These types of beliefs can imprison your mind and prevent you from being able to unlock the potential residing within your team.

In 1883, George F. Pentecost published a religious essay entitled "The Angel in the Marble." In this essay, the author recounts a story from his childhood, where he is having a dialogue with a sculptor who has acquired a large block of marble and placed it in his studio. When the young George asks the sculptor what he plans to make with the marble, he answers that he is not going to make anything with it. Rather, he is going to find something within it. The sculptor says:

> *"There is a beautiful angel in that block of marble, and I am going to find it? All I have to do is to knock off the outside pieces of marble, and be very careful not to cut into the angel with my chisel."*[2]

This story reflects what I have discovered in working with my team to bring about a Lean management transformation within the organization. When the transformation really starts to take hold, you may find talents and abilities being unleashed within your team for the first time. You will then realize that these talents and abilities were there all along, residing within your people—but you just couldn't see those talents and abilities because you weren't looking for them. This hidden potential is the benefit of Lean management. Unlock this potential, and you unlock other tremendous benefits as well. You will develop a new culture within your organization that likely looks very different from what exists today.

The people will believe that they have the ability to challenge the status quo, and that management actually cares about their ideas and input. The people will bring forward ways to innovate that will amaze you. They will embrace metrics and measurement, and the organization will learn how to better manage parts of the business in doing so. But first, you, as the senior leader, may need to free your mind.

The 1999 movie The Matrix envisions a post-apocalyptic future where artificial intelligence and machines have taken over the world. Humans are imprisoned from birth and held in slavery to serve the machines. The machines keep the human prisoners pacified and unknowing, using an elaborate virtual reality simulation to hide the actual world. But some humans have been freed from the slave existence and are waging a war of rebellion against the machines. One character, Morpheus, works to free the lead protagonist, Neo, in the hopes that Neo can lead the rebellion to victory.

But first Morpheus must convince Neo to reject everything he thought to be true. Neo struggles to accept his new reality, that the world he thought he knew for his entire life, was completely artificial. After telling Neo that he has been living his entire life in a dream world, Morpheus tries to explain that he is trying to help Neo, but Neo has to make the personal choice to accept and believe the truth:

> "I'm trying to free your mind, Neo, but I can only show you the door. You're the one that has to walk through it."[3]

I wonder how often as senior leaders we look at the people on our teams simply as the tools needed to accomplish an end. We do insist on calling them "resources" after all. I found that I needed to free my own mind from the invisible prison I had constructed for myself, in order to be successful as a Lean champion for my organization. This mental prison affected how I viewed my own role as a leader, my source of leadership authority, and how I viewed the people on my team. Only once I was able to transform myself was I able to effectively help to lead the transformation of my team. It will likely be the same for you as well. Don't worry, it can be done.

Many organizations recognize that they have inefficiencies, that they could greatly improve how they operate. Often, leaders of these companies want to solve their organizational problems with solutions of structure, systems, and tools, instead of addressing the problems of human behaviour. But it is human behaviour that will dictate the success or failure of our solutions. We need to stop pretending that behaviour can be trumped by structure—it's a fallacy.

Understanding human behaviour during an organizational transformation, during a culture change, is absolutely crucial. If you want your people to change, then you must appreciate that the leadership plays a defining role in setting the stage for the culture change of an organization to be either successful or a failed attempt. It is my firm belief that it is a waste of time to unleash the tools of Lean upon an organization where management does not yet understand the appropriate framework of leadership behaviours that will be supportive to the cultural journey. It would be like scattering seeds upon concrete—the tools will not have a nourishing environment in which to demonstrate their usefulness. Although in most cases it would be completely inadvertent, the behaviours of the leadership that are contrary to the desired innovative culture will extinguish attempts to advance that cultural transformation. The things that the leaders would say and do, in keeping with how they behaved in the past, would pour cold water on the trust in the leadership that the staff need to develop before they can truly engage in innovation.

Most of the information that is written about Lean management seems to me to be written to help mature organizations improve even further. But I believe that very little literature exists to help guide people who are on day zero of their transformational journey—that is why I chose to write this book. There are many organizations where the existing culture is so out of alignment with the approaches of Lean that the introduction of the Lean toolkit, without first addressing the leadership behaviours, would be a complete failure. This book is for the senior leader who wants to start their organization down a path of culture change involving operations excellence, but today, the organizational culture is oblivious to the potential benefits. They may not know anything about what Lean management can do to positively transform a company and its people.

In my experience of starting the Lean journey at Manitoba Housing, I had to start something from nothing. I quickly found that this was very different from taking over as the Lean champion in an organization that has already had a Lean culture in place for some time. I need to be very clear that I am not writing this book in an attempt to advertise to its readers my lifelong perfection as a leader. Some things I got right the first time, but there are plenty of things that I came to realize I was doing wrong. I have written this book in an attempt to help others to avoid the mistakes that I now realize can be very common, and very detrimental to your success as a Lean leader. In order to be successful, I found that I had to change many aspects about myself as an individual, and as a leader, that had taken my whole life to develop. I don't consider myself to have any special magical powers—if I can change, anyone can. But I can only show you the door. You have to be the one to walk through it.

---

## UNDERSTANDING YOURSELF

*"The things that have been most valuable to me I did not learn in school."*

**Will Smith**
*actor*

For some reason, I had believed since I was a young child that my purpose in life was to be an engineer. I wanted to be someone who designed things, someone who solved technical problems using applied science. I thought that one day, I would design airplanes.

After high school, I completed my Bachelor of Science degree in Mechanical Engineering from the University of Manitoba, and immediately followed it up with a Master of Science degree, specializing in heat transfer and fluid dynamics. Before I completed my master's thesis, I was hired as a facilities engineer at a major aerospace company in Winnipeg that overhauls gas-turbine engines. I got to learn from some incredibly knowledgeable engineers, and I had the great fortune to be sent by the company to various corporate sites in North America, and even in Europe, as a technical expert.

After a few years, I was promoted to be the engineering manager of a functional team that supported the corporation's engine test facilities. I was responsible for a team of sixteen engineers, technologists, and technicians, a team with a combination of mechanical, computer, and electrical specialties. I continued to travel a lot with the team as they supported some major projects at sites around the world. Along the way, I developed expertise in project management.

After nearly four years in that role, I was suddenly promoted to acting director of engineering for the department, as the incumbent was seconded to be the lead on a major corporate project. Along the way, I obtained my Project Management Professional designation, and I even developed a project management training course that I taught at various locations around the company. I held a couple of more senior technical leadership positions, the final one being the director of engineering of the company's largest business unit, before moving on to a new organization for a different challenge.

In 2012, I joined Manitoba Housing as the executive director of asset management. Manitoba Housing, a crown corporation of the Manitoba Government, responsible for social housing across the province. When I started, I was responsible for team of sixty-five individuals, and a capital project budget of over $80 million. My capital project management experience from the aerospace world was what made my transition from private-sector employment into the public sector possible.

After a couple of years in that role, in a series of domino moves starting with the retirement of the CEO of Manitoba Housing, I was asked to take on the role of acting chief operating officer. I was now responsible for over 400 staff, and an annual budget of over $100 million. Several months after starting as COO, I was tasked to be the Lean champion as Manitoba Housing began a new chapter of the transformation journey on which it had been travelling since 2008.

But there was only one problem—I had for years been developing into a leader who believed that his authority came from having all the answers. I would have to change this aspect of who I was in order to become a true Lean leader.

As a senior leader, you need to ask yourself what the true source of your leadership authority is, and what makes you valuable to your organization. If you answered, as I did for many years, that it is your subject-matter expertise, then you have some soul-searching to do. This kind of belief will hold you back from being truly able to use Lean management methodologies in order to free the hidden additional potential residing within your team. You need to think hard about what kind of leader you are, and I encourage you to think about the journey you took to get to be the kind of leader you are today. It took me over forty years to become the kind of leader who 'had all the answers,' but it only took a year to make the significant changes in my approach that made me the leader I am today.

First, I had to free my mind from the some of the imprisoning beliefs that I had constructed for myself as a leader. Only then could I truly begin to succeed in leading the Lean journey at Manitoba Housing. You may also need to make changes about yourself as a leader before you can begin to succeed at leading your own journey. It won't be easy. But I promise you, if you are sincere in your commitment, it will be a truly rewarding experience.

## WHY WOULD YOU WANT TO BOTHER?

*"The greatest waste in America is failure to use the abilities of people.*

**W. Edwards Deming**[4]
*management consultant and pioneer of the modern quality system*

Why would any senior leader have interest in getting started in Lean management? Well, you need to decide that answer for yourself fairly soon because if you decide to embark on this journey people will ask you that question—and you will need a good answer that you can state confidently. But it might be hard to be confident if it's something that you've never tried before or even seen in practice.

I think you need to also identify what attracted you to the concept in the first place. Maybe you had been on a tour of an organization that had adopted Lean management practices, and you liked what you saw and heard. Perhaps you saw a presentation at a conference, and the ideas resonated with you. Maybe you know someone who works in an organization that follows Lean management principles and what they told you was inspiring. Or possibly you started reading some literature on Lean management on your own, and you saw value in the concepts.

I'll tell you why we got started with our operations excellence Lean program at Manitoba Housing: it was that the CEO and I felt that something was missing in the organization. At first, though, it was hard to quantify what was that "missing" thing.

## FROM AN AEROSPACE COMPANY...

The aerospace organization at which I worked before joining Manitoba Housing had adopted Lean management practices before I had joined the company. I got to "grow up" in an organization that embraced change and continuous improvement from the first day of our induction training as new employees. I got to experience what standardized work was supposed to look like, and I saw visual management boards mounted on walls in each area of the building that included various charts of team performance. I saw daily production stand-up meetings to kick off each work day, and I regularly saw parts of the business undergoing transformation in order to optimize production flow. I worked every day in an environment where the leadership made sure every place was kept to the same standard of upkeep: brightly lit, a nearly-white painted floor, large signs indicating what each production cell was called, and everything clean and in its place.

Everyone in the organization was trained in the importance of focusing on the customer at all times, whether the customer was the person buying the service from the company, or an internal customer who used your output to start their workflow. Many of us were trained in basic Lean techniques, like process-mapping, using fishbone (or Ishikawa) diagrams for root-cause analysis, developing Pareto charts to prioritize issues by frequency of occurrence, and developing swim-lane diagrams and spaghetti maps to show how far a piece of product "traveled" and the hand-offs involved during a process. We were trained, like all staff, in the basics of how to read business financial statements.

We watched the company develop a communication philosophy that involved sharing as much information as possible regularly with all the staff, regardless of their position. Challenging the process, respectfully of course, was not considered forbidden; rather, it was expected and celebrated.

Management believed in its people and invested heavily in training and development for everyone. Every employee, upon arrival, was soon given a copy of their own training-development plan—a document that identified for each specific job the different learning experiences, mentorship steps, and training courses that the employee needed to complete and have signed off by their supervisor in order to be considered fully-capable in their role. Every year, the employees received an individual performance review from their supervisor, and afterwards both employee and supervisor together created a learning development plan for the upcoming year.

Senior and executive management were known out on the shop floor, and they knew the names of many of the staff. There was a tremendous sense of community within the organization—company intramural sports leagues, especially hockey, were popular pastimes, with business units, and even the executives, each supplying their own teams to play against other business unit teams in the evenings. Being a part of this organization, you felt like you were a part of a large family.

When the company began expanding rapidly, starting shortly after my arrival in early 1997, they did not hire large teams of external consultants to help set up the new sites—instead, they sent experienced leaders and front-line staff to form a project team to set up each site. Changing or supporting these sites often involved travel from experienced staff. I was fortunate enough to have been a part of this experience for many different sites. Because of this approach, I travelled extensively, and often multiple times to sites all over the United States, Canada, the United Kingdom, and the Netherlands. Most of these facilities were initially obtained through corporate acquisitions, but because they were set up by our people they were set up to follow the same design formula. When you went from the Winnipeg facility to the San Antonio facility, you felt at home right away—the same lighting, floor paint, signage, metrics board, and level of cleanliness. And you would see a similar thing in each facility that you visited. But each site had its own variations, especially in the culture and organizational traditions. While every site looked the same superficially, those of us who had been around a while, and who got to travel between locations, could identify the cultural differences and appreciate them.

Eventually, at each site that was brought on line, the staff developed to the same level of production efficiency and effectiveness. They learned and absorbed the company philosophy of continuous improvement, and Lean management, using business metrics to look for areas to improve, and through understanding operational data. And you could feel it when you walked through each facility and talked to the people. You were a part of a mature organization that really knew how to improve itself and perform.

## ...TO A GOVERNMENT SOCIAL HOUSING PROGRAM

Prior to 2007, Manitoba Housing was a very different organization than it is today in 2018. In 2007, an external auditor report was made public, which impartially outlined the significant problems that Manitoba Housing was facing at that time, including the significant capital investment shortages and the critical state of the properties. In the initial stage of addressing the findings of the audit, there were significant changes in personnel within the organization.

A new CEO was hired from Saskatchewan, the former CEO of that province's government social housing corporation. After he started, he worked to bring in other leaders to effect positive organizational transformation. This CEO struggled to handle the day-to-day operations while dealing with the strategic and external factors facing the organization. He brought in from another department a senior leader that he made the general manager, the role that later was changed to the COO. The general manager worked very hard to establish a higher level of accountability within the leadership levels. A few reorganizations took place over time, and some groups separated from larger ones in order to allow for more focused development.

Manitoba Housing was the largest property owner in the Province of Manitoba, with over 3,000 buildings, for a total of over 18,200 units of housing. However, the external audit report clearly indicated that many of these buildings were in desperate need of capital repairs. When the government clearly understood the magnitude of the problem, they responded.

They committed to a massive capital rejuvenation plan for Manitoba Housing. In 2008, the annual capital funding increased from $7 million to $12 million. In 2009, it doubled to $24 million—this was the year that the professional services unit, a group of engineering and architectural staff that supported capital projects for Manitoba Housing, was first developed. The CEO hired the director of the team from outside of government, an engineer from the aerospace sector.

In 2010, the capital funding allocation jumped to $48 million. Not long after that, the director of the professional services unit was promoted to the role of executive director of the asset management branch. This branch was responsible for the capital planning unit, the professional services unit, and the new procurement unit that was borne out of the recommendations of the 2007 external audit to bring control and standardization to the organization's procurement procedures.

The annual capital funding allocation continued to increase until 2012. Eventually, the COO retired and was replaced by the executive director of asset management. I applied for the vacant executive director position and was hired by the CEO in May of 2012. That year, the capital funding allocation reached $82 million, and was $96 million the year after that—a tremendous increase from the $7 million per year that was the norm only five years earlier. But the systems for managing capital work had to mature to catch up with the increased demands from the new funding.

Although the organization had made tremendous strides forward in its organizational evolution since 2007, the COO and I noticed a few things about Manitoba Housing that were different than the aerospace sector from where we had both come. For one, there was a lack of standardized work. Every site office seemed to have its own way of things, and this fact, for some reason, seemed to be celebrated.

Although financial reports had for some time been available for each property manager and branch leader, few other metrics were used in the management of the program as a whole. Daily or weekly meetings between staff and management to review the business of the week often didn't occur. Many managers did not meet regularly one-on-one with their own staff. Very little information about the business flowed from the executives to the staff. To me as a newcomer, numerous business processes appeared to contain tremendous inefficiencies and unnecessary steps. To make matters worse, the staff still appeared to significantly fear the senior leadership of the organization. There was still a lot of room for the corporation to grow in terms of overall organizational maturity.

In May of 2014, a few months after the CEO had retired, the COO was appointed acting CEO, and I was appointed acting COO. We had a new deputy minister to whom we reported, and we worked hard to build trust with him. He was a great guy who valued a lot of what we were trying to accomplish with our organizational transformation efforts, and we learned from him as well. We invested time talking to him about starting a Lean program at Manitoba Housing, and he got on board with the idea.

We started pitching the idea to the other executives that formed the management board of directors for Manitoba Housing. We reached out to some consultants in Winnipeg and ended up awarding a consulting contract to an individual Lean consultant. He was a perfect fit for the staff of Manitoba Housing. Unlike some consultants, he never bragged about his knowledge, was extremely humble, was eager to learn, took accountability to complete jobs, and didn't hesitate to get his hands dirty out in the field. The staff loved it any time someone from head office was willing to get out into the field.

Our consultant's mandate from us was simple: guide us in developing our Lean program, and work to replace yourself with someone internal to Manitoba Housing within eighteen months. He did a great job and fully lived up to his objectives. He spent a lot of time getting out into the field to meet staff. He wanted to learn the operating environment from the front-line staff perspective, and he also wanted to build trust relationships with staff. He started training his replacement at Manitoba Housing soon after he started as our consultant.

In our organization, we had two positions with the job title of operations analyst—one reporting to the COO and one to the CEO. Part of the role of the operations analyst was to serve as a project manager for strategic projects that crossed divisional boundaries. The other primary duty was to serve as a Lean practitioner. In Manitoba Housing, the Lean practitioner was an individual who had received more extensive Lean training than most of the other staff and served as a coach for our trained staff facilitators. In our case, the Lean practitioners received "Lean Green Belt" training certification within a year from each of their start dates.

Our consultant worked very hard to learn some of the pain points in our processes from the front-line staff so that he could get a few ideas of areas in which to start continuous improvement activities. He also invested in learning the language and terminology of the organization. From this research, he started to develop a basic introduction to operations excellence presentation, so that we could start at the very beginning to introduce our staff to what this new part of our culture was all about.

Shortly after, our consultant began to develop "Lean 101" training material for our staff, to try to demystify what Lean was all about. We ran an introductory session for the executive leadership of the department, and it was a huge hit. We committed to provide this training to every staff member at Manitoba Housing, even though that would take a few years to do.

Our consultant helped facilitate our first continuous improvement event, with the pest-management group, where the goal was to reduce the time from client notification of pest activity to treatment by twenty percent. There was a bit of trepidation around this first event, and not everyone at the staff level felt they could yet be as free and open about discussing the process problems as they needed to be, but it was a good start.

The consultant worked hard to make sure that everything was in place for this event to run smoothly, and it did. He had to manage some group dynamic issues, and the leadership wasn't sure how they fit into this event, but that was to be expected. Overall, the event was successful and a fantastic start to our operations excellence program at Manitoba Housing. There would be many more continuous improvement events to come, which I will describe more in the book.

## SO, WAS IT WORTH THE EFFORT?

Absolutely it was worth the effort. The CEO and I also learned a lot along the way, perhaps more than our staff did, which we didn't expect. Lean, for us, quickly became more of a style of leadership and a mindset, than a toolkit. I think this is where many organizations get it wrong—they think that Lean *is* the toolkit of process flow mapping, root-cause analysis, and so on.

Once each month, as COO, I would meet with all of my senior leaders in operations—this included all directors and executive directors. I called this my SLT, or senior leadership team meeting. A few years ago, I wanted to develop a rallying focal point for operations, something that tied to, or complemented, our corporate mission statement. After months of discussion and iteration, we developed the graphic shown in Figure 0.1.

This graphic shows the corporate values of Manitoba Housing around the perimeter, and the three interlocking circles in the middle represent the operations stakeholder groups. For many years, our operations team had been faithfully focusing on the "clients and communities" that they served—they did not need me to tell them to do that at all, as it came naturally.

But we had now added the concept of balance to our decision-making. We would also focus on looking at the impact of our leadership decisions on "the public," whom we served as public servants—the citizens that have entrusted us to be good stewards of public assets and resources. We would also start to recognize the importance of evaluating the impact of our leadership decisions on "our people"—our staff, who had rarely been recognized as stakeholders by the organization before.

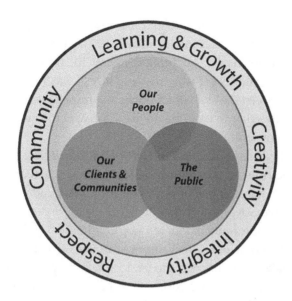

**FIGURE 0.1**   Manitoba Housing Values and Stakeholders Wheel.[5]
Copyright 2015, Manitoba Housing, used with permission.

I think the launch of this graphic across Manitoba Housing was a small, yet important, milestone in its own right. As we publicly declared our commitment to our people, we were also giving our people the ability to hold their leaders accountable to this proclamation.

For us, there was a very crucial aspect to our Lean transformation—it was about changing the culture of our organization. Lean was about the leadership respecting the input and guidance from the front-line staff on how to improve the corporation's processes. Lean was about the leadership becoming coaches, rather than serving as the experts. It was about the leaders "going to *gemba*," going to where the problem was, to see for themselves what was going on and then organizing some staff to help fix it. Lean was about reducing variation in our processes through standardized work. It was about measuring results and working as teams to improve our performance for our clients.

When our teams started getting more productive, efficient, and effective, both the clients and the public would benefit, and our staff benefited from the engagement and empowerment to make a difference. Lean was about trusting our people and maturing together into a more professional organization.

After only about eighteen months, our Lean program at Manitoba Housing was looking very successful, despite its short life. The first Lean practitioner that our consultant had trained was doing a great job, and, in many cases, was able to act independently to coach our staff facilitators. Our Lean practitioner was providing the Lean 101 training by himself to our staff, and the staff were fully trusting him. I was really enjoying the partnership between the Lean practitioner and myself (as Lean champion), as we worked together to continue to drive forward the culture change of Lean into the corporation.

Although the Manitoba Department of Health had been working with Lean for some time before Manitoba Housing had started our program, we were rapidly become one of the most prominent leader-organizations in the Manitoba Government. Not too bad for an organization that few people would have wanted to join ten years earlier.

I do need to point out something. Manitoba Housing's evolutionary journey had taken over ten years to get to where they were in 2018, given the point from which the transformation had started. They likely could not have started a Lean program in 2007, until some basic fundamentals of control had been put in place. The organization just wasn't ready for it before we launched our operations excellence program in 2014. There is still have a long way to go for the corporation, but I have great confidence in the people, and their future.

# Acknowledgements

Who I am as a leader today, as I write this, is not due to my inherent talents but is due to the influence of others upon me. In my private-sector employment, I learned from principled leaders, such as Paul Soubry, Jr., Ian Smart, Verna Taylor, Brian Lanoway, Bruce Clarke, Kerry Boucher, Kim Olson, Alex Yoong, Wayne Thomas, Brent Junkin, Brian McMillan, Danny Gonzales, and many others. I am deeply indebted to all of these individuals for the coaching that they provided me, both directly, and through their examples. I would especially like to thank Paul Soubry for reviewing my manuscript and contributing the Foreword to this book—it was an honour for me to be able to include Paul's thoughts along with my own.

In my time in the public sector, I feel that I've learned just as much about leadership as I did in the private sector. I've had the privilege to get to know and learn from talented, thoughtful workers and leaders, who through their actions every day defy the unfair negative stereotypes of the "civil servant." Many of these people were a part of the journey of evolution within Manitoba Housing, or within the Department of Families, and they have been tremendously supportive to my development as a leader. I am grateful to the hard-working staff and leaders of Manitoba Housing, past and present, who taught me so much, and to the fantastic leaders and innovators that I have met across the various departments of the civil service. I would also like to thank for their support and consideration to write this book a few leaders from within the Manitoba Government: Jay Rodgers, Deputy Minister of the Department of Families; Nancy Carroll, former Civil Service Commissioner; and Fred Meier, Clerk of the Executive Council.

There are some individuals that I feel compelled to single out due to their direct contributions to me in the development of this book. Steven Spry, the former CEO of Manitoba Housing, and my good friend, has traveled a similar personal leadership journey alongside me, and many chapters in this book outline something that we discovered together over the years. I greatly appreciate the steadfast support of Steve over the years. Carolyn Ryan, thank you for your patience, advice and guidance—many parts of this book were refined through our reflective discussions together over the years. The first Lean practitioner in Manitoba Housing, Adrien Sala, was the one who inspired me to write this book over two years ago. Adrien, thanks for your deep insights and reflections, and for your dedication towards the principles of Lean leadership.

I am so grateful for the many people within my Lean community with whom I have shared questions and thoughts; it is from you that I have learned some of the science behind the methodology. I'm very thankful for what I have learned from my close friend Rick Porayko, and many other Lean experts with whom I worked during my career in the aerospace sector. I'm indebted to my Lean Blackbelt instructors, Ian Marshall of Canadian Manufacturers and Exporters, and David Chao, the many Government of Manitoba Lean practitioners, the brilliant authors of the Lean and leadership literature which I have referenced in this book, and most recently Mike Rother, whom I was privileged to meet in 2018. Kurt Shaw, our Lean consultant, was the one who truly started my journey as a Lean leader by coaching me to realize that we leaders need to be prepared to change first before we can expect our people to change, which became a key foundation for this book.

It should not be that only the employees learn from their leader, but rather that leaders should also learn from their employees. I am no different. I learned countless lessons from every one of the many employees that I have had the privilege of leading, in both the public and the private sector, including how to be a better leader. I wish I could proudly state that I have always followed every one of these principles, but I can't. Some of them I learned along the way from my staff and leadership team members. Thank goodness they had patience.

As a first-time author, I reached out to some publishers, hoping that one would want to work with me on this project. I was so pleased that Productivity Press of Taylor and Francis responded to my proposal with a contract. I'm very grateful to Michael Sinocchi, my editor, to Katherine Kadian, editorial assistant, and to Andrew Corrigan, my project manager from Deanta Global, for patiently guiding me through the process of publishing a book.

To my family and friends, thank you for your support and encouragement during the countless hours of writing, editing, and editing again. My parents, Don and Ruth, have always been tremendous supporters of me as a leader. My late grandfather, Jaring Timmerman, modelled for me through his behaviour an incredible example of "acting with respect for people."

Of course, those closest to you make the largest sacrifices when you undertake a project like this. To my wife Trish, I couldn't have done this without your love and support and reassurance. To my children Mark and Breanna, whom I love very much, it's all done—let's have some fun!

# About the Author

 **Brent Timmerman**, worked for 15 years in the aerospace industry in a variety of engineering and leadership roles, travelling extensively to various international corporate facilitates. In 2012, Brent moved to the public sector by joining Manitoba Housing (the social housing crown corporation of the provincial government) as an Executive Director. Brent later became the Chief Operating Officer of the corporation. In that role, he worked with the organization to introduce Lean management principles. In 2018, Brent became the Chief Innovation Officer for the Manitoba Government Department of Families, championing the deployment of a Lean transformation strategy that focuses on leadership and employee engagement to create a culture of improvement and operational excellence. Brent has a Master of Science degree in mechanical engineering from the University of Manitoba. He is a registered Professional Engineer, a certified Project Management Professional (PMP) with the Project Management Institute, and a Lean Blackbelt Champion with Lean Sensei International. Brent is passionate about leadership and continuous improvement, and he believes that Lean approaches can be applied in any organization, public-sector, private-sector, or non-profit.

He is married to Trish and they have a son and a daughter, both of whom are active in sports and music. Brent and his family live in Winnipeg, Manitoba, Canada.

# Part I

# Understanding the Spaces
# of Lean Transformation

# 1

## Introduction

*"A man has made at least a start on discovering the meaning of human life when he plants shade trees under which he knows full well he will never sit."*

**Elton Trueblood**[1]
*author*

This book is written as a guidebook for senior leaders looking at starting a Lean journey in an organization that has little or no experience with the methodology and philosophy. It is also intended as a troubleshooting tool for leaders who have already started a Lean journey but recognize that they are struggling with getting aspects of the culture change to stick.

Part 1 of this text sets the stage for how the framework of the book is intended to work, according to a model that I call the "Three Spaces of Lean Transformation." The next chapter defines and describes this model, and each of the spaces, and then Chapter 3 defines some of the terminology that I use throughout the book to provide some clarity. Chapter 4 describes the roles that are played by the different "characters" within the Lean management team, and it also outlines the duties that each of the characters have in each of the Three Spaces of Lean Transformation in order to properly support the desired culture change.

The next three parts of the book are dedicated to outlining the set of principles that the organization's leadership team must follow in order to provide a supportive leadership environment for the tools of innovation to work. Each space of the model contains its own relevant group of leadership principles and is described in its own dedicated part of the book, such as Part 2 Understanding the Space of Trust, Part 3 Understanding the Space for Change, and Part 4 Understanding the Space for Continuous Improvement. Each chapter is kept quite short, some just a couple of pages long, in order to keep the reader focused on a single principle. Each chapter in these three parts describes a single leadership principle, and the titles of these chapters label each principle in plain, jargon-free English, in order to try to introduce to the reader simple terminology that I have found resonates well with people on a journey like this.

The final part of the book, Understanding the New Way, is a summary of what is intended to be accomplished by putting in place the model of the Three Spaces. It also includes a challenge for the reader in terms of taking the concept of modelling the way of these leadership principles beyond the workplace. The final two chapters illustrate for the reader that idea of how the change in organizational culture will start to "feel," when it begins, and the criticality of the role of the leader in this transformation.

Taking your organization on a journey that involves the transformation of the organizational culture is both exciting, and scary, for everyone involved. But there is tremendous value in taking your organization going down the path of a Lean journey, especially if every senior leader is prepared to ask themselves, "What if part of the problem is me?"

# 2

## The Three Spaces Model

*"Progress cannot be generated when we are satisfied with the existing situation."*

**Attributed to Taiichi Ohno**
*founder of the Toyota Production System*

The conceptual model of the Three Spaces of Lean Transformation was something we developed at Manitoba Housing in 2016 to attempt to represent to outside audiences why we were successful with our Lean program so quickly, when other organizations were struggling to gain traction with their efforts. In order to graphically show the model, I had the following simple diagram developed by a staff member at Manitoba Housing, Figure 2.1.

This graphical illustration showed our belief that there are three spaces that need to be developed during an organization's Lean transformation, in order for it to be successful. These spaces should not to be confused with phases, or sequential steps, that occur one after the other. In fact, there is substantial overlap between the development and "shaping" of these spaces. And each space really does need to be shaped.

In 2016, I developed material that I would jointly present alongside our CEO in October at a Lean conference.[1] I started working on the presentation in August, along with our Lean practitioner.

When we started thinking about this presentation, we had no idea that we would develop a conceptual model at the end of it. The CEO and I had given well-received presentations in the previous months to several different audiences, but I felt that there was something new at this point in our journey, a new facet to our story. We had learned more in recent months, but I wasn't exactly sure how to describe the new approach that we had been learning.

**FIGURE 2.1** The Three Spaces conceptual model.[2] Copyright 2016, Manitoba Housing, used with permission.

In our first brainstorming meeting about this presentation, the Lean practitioner showed up in my office with printed copies of all of the previous presentations that we had given about the Manitoba Housing Lean program. I asked him to turn them face down on the table. I didn't want any of them to hinder us from really innovating on a new concept. So, I had us, for almost two hours, simply focus on the three take-away points that we hoped our future audience would remember after the presentation. We doodled on my whiteboard, just trying to come up with three simple bullet-points. Our first draft looked like this:

- Recognizing the role you can play as the senior leader in being an obstacle to the success of Lean;
- Recognizing the importance of change management in Lean; and
- Recognizing the importance of setting boundaries around *kaizen* events, to organize them for success.

We repeatedly updated and reworked the language of these three points. We came back another day and shared with each other what we had developed over the evening. I eventually suggested that we find a way to incorporate the wording of "spaces" into these three points.

Since I was a huge fan of *The Speed of Trust* by Stephen M.R. Covey,[3] I really wanted to describe the first bullet using the word "Trust" to describe the change of mindset that the senior leadership needs to adopt in order to avoid being a barrier to the process. This point morphed into "The Space of Trust."

The second point didn't take long, given the wording convention that we had started to adopt, to become "The Space for Change."

The last point took us some time and a few more iterations. I had actually wanted at first to call it "Shaping the Working Space," but that phrasing didn't align with the first two points. It was the Lean practitioner that suggested the tried-and-true Lean terminology of continuous improvement, and so the final space was renamed into its final form of "The Space for Continuous Improvement."

We had been, at the same time as we were working on the wording, trying to think of a graphical representation of our three points. We had a few variations of graphics on the side of our whiteboard. One of them was a funnel shape with segments to match each of the three points, but that looked too much like it was indicating a purely sequential approach to these three points. When we adopted the spaces language we quickly moved to three concentric circles, the graphic shown at the beginning of this chapter. It was simple, and since Lean methodology often celebrates simple as better, we went with it.

Back to the conceptual model, the idea was that we felt that each space needed to be "shaped" from what they currently look like in the organization today. Not only does each space need to be developed and shaped, but each also needs to be maintained. We believed that if the organization neglects the leadership duties to maintain the spaces that have been shaped, then these spaces will degrade and hinder, halt, or even reverse some of the progress that has been made in developing the Lean culture.

In Manitoba Housing, we found that a key partnership that worked well was the pairing of the senior leader, the Lean champion for the organization, and the Lean practitioner. In the next chapter, I will attempt to explain in more detail the roles of each of the "players" on the Lean team.

In Manitoba Housing, the CEO and the I (the COO) distinguished our strategic duties in the following simple way:

- The CEO would focus "outward and forward." This role focused on the strategic elements of the corporation moving outside to the bigger government environment, and it also focused on strategic business planning for the future.

- The COO would focus "inward." It was my role as COO to focus on operationalizing, making into a working reality, the strategic goals of the corporation. As such, when our new Social Housing Rental Program policy set was developed and approved, it was then handed to me to plan and manage the implementation of the policies into operations. Similarly, making Lean a part of our organizational culture at Manitoba Housing therefore also fell into my purview.

This isn't to say that I wasn't involved at all in strategic planning or that I never worked with other government departments, but the CEO took the lead on these areas. Conversely, the CEO was also involved with Lean, and attended as many continuous improvement event team presentations as possible. He spoke alongside me at conferences, and always steadfastly preached support for Lean management principles to staff or other leaders across government any chance he got.

In this model, *The Space of Trust* is the essential foundational space that needs to be in place before the Lean transformation has any hope of being successful. This space refers to the overall leadership environment, the "universe" which encompasses all of the people of the organization. It involves building and maintaining solid trust relationships between the senior leadership and the staff.

*The Space for Change* is a smaller space, encapsulated within the leadership universe, *The Space of Trust*. This is the space where change happens, and it involves the part of the organizational culture that makes people willing to change and to even participate themselves in making some of the changes happen.

*The Space for Continuous Improvement* is yet another smaller space, set within *The Space for Change*. This space is every individual improvement event in your Lean transformation. In order for each Lean event to be successful, the Lean champion and the Lean practitioner must work together, in advance, and fulfill their individual duties. Each Lean event needs careful shaping and planning beforehand to ensure that the team members are able to succeed.

Of course, there are more than just two players on the Lean management team, and each of them has a significant role to play in making sure that the Lean program is successful. But first, some key terms deserve to be defined for clarity.

# 3

## Defining Some Key Terms

*"Earn your leadership every day."*

**Attributed to Michael Jordan**
*former NBA star*

### SENIOR LEADER

This book is developed as a "Senior Leader's Guide," so it is probably worth stating what I mean with this term. From my perspective, I intend this term to encompass leaders from the most senior leader in the organization and down one or two layers of management. As a result, the term senior leader might involve people with the title of director, executive director, vice-president, executive vice-president, chief-whatever-officer, and so on.

### LEAN

This is a somewhat generic term that refers to a process management system derived from the Toyota Production System. Lean often focuses on reducing waste and maximizing efficiency. It is now a global movement that is widely embraced by service- and manufacturing-sector companies, and it is also gaining popularity in public-sector organizations looking to improve efficiency.

## OPERATIONS EXCELLENCE

This is a term that I often use (somewhat incorrectly) interchangeably with Lean, as it is what we branded our Lean management program at Manitoba Housing. In some applications in the business world, operations excellence is considered to add a strong element of focus on organizational and leadership culture to sustain continuous improvement and meet performance metrics.

## CONTINUOUS IMPROVEMENT

In my context, referring to continuous improvement usually is synonymous with Lean, although other people may use it to mean things such as Agile, or Lean Six-Sigma.

## KAIZEN

This is probably the most frequently used term in this book. It is a combination of two Japanese words, *kai* (which means "change"), and *zen* (which means "good"). Although a *kaizen* can take many different formats, my intent with the term is to describe an event lasting between two and five days that is designed to develop incremental efficiency improvements to a specific business process. This event is led by a Lean facilitator, who is the person charged with leading the *kaizen* team through the structured process from beginning to end to optimize the business process.

The *kaizen* event is planned in advance, and a simple project charter is developed and agreed to by the relevant senior leaders responsible for the affected business process. The charter describes clearly the problem that the team is to solve, and it also outlines the efficiency improvement goal in measurable terms. The charter also outlines any constraints to the problem.

The *kaizen* team is a collection of staff subject-matter experts familiar with the business process, although I do later describe the benefits of adding outsiders to the team.

The *kaizen* event usually consists of the facilitator leading the *kaizen* team through a structured process to develop a map of the current process, identify problems, look for waste in the process, and then develop ideas on how to remove the waste and increase the process efficiency.

The beginning of each *kaizen* event usually has the senior leader responsible for the process kicking off the project and "deputizing" the staff to help improve the process. At the end of every *kaizen* event, the senior leadership attends a closeout presentation where the *kaizen* team presents their findings and their solutions to improve the process.

Note that a *kaizen* event is usually intended (in my context) to produce an incremental improvement in performance of a particular business process. The assumption, of course, is that the business process in question is working at a basic level, but it is recognized that the process has waste and inefficiency that can be removed.

A *kaizen* event is not suitable for major business transformation that involves completely rethinking business processes—Lean has a term for this approach, known as *kaikaku*, which means "radical change" in Japanese. Sometimes the term *kakushin* is used to mean transformative change. Nonetheless, Lean tools, such as value-stream mapping, are still relevant in radical change projects, such has *kaikaku*. These types of larger project concepts are outside the scope of this book and are not something that you would usually want to take on at the very beginning of your cultural transformation with your staff. Instead, you need to focus on building trust through engagement with your people—I believe that this is much easier with small, manageable change projects, rather than large, disruptive ones.

# 4

## The Lean Management Team

*"We cannot change what we are not aware of, and once we are aware, we cannot help but change."*

Sheryl Sandberg[1]
*Chief Operating Office, Facebook*

### THE MOST SENIOR LEADER

This individual has a simple, but simple job with regards to the continuous improvement transformation. The most senior leader must regularly, and publicly, endorse the operations excellence or Lean program, and the Lean champion, every chance they get. They must hold everyone on the executive team accountable to drive forward with progress towards the different milestones. This person needs to be able to sign off on reasonable requests for resources and to help remove obstacles to the program when required.

The most senior leader does not necessarily need to be deeply schooled in Lean management methodologies, but early in the program this person does need training on the fundamentals of Lean so he or she can be at least conversant. Lean for Leaders training early in the journey would be beneficial for this person, if at all possible.

One key factor to remember is that you *cannot* make this person necessary to sign off every process change. Ideally, you need to delegate the authority for process changes to the executive team. The reason is that, for many larger organizations, the most senior leader is, quite often, far too busy to be able to be present when needed, and that is frequently, when this program is moving along. Keeping the authority for everything locked up tightly with the most senior leader will choke the progress of the operations excellence program.

## THE OTHER EXECUTIVES

The executive team will obviously look very different in each company, depending on the organizational structure. These people need to be on board, and also must be prepared to regularly, and publicly, endorse the operations excellence program. You need to invest in training for these people in the fundamentals of Lean immediately before the program kicks off, so that they can speak with some knowledge when asked by staff about what Lean is all about.

You need to get these people into "Lean for Leaders" training as soon as you possibly can. These people need to be prepared to work together to remove obstacles during a process improvement event. One of the executive team needs to be selected as the Lean champion.

### The Space of Trust

In the *Space of Trust*, the other executives in the organization have a simple, but very important role. They have to support the Lean activities and the management approach, and they can *never* give any indication to the hierarchy below them that they don't agree with it. If an executive hints to the team that he or she really isn't onboard, then that executive's part of the organization will very weakly, or not at all, engage with the transformation. When a *kaizen* team reaches out across silo walls wanting help from that executive's part of the organization to implement changes, the team might be stymied or stalled.

Every executive needs to be visibly onboard with the management approach and must be consistently applying the fundamentals. They all need to be conversant in the Lean toolkit, and they should be able to explain in simple words what Lean is all about, but they don't all need to be experts. But they do need to be supportive and congruent.

### The Space for Change

The executive team has to be on board with the principles of organizational change management. They need to support the communication vehicles between the senior leadership and all levels of the organization. The biggest commitment at Manitoba Housing, by far, was the commitment of the executive team to the monthly Housing Leadership team meetings (described in Chapter 38, Change Principle #5: Communicate everything you can), as each executive had to prepare their piece of the presentation every month, without fail.

Most importantly, the executive team needs to commit to the philosophy of communication transparency with the staff: *that they will communicate information to the people unless there is a compelling reason not to do so.* For some leaders, this will be frightening, and it may even feel threatening.

Information is not something to be protected and hoarded, to make an individual indispensable, but rather information is a tool to be shared so that everyone on the team can be more effective. If you don't know every single factor surrounding the issue, that's okay. Tell the people what you do know and commit to filling in the gaps later. They will appreciate you for it more than you may appreciate it.

## The Space for CI

In the *Space for CI*, the executive team, as always, need to continue to be supportive when speaking to the staff and leadership about the program. If a *kaizen* event involves a process in the responsibility area for any of them, that executive should attend the closeout presentation, and ideally, also the *kaizen* kickoff presentation. The executive team members all need to be prepared to celebrate all the successes of the culture change with the staff.

# THE LEAN CHAMPION

This person must be an executive. This crucial role absolutely must not be delegated to a lower-level leader if you actually want your Lean program to succeed. I've seen this done in many organizations because the executives think that they are far too busy to dedicate the time to it. That may be the case, but then spare your team the disappointment and don't even bother with a Lean program.

If an executive can't dedicate the time to be the Lean champion, then quite simply it will not work. You will be sending the message to your staff that you want them to dedicate time to this initiative, but the executives can't be bothered to do it themselves. This incongruence will hamper you every step along the way.

The best choice for your Lean champion, in my opinion, is the executive who controls a large piece of your operations—that is where the biggest process improvements are going to take place anyway. The Lean champion must be a listened-to peer of the other executives. Avoid setting up a functional leader to be the Lean champion, as that person will be swimming against the current trying to get operations people to change when they don't feel as though they are able to control their own destiny. Whoever is selected as the Lean champion needs to be completely on board with the approach and must be prepared to preach it out loud to every staff member and leader.

At Manitoba Housing, we called our program operations excellence, and we made me, the chief operating officer, the Lean champion. Our organizational structure was set up so that I had responsibility for approximately two-thirds of the staff. I think that, although efficiency improvements can be made in the functional areas such as finance, HR, procurement, engineering, or IT, the biggest wins to be made, and those that impact the client, are often in operations.

Throughout my career, I've often seen the sometimes-subtle, but sometimes-blunt, conflict between operations staff and functional support staff. At times, the operations staff appear to wish that the functional support personnel understood what it was like to work "on the front lines," or how things worked "in the real world." On the other hand, the functional people sometimes look at the operations staff as anarchists who would run wild without heed of proper process. This is one reason why I would be very hesitant to assign the role of Lean champion to a functional executive. In many cases, this person might be pushing uphill trying to gain credibility with the operations staff.

The Lean champion needs to be prepared to work collaboratively with other executives to assign resources as needed for Lean activities, and also to remove obstacles or barriers to process improvements when necessary.

The Lean champion needs to be prepared to devote a *lot* of time to this program, especially in the first year. As the Lean champion for Manitoba Housing, I made the time to attend every *kaizen* kickoff event, and every closeout presentation made by the staff. I spent countless hours visiting operations staff one-on-one in the many field offices across the province, and with each person, I would explain what our operations excellence program meant and why I thought it was important.

The Lean champion needs to really *believe* in the approach. I can't stress this point enough. If you don't believe in it yourself, then you can't make others enthusiastic about the journey either. Not only do you need to believe, but you also need to get truly excited about the possibilities for your organization.

If you take the time to tour some other organizations that have successful Lean management programs up and running, you will see what is possible, and these types of tours can be very uplifting and inspiring. You will face some tough challenges and setbacks in the days ahead, so you will need that optimism to carry forward not only your team but yourself as well.

The advantage I had in this role was that I had spent fifteen years in an aerospace organization that had embraced a culture of continuous improvement even before I had arrived. I "grew up" in the environment of Lean, so I knew what the future could look like, and how it could benefit my team. This knowledge was important because it helped me to work with our consultant to continually update our strategy and to determine what we next needed to focus with our staff.

The Lean champion will need to be prepared to learn beyond the "Lean for Leaders" training. They will need to read and study, on their own, to learn about additional pieces of the vast Lean toolkit and work out a strategic plan with the consultant to adapt and introduce these tools into practice with the team.

This person also needs to be knowledgeable in the field of organizational change management, so that they understand the proper methodology to effectively embed change throughout an organization.

More than anything, this person will need to be able to embrace the coaching leadership style. If this person is highly dependent on being the subject-matter expert, or on centralizing decision-making to themselves, then he or she will simply not be successful as the Lean champion.

This role depends on the individual wanting to help others find the answers themselves, and not being the person to give out the answers. You must be willing to support experimentation, trying new ways of doing things, and be willing to tolerate mistakes made in good faith in the process. Patience will definitely be a virtue.

## The Space of Trust

In developing and shaping this space, the Lean champion has the lion's share of the work. The Lean champion has to get familiar with the fundamentals of what Lean is and be able to speak about it in simple terms whenever asked. This person must be prepared to repeat some of the same verbiage many times to convince staff, and other leaders, of the sincerity of the new management approach. The champion must remind them that, while the traditional way of changing processes was for the big boss to make the changes and instruct the staff to follow them, things are different now.

In Lean, during a *kaizen* event, front-line staff are assembled to form a team of subject-matter experts. Management trusts these people to come up with better answers to fixing the process problems than the leadership might develop. Be prepared to get some skeptical responses from people at first. Don't be bothered by it, just smile and accept it, but know that they will eventually change their minds when you really get going.

The champion needs to be able to get out of their office and devote time to talking to staff, and to listening to what they have to say about how to improve the business processes. The Lean champion needs to have self-awareness of his/her own behaviour, and also needs to be willing to accept that he/she may be the problem in some cases. For some people, this may be an impossible challenge.

When you visit an office, talk to everyone in the office one-on-one if you can, but be very careful not to violate the leadership chain of command. Make sure to communicate to the leadership about your site visits, and the purpose, before you go. Ask each person about their job, find out about their background, how long they've been with the organization. Tell them a bit about yourself if they ask. But work hard to listen to them.

Use questions to get them to tell you more. Ask them if they have any ideas about processes in the organization that need fixing, ones that seem broken. If you are told any, write them down and work with your consultant and Lean practitioner to try to work on one of them in an early *kaizen* event. If you do, make sure you let the originator know that you took their advice and thank them for the idea. Show them later what the organization did differently as a result of their suggestion. Don't forget to keep your eyes open for other process problems that might fit a future *kaizen* event. Keep a list if you need to.

Remember that when you start visiting front-line staff to build trust, then you can't stop later on when things seem to be going well. This will be something you will need to keep doing without stopping, although you can likely reduce the frequency a bit after the initial push.

You will need to keep watch on the other executives and leaders, to make sure that they keep doing their parts to develop the trust environment in the organization. If you see problems developing, where people are not demonstrating the correct behaviours as leaders, you will need to step in and address these issues right away. This may or may not be difficult, depending on the individual that you need to confront.

These types of conversations alone can be just as challenging as some of the other major problems in an organization, and figuring out how to ask a peer, or possibly someone senior to you, to change their leadership approach takes a lot of patience, courage, and planning. You want to get the behaviour to change, and your goal isn't to get the person to simply feel bad about themselves. How to get the person to really internalize what you are trying to say takes a strong trust relationship between the two of you. You may need to build up these relationships between other leaders before you can approach them about changing their approaches.

But the hardest role that the Lean champion has in this space is personally monitoring their own behaviour. You have to be willing to have the Lean consultant, or your Lean practitioner, come into your office and tell you that you did something wrong, or that you spoke in the wrong way. You have to be prepared to accept this type of feedback from a subordinate and say "Thanks for letting me know... I hadn't realized that I said it that way. I'll try to clarify things tomorrow for that staff member and be more careful next time."

As the Lean champion at Manitoba Housing, I came to greatly value my closed-door discussions with our Lean practitioners and Lean consultant. I really appreciated the fact that they felt comfortable enough to confront me about things and to raise innovative ideas with me as well.

## The Space for Change

In this space, the Lean champion needs to work to get many new communication channels set up and moving. This will be hard if such ideas are foreign to the culture of your organization. But the dedication to set up these communication streams is going to be a tremendous investment that will pay off in spades. And the payoff won't be years down the line. Inside one year of continuous commitment to developing and maintaining the *Space for Change*, you will already feel that the culture of your organization has changed for the better.

The Lean champion needs to be prepared to be the coach for the evolution of the organization. You need to understand that tremendous persistence on your part will be needed to change the inertia of the bureaucracy, and the bigger the bureaucracy, the harder that will be. You need to expect pushback from your people, and to handle it appropriately—to look for the underlying root causes, and to try to address them with the staff and the leadership so that you can continue to move forward.

Find the pace of that evolution that your organization can handle, and then try to nudge it a little faster. Just remember that none of these challenges mean that there is anything wrong with your people—from their perspective, the problem will be you. Be prepared to listen to your staff, your leaders, and to your Lean practitioner about what you need to do differently.

## The Space for CI

This space will require an important partnership between the Lean practitioner and the Lean champion. Together, these two should be selecting the team members, along with the senior leader responsible for the affected process. As well, the Lean champion will be responsible for taking whatever action is necessary, including working with other executives or senior leaders, to remove barriers that are identified by the Lean practitioner during the Lean event preparation stage.

The Lean champion will be involved with approving the project scope, along with the senior leader that owns the process. Making sure that the scope is carefully defined, so that the recommendations that the staff produce can be celebrated and implemented, is absolutely essential. Remember that a *kaizen* event is truly an exercise in the delegation of authority of the senior leadership to the staff.

Defining the project scope to ensure the team can be successful in the time allotted is important as well. Be careful not to overshoot on the breadth of the project scope, as you want the team to produce by the last day results of which they can be proud.

Finally, the Lean champion needs to recognize and celebrate the team. You will need to attend the kickoff of each *kaizen* event, and thank the team for trusting in the process, and then leave the room. The team won't really feel that they can really start working until you and the other leaders leave them alone.

A few times at the beginning of *kaizen* events, I had hung around for a bit after giving my kickoff speech. I could tell that the team was somewhat uncomfortable with getting going, so I would quickly suggest that they might feel more free to get to work without me around—the nervous laughs that my comment received confirmed my thoughts.

When I would ask the facilitator how things went after I had left, they always admitted that everyone relaxed, and things started moving freely after I had left.

When the *kaizen* is complete, you need to attend, along with the other appropriate senior leaders, the team's presentation on their conclusions about how to improve the process and thank them for their hard work.

## THE LEAN PRACTITIONER

The next most important team members are the Lean practitioners. Depending on your team's size you may only need one, or you may need more. The practitioner needs to be a person with superb interpersonal skills, and capable of being a true facilitator—someone who can lead people to the answers without dictating the answers.

Look for the people skills first, and the ability to learn the Lean toolkit later, as long as they have the inherent aptitude. It's much harder to learn the people skills if you don't have them at the start. The practitioner needs to be someone who can be at ease with people at all levels in the organization, from the top executives to mid-level leaders, to front-line staff, and they must be trusted by people at all levels. Confidence, but not arrogance, is crucial.

This person needs to be a top-notch facilitator, but even more, this person needs to value the coaching leadership style. The practitioner will be the coach of the staff-level Lean facilitators. These facilitators won't have the frequency of Lean activities that the practitioner will have, and so they will need a more experienced Lean support person, and that person is the practitioner. A balance between confidence and humility is definitely required.

The practitioner will also need to have a level of political acumen beyond that of your average staff Lean facilitator, since they will often be the bridge between the staff and the executives across the organization. A solid understanding of organizational change management and project management theory and principles will also be crucial.

The practitioner needs to have a solid, trusting relationship between themselves and the Lean champion, and the other senior leaders in the organization. The practitioner will need to feel comfortable and confident enough to walk into the Lean champion's office, close the door, and let them know (respectfully of course) that they made a mistake that day. This is a tough duty to have, and it's definitely not for the faint of heart, but it's absolutely critical that this person is able to navigate the spaces between the executives and the staff in the various silos of the organization.

I think that it is best if the practitioners report to executives, and ideally, one of them needs to report to the Lean champion. One of the practitioners needs to be very knowledgeable about the context of the operating realities of the front-line staff.

The practitioner will need to have the equivalent of "Lean Green Belt" training, at a minimum, to take them to a technical level of expertise beyond that of the typical staff Lean facilitators, simply because they need the additional expertise to serve as the coach of the facilitators.

## The Space of Trust

In this space, the Lean practitioner needs to get out to the front lines and meet with staff one-on-one to build his/her own trust relationships. This person will start showing up in future *kaizen* events and will likely start giving "Lean 101" training sessions to staff, so the staff need to trust the person in this role.

The practitioner will need to keep an ear close to the ground to make sure that the leaders, and the Lean champion, are correctly portraying the messages about Lean to the staff. As well, it is important to learn if the messages are being properly understood by the staff. When problems arise, the practitioner needs to be able to have that frank conversation with the Lean champion so that the messaging can be tweaked to help properly develop that *Space of Trust*.

The Lean practitioner should also be constantly on the lookout for opportunities for future *kaizen* events.

## The Space for Change

The Lean practitioner should be developing and learning through hands-on coaching from the Lean consultant about how to be the best possible coach of Lean facilitators. This needs to be done concurrently while working to develop the first, and perhaps second, generation of Lean facilitators. It will be performed during actual *kaizen* events, and it will be stressful, as everyone is trying to figure out the routine, and the expectations for each person in their role.

The Lean practitioner needs to be there to be there to support the Lean champion in their efforts to coach the evolution of the organization. And they need to work with the Lean champion to understand all of the objectives that they are trying to achieve when setting up those communication protocols through the organization.

The Lean practitioner needs to be prepared to walk into the champion's office and tell them what is working, and what isn't, and what, if anything, the champion needs to do differently. One of this person's duties is to help the Lean champion be successful in developing the *Space for Change.*

## The Space for CI

The Lean practitioner is definitely working at their busiest pace in the *Space for CI.* This person will be working several weeks in advance of each event to pave the way for success for the Lean facilitator and the team. They need to be on the lookout for roadblocks, and to bring these barriers to the attention of the Lean champion for resolution. They need to ensure that all of the key senior leaders are informed of the project, and on-board with the project scope as well.

The practitioner needs to work to make sure that everyone understands their role, from the Lean facilitator to the champion, to the senior leader who owns the process, to the other leaders and the selected *kaizen* team members. The practitioner should be involved in selecting the *kaizen* team with the champion and the process-owning senior leader—make sure that all of the key areas of expertise are properly represented. This takes careful analysis and some research long before the *kaizen* event happens to properly understand how the process works. In this way, you can make sure that you don't neglect to invite a key subject-matter expert onto the team.

The practitioner will serve as the coach for the Lean facilitator. It is the role of the practitioner to ensure that the Lean facilitator shines and is successful. This means everything including helping the facilitator to prepare the agenda, including time durations for each piece, coaching the facilitator on how to handle different situations in advance, and making sure the facilitator is comfortable with the *kaizen* approach and the Lean toolkit.

It also involves making sure that the facilitator is prepared with contingency strategies on how to handle personnel conflicts or challenging team member behaviours.

At Manitoba Housing, the practitioner would attend each *kaizen* and would sit at the back during the event. The facilitator would be the one at the front guiding the team through the *kaizen* agenda and using the Lean toolkit, but the practitioner would be watching the team members and would provide quiet guidance to the facilitator at the first opportunity, such as a break. Occasionally, the practitioner might speak up from the back, but only to nudge the team towards an answer they seemed to know already, if they were hung-up on some irrelevant detail. At all times, the practitioner needs to remember that their goal is to help the facilitator be successful.

The Lean practitioner needs to work with the facilitator and the accountable senior leader after the event to make sure that the actions all get completed. This will be a very challenging, and at times, frustrating exercise. Track all of the open action items on a tracking sheet that is posted publicly for clear accountability. The practitioner should work with the champion and the responsible senior leader to drive to completion all remaining items so that the *kaizen* improvements can all be fully implemented.

## THE LEAN FACILITATORS

These people will be the facilitators that help your front-line staff arrive at the process improvements. These people need to be trusted by their peers to listen to the group and to help lead the team to a consensus, without being dictatorial or over-bearing. Good people skills will be essential, obviously.

These individuals will all need to be put through the Lean facilitator training program developed by the Lean consultant.

When we first got going, the CEO and I selected our first group of Lean facilitators, with the advice of our Lean consultant who had spent a lot of time in the field meeting staff. We wanted this first group of Lean facilitators to be the "right" group with the desired character traits to be successful in the roles, and also to work effectively with staff from different areas. As you can imagine, every organization has some very intelligent individuals that just would not be appropriate for the Lean facilitator role—they just might not have the right combination of interpersonal skills.

Even with this initial selection method, we of course had to get the endorsement of our branch leaders for these people to be signed up as facilitators. A few times, we had branch leaders volunteer to be facilitators. In retrospect, I would have avoided making a branch leader or a team leader a Lean facilitator because their positional authority may act as a barrier to innovation.

If a team of staff is working to improve a process, and the manager responsible for that process is leading the *kaizen*, the staff may be apprehensive about being honest and forthright about the shortcomings of the existing process, especially if the manager helped to develop the process. I think having front-line staff as the facilitators is the best situation possible, as the question of possible interference of authority is removed. People tend to be open and honest around their own colleagues.

## The Space of Trust

In this space, these people initially won't have been identified yet. As you are first developing the *Space of Trust*, you will be working with your consultant, your practitioner, and your senior leadership to try to select the right people for your first batch of Lean facilitators.

I would be cautious of the open casting call at first because people really don't know what Lean is all about right away. Don't be afraid to be a little more directive in selecting, with your leadership team, the first Lean facilitators based on what you know about your people. But for your second round of selection, think of a way you can open it up to all staff to voice an interest in the role.

## The Space for Change

In the *Space for Change*, the Lean facilitators will just be getting going into their roles. The training of the first team of staff facilitators should be completed early on in the development of this space. The planning of the first *kaizen* events will begin in this space, and the first facilitators will be selected to lead these events. They will work with the Lean practitioners to plan these items out in advance, using the approaches that will be further explained in the *Space for Continuous Improvement*. These folks will be starting their roles in a functional area that will likely be foreign to them, so they will need to trust in the processes that they have been taught during facilitator training.

## The Space for CI

The Lean facilitator needs to research the process that the *kaizen* will address by going to see the process in person, and start talking to the leaders in the area affected by the *kaizen*. This person needs to become conversant with the process under review, and also with the terminology associated with the process so that they can properly understand the language that will come up during the *kaizen*.

The facilitator also needs to be confident and comfortable with the Lean toolkit that they will be using during the *kaizen* event. They should be prepared to ask for help from the coach (the Lean practitioner) before, during, and after the *kaizen*.

The facilitator will need to work to make certain that the team is successful during the *kaizen* event. The facilitator is not there to be the subject-matter expert, but rather the expert on the *kaizen* methodology and the Lean toolkit. The facilitator should work to help the team get to the answers, rather than telling them the answers.

Making sure that all team members voices are heard and that all input is appropriately considered is important, but keeping to the agenda and delivering a finished product of process improvements by the closing time of the *kaizen* is also crucial. The facilitator will need to budget enough time so that the team can feel like they achieved what they wanted to during the event, and enough time needs to be budgeted to also allow the team to prepare and rehearse the final presentation for the senior leadership. Although the facilitator might start off the final presentation, it is important that several team members participate in delivering the presentation to the leadership.

## THE OTHER LEADERS

The other leaders in the organization simply need to be brought on board with the Introduction to Lean training right away and then given "Lean 101" training later. They need to understand from their executives that they need to convey support for the operations excellence program at all times, and that any concerns need to be elevated, in private, to their supervisor.

## The Space of Trust

In this space, these other leaders simply need to be up to speed on what Lean is all about, but they don't need to be experts. They need to be willing to put up their hands when they have questions, but above all, they need to be supportive of the program to their own teams. Only once over my career, did I need to have a stern conversation with a leader about one of their managers—this person was complaining to their team that they couldn't afford the time for the staff facilitator, who reported to the manager, to go work on a *kaizen* event. My message to the leader was simple: "Complaints should go up, not down, the organizational structure." If your manager has a concern with a new initiative, he or she needs to tell you in your office, but he or she cannot complain about the initiative in front of the staff.

## The Space for Change

In the *Space for Change*, the other leaders simply need to show support for the new communication channels, and the associated time requirements of each one. They need to be able to support the principles of organizational change management and to play their parts in leading and supporting change throughout the organization.

Most importantly, they will need to buy in to the philosophy around openness and sharing of important information, instead of guarding it and controlling it. Not every leader will be comfortable with their roles in this space. You may need to have "tough chats" with a couple of them. Some may move on to other opportunities if they become truly uncomfortable with the new direction that the organization is going. That might be what is required, depending on the situation.

But it also might open up a new opportunity for another leader to step in with a fresh viewpoint, and it might also present a development opportunity for a staff member with the right capabilities and energy to be promoted. Sometimes change like this can be rejuvenating.

## The Space for CI

The leader who owns the affected process should participate with the Lean champion and the Lean practitioner in recommending team members for the *kaizen* event as well as to define the project scope and boundaries.

Leaders who may not own the process, but are affected, should also be consulted by the practitioner as well.

The other leaders will have to understand that although they might think that they have all of the answers to fix the process, during a *kaizen* event, they may need to leave the room once it starts. This will be very challenging for many leaders to do, but it will be essential for the team to feel as though they have the manoeuvring room to be able to really make a change to the process. If the manager is still in the room, the team may automatically feel as though they need to just defer to whatever the leader says.

## YOUR LEAN CONSULTANT

Unless you are well schooled in the Lean management methodologies, and have a Lean Black Belt certification, you likely will need the support of outside help, in the form of a consultant. Our Lean consultant at Manitoba Housing was absolutely fantastic, and he worked out so well for us. Our staff loved working with him, and I think his extremely humble personality had a lot to do with that. The working approach of your consultant will have a lot to do with whether or not your team buys in to the new approach early on in your program.

Knowledge is very important, but truly, it's not the only thing. You do want your consultant to be qualified. The "Lean Black Belt" certifications for consultants are somewhat ubiquitous nowadays, and it can be very difficult to figure out which certification programs have true legitimacy, and which are "thin." It's worth at least doing some research online to figure out which type of Black Belt certification your consultant has before signing on. References from people who worked with the consultant are important to check. You want a consultant who has had a lot of experience in working with a wide variety of groups, including pure office staff groups—this will be a good indicator if they can make the transition to working outside of a purely industrial environment.

I think many employees are wary of consultants because they have seen so many of them come and go over the years, in some cases, leaving behind little in the way of tangible value that "sticks." Sometimes, these consultants come in with brash, know-it-all, type-A personalities, and in many cases this is a huge turnoff for many staff members. When trying to attract your people to the notion of using Lean or operations excellence to improve processes, it takes a lot of trust between senior leadership and the staff. And the staff will view the Lean consultant as simply an extension of the senior leadership. When our consultant came on board, his approach of modelling the value of respect for people was exactly what was needed to help us introduce this program.

He spent his first few weeks going out into the different field offices, talking with people one-on-one, asking them about their jobs, and their challenges. He didn't show up acting like he was a person with all the answers. In fact, he acted as though he wanted to help bring to reality the answers to process problems that resided within the staff, and the people really appreciated him for that. His initial time out in the field also helped him to learn some of the terminology that everyone used, so that he could adjust the training that he would develop into language that everyone would understand.

When he was explaining what operations excellence was all about, he used simple language and was careful not to use complicated terminology that might confuse and alienate the staff. This adaptability of his approach to Lean methodology was also very important. He knew when Lean terminology should not be changed, but he also knew which battles weren't worth fighting over when trying to get everyone moving on the upcoming journey.

The Lean consultant will likely be the one who develops your training programs. The following training courses will be important, although names may vary:

- Introduction to operations excellence—a very short presentation that speaks to the fundamentals of what the program involves, WHY you are doing it, and defining some terminology, like "*kaizen.*" Although this may be an in-person presentation for as many of the staff as possible early on, you may want this training to be available online for people in a self-serve format;
- What is 5S—a short and simple presentation-style course to explain what the concept of 5S (explained further in Chapter 48, Change Principle #15: Realize that in an office, 5S doesn't just mean cleaning off your desk) means, and how it is actually applicable in an office environment. This lends itself well to online self-serve delivery as well;
- Lean 101—we made this a half-day training class, mixed in with group exercises and activities, to explain to people more about the steps

involved with a *kaizen*. The exercises are physical activities, such as passing balls around, that help to demonstrate such concepts as why single-piece process flow is more effective than batch-processing. In-person delivery is much better for this type of training;

- Lean for Leaders—this training is much more extensive and is designed for senior leaders. Held over multiple days, it involves an advanced level of detail around how value-stream mapping works, and also shows the senior leader how they can use the Lean toolkit for strategic objective planning;
- Lean Facilitator Training—this training is specifically designed for your staff-level Lean facilitators. It involves teaching them the introductory Lean toolkit, especially focusing on how to develop process maps, Pareto charts, opportunity value charting, the 5-Why method of root-cause determination, Ishikawa or fishbone diagrams, etc. This training also provides instruction on how to facilitate group activities, such as the *kaizen* events. Our training course was considered equivalent to "Lean Six-Sigma Yellow Belt" training; and
- Green Belt training—this is the more advanced Lean training that you will need to put your Lean practitioners through if they don't already have it. In our case, we put our practitioners through a "Green Belt" training program with an external organization.

I think the important thing to remember when selecting your Lean consultant is that you are not buying a commodity or a set of services— rather, think of it as investing in a relationship. Not only you but your people have to trust in this person to help take you down a new path. If your people won't trust your consultant, then you are going to have an uphill struggle to bring them along on the ride.

## The Space of Trust

In the *Space of Trust*, the consultant needs to get out into the front lines of your organization and do a lot of listening to the staff. He or she will need to build trust with the staff so that everyone will feel comfortable opening up to share the organizational problems.

The consultant will also need to be able to confront the Lean champion with truthful observations about where the problems exist, and also about what the Lean champion is doing wrong. Of course, the Lean champion needs to be prepared to hear it. The consultant needs to equip the Lean

> *It may take many months, or a few years, but the measure of success of the Lean consultant will be to ensure that they have properly worked themselves out of a job.*

champion to be able to go out onto the front lines to talk to staff in plain language about what is coming in the future with the Lean transformation.

## Space for Change

In the *Space for Change*, your Lean consultant needs to help you develop your training material to help to explain the WHY to your people. This individual should be working to train your Lean practitioner and should be serving as the coach in that regard, in a "train the trainer" model.

Most importantly, the team of staff Lean facilitators need to be selected and trained on the tool kit that will be used in *kaizen* events, and in facilitation skills. To be honest, our facilitator training involved a very limited skill set at first, and this might be different than typical Lean facilitator training approaches. Because it was so new to our people, we felt that getting them comfortable with a limited and simplified toolkit was best at first, and then we would add sets of tools to the tool kit in subsequent phases of the operations excellence journey. We trained them on how to develop a simplified project charter for a *kaizen*, how to work with a team to assess the SIPOC elements (Suppliers, Inputs, Process description, Outputs, Customer), and how to perform value-stream mapping for a process. We also trained them how to plot opportunities on a chart of improvement value vs. effort, how to set up a closeout presentation, and facilitation skills.

The key areas on which the Lean consultant should be focusing the training of the Lean practitioner should be how to coach other Lean facilitators, and how to guide the Lean champion towards what is happening at the staff level.

## The Space for CI

Here, the Lean consultant needs to be continuing to train the Lean practitioner on how to be a coach for the Lean facilitators. The Lean consultant should be working to make the Lean practitioners, the Lean champion, and the Lean facilitators self-sustaining. It may take many months, or a few years, but the measure of success of the Lean consultant will be to ensure that they have properly worked themselves out of a job.

# Part II

# Understanding the
# Space of Trust

# 5

## The Space of Trust Explained

*"It's a terrible thing to look over your shoulder when you are trying to lead and find nobody there."*

**Franklin Delano Roosevelt**[1]
*32nd President of the United States*

Without trust, you aren't going anywhere in your journey—you will be stopped before you ever get started. I found that recognizing and assessing the state of the trust relationships between senior leadership and the staff was extremely important for me as the organization's Lean champion. When I previously described the concept of the Three Spaces model, I referred to the *Space of Trust* as the "universe" in which the organization operates.

If you, as the senior leader starting your transformational journey, are prepared to spend a lot of time focusing on changing the feel of your organizational "universe," that leadership environment, you will find that you are setting the foundation for your journey to be successful. Without the foundation of trust in place, you will not be able to set up the next smaller space inside of it, the *Space for Change*, and you certainly will be in a poor position to be able to facilitate any successful Lean improvement events.

To be able to start understanding some of the fundamentals required to develop this necessary *Space of Trust*, you will need to consider your own leadership mindset. In many cases, I believe that the failure of a Lean management program results from a failure at the senior leadership level, not with the people of the organization. Yet, I believe that it is rare that the senior leaders of these organizations recognize or acknowledge this fact. Rather, they blame others—often the staff, the very people whom they were trying to help.

In order for a Lean journey to be successful, you need to develop within your organization the trust environment between the staff and the senior leadership. But the hardest part of this task will be that, in many cases, the senior leaders will need to change themselves. As a senior leader who needed to change himself, I can attest that this is not easy. But it can be done. You will need to be prepared to reconsider how you view and handle leadership authority, how you view your people's motivations in the workplace, how you handle situations when your people make mistakes, and your role as a leader—is it a coach or a subject-matter expert? You may need to experience within yourself a reckoning about one, some, or all of these areas before you are able to successfully shape the *Space of Trust* within your organization.

But I need to state this again—the senior leader cannot delegate a Lean program to a lower-level leader and expect success. Without the senior leadership working actively to build trust with the staff and to also model the correct behaviours throughout the journey, the Lean program will never have a chance.

If you are a senior leader who is having problems trying to build an organizational culture of continuous improvement, you need to consider this: what if the problem is you?

# 6

---

## Trust Principle #1: Know That Culture Change Is the Goal, Not the Implementation of Lean Tools

*"Customers will never love a company until the employees love it first."*

**Simon Sinek**[1]
*leadership Author*

Over my career, I have met many people tasked or entrusted with the objective to start, or to further enhance, an organization's continuous improvement transformation. Given that I have also taken on this role myself, I believe that I can speak from some experience when I say that I've seen many people develop the wrong the leadership mindset. Many Lean or continuous improvement people focus on the implementation of the Lean toolkit across the company, when instead, I think they should instead be first focusing on the transformation of the organizational culture.

I think I know why Lean people like to focus on the toolkit—it's because these items can be easily taught and learned. You can develop training material, read books, take classes, hire consultants, and so on. When you do this, you can start to post metrics to demonstrate the progress of your continuous improvement transformation, such as the increasing number of people who have had Introduction to Lean training. Changing an organization's approach to leadership is very hard. And it's hard for continuous improvement experts to do anything without having executive leadership authority. A growing number of staff who have had Lean training does not mean that your organization is embracing the concepts to the core. I believe that only comes when you take a different approach, and that is to focus instead on embedding the proper leadership principles across the organization.

When you apply the toolkit across the ranks of a company, but the leadership doesn't properly follow a comprehensive set of principles for leadership, the tools won't seem to make sense in many cases. They won't make sense to the staff, and often they won't make sense to the management team. And worst of all, if the management team doesn't get it, they won't consistently apply the toolkit when you aren't around to force them. In other words, the transformation won't "stick."

I attribute this lack of "stickiness" in many organizational continuous improvement transformations to a shallow, but all-too-common focus on the Lean toolkit instead of the proper leadership principles. Using a leadership principle set as your strategic focus, I believe, allows you to create a proper foundation to begin to truly change the organizational culture over time.

People in the Lean community of practice often revere Toyota, and rightly so, as the birthplace of the Toyota Production System, which gave rise to the Lean movement. The interesting thing is that Toyota regularly allows outsiders to tour their production facilities. In the highly competitive manufacturing environment, why would they do this? They invited American car manufacturers to tour their shops years ago, knowing that the American companies might attempt to copy their practices, but that they would never duplicate their results.

> *"Many good American companies have respect for individuals and practice kaizen and other TPS {Toyota Production System} tools. But what is important is having all of the elements together as a system. It must be practiced every day in a very consistent manner–not in spurts–in a concrete way on the shop floor."*
>
> **Fujio Cho, President[2]**
> *Toyota Motor Corporation,*
> *The Toyota Way, 2004.*

Toyota, when questioned about why they can achieve results that others cannot, despite following some of the same practices, often provides the answer that they have everything working together in a "system." But this sometimes doesn't make sense to North Americans. We often look at systems as commodities that can be purchased, things that we can take training courses to understand, and things that we can copy and implement ourselves.

But when we do this, and we don't get the same performance as Toyota, we are confused. But what if we replace the word "system" with "culture"? To me, that is language that, in North America, better speaks to what we are trying to accomplish with a Lean transformation. At least in North

America, we can appreciate that you can't simply copy practices and change the culture. Usually, we recognize that culture change is difficult and that it takes significant effort.

If you are able to really change the culture, that is when the use of the tools will become second nature across the organization. The leadership and the staff will see the value in the Lean tools, and they will use them regularly when the needs arise.

If you adopt the approach that you initially are beginning the Lean management journey for the benefit of your team, then you need to realize that you are shaping a new culture. But before you can begin to do that as a leader, you need to know what the culture looks like in that future-vision state. Having worked in both the private sector industry and the public-sector environment, I believe that I can describe the picture of the culture for which you are striving with your team.

In the new culture, the leadership needs to be humble and be willing to admit their mistakes to their teams.

The new culture should have the senior leadership known among the front-line staff and the managers because they go out to the front lines and ask the staff about their successes, and their challenges. When the leadership goes out to meet with staff, they go out with the intent to listen and to talk about important corporate initiatives in plain language. And the staff are grateful when the leadership visits, not afraid.

You want a culture where the staff trusts the leadership, and the leadership believes in the staff. You want a culture where the staff feel that their opinions matter, that the leadership are willing to listen to the advice of the staff (those who do the front-line work every day) about how to make the business run better.

You want a culture where the leadership recognizes and uses their authority properly, and justly, but is prepared to fully and completely delegate some authority within prescribed boundaries to the staff so that those doing the work every day can make process improvements. And where the leadership thank the staff for their efforts and adopts those improvements into everyday practice.

You are trying to build a culture where the staff recognizes that it is safe to respectfully challenge the process and that the organization is always prepared to consider adopting better ways to do things. A culture where no one says, "Well, that's the way we've always done it," as a defense for the status quo.

The new culture should allow the staff to feel safe to experiment, with some structure, of course, on new approaches. Mistakes made in good faith are not punished by the leadership, but rather are looked at as opportunities for learning.

You want a culture where the leadership see themselves as coaches for their teams, instead of subject-matter experts. They recognize that their primary job is to help each of their people become better in their roles and to develop them for potential advancement within the organization.

The new culture should make it the norm for leaders to meet individually with each of their staff at least once a month, to talk about each staff member's successes, challenges, goals, and improvement areas. And the leaders should regularly give individual recognition, in private, to each staff member for a job well done.

The culture should be reflected in the organizational values, and these should be posted visibly throughout the offices. The leadership should be expected to model those values at all times in their behaviour. The leadership strive to achieve consistent congruence between their actions and words, to walk the talk at all times.

You want an organization where measurements and metrics are not feared but are just a normal part of assessing how each team is doing. The metrics are never used for performance management of individuals but instead are used to identify areas for improvement for teams. The desire for better and better data and measurements should become integral to the organization, and not seen as a one-time effort, but rather, as a part of the culture.

You are striving for a culture where the team leader gets together with their staff on a regular basis to talk about what is going on in the business, and to talk about improvement opportunities. Collaboration is real, and not just talk.

The new culture should include regular communication from the executive down to the front lines of the organization frequently. And the executive should trust the front-line staff with all relevant information unless there is a truly compelling reason not to share something in particular. Information should not be hoarded or controlled as a source of power by anyone in leadership.

You want a culture where the senior leadership develop a long-range strategic plan that is both a stretch, yet achievable, and this serves as an energizing "true-north" compass for the entire organization. The executives engage the other levels of leadership in developing the cascading levels of the strategic plan, so that every division, branch, and team has their own piece of the strategic plan that is meaningful to them, and it gives them a course heading that is aligned with everyone else in the corporation.

This list is not by any means exhaustive, but it should start to paint a picture for you of where you are trying to go when you are taking on a Lean transformation for your people. If you can bring about these elements of culture change, I assure you that you will start seeing the associated side benefits of improved efficiency, increased program effectiveness, better client service, and yes, cost savings.

It is my fervent belief that in order to change the culture of an organization, you first need to adopt the proper leadership principles across the management ranks, starting from the very top. When this

> *"Culture eats strategy for breakfast."*
> **Peter Drucker[3]**
> *Management Author.*

happens, Lean will truly become a part of the organization, because it will have become a part of the culture. The Lean tools will naturally come along for the ride.

# 7

## Trust Principle #2: Trust That Your People Are Not the Problem. You Are

*"Bad leaders believe that they have to project control at all times."*

**Simon Sinek**[1]
*leadership author*

## DO ANY OF THESE SOUND FAMILIAR?

If it wasn't for Jim over there, the project would have succeeded. He deliberately torpedoed the whole thing.

The work environment is poisonous. There are a bunch of bad apples mixed in with everyone—it spoils everything.

My plan was perfect, but my staff couldn't handle the execution. You know what they say, if you want something done right, you've got to do it yourself.

What do you mean John didn't follow the new procedure? He sat in the training session last Friday, and I've got his name on the sign-in sheet to prove it. That will be Exhibit A at the grievance hearing for his upcoming suspension. I'm going to nail him to the wall this time.

It seems like every time I turn around someone is trying to pull a fast one here. I'm almost afraid to take a vacation. The team would turn this place into the O-K Corral the minute I left the office.

Why do the staff keep complaining that they need to know everything? They should just worry about doing their jobs and let me worry about what information they need. Giving the staff extra information just causes distractions.

Why should we bother with information sessions for all of the staff? Half of the people don't need to know this stuff anyway to do their jobs anyway. Why does a clerk need to know about the finances? That's for directors to worry about.

If we give the staff too much information, we may as well just give it to the media. We can't trust these folks with this material.

The complaint to the CEO said that the staff did what? Seriously? Man, we just can't get our people to do anything right. Well, time for me to go in and show the staff who's boss.

Another methodology for business transformation? You've got to be kidding me! We are barely holding things together as it is. We don't have time to send anyone for Lean training, or any other type of training for these fly-by-night management fads. The Board might support this, but this looks like a waste of time to me.

## IF YOU ARE NOT A SENIOR LEADER

You have a big challenge in front of you. Well, maybe you do. It's possible that you work for a senior leader that already has the right mindset for this type of organizational transformation. But I think that these people are in somewhat short supply.

There are lots of well-intentioned leaders who do the wrong things and have the wrong perceptions of their team members. There are lots of other leaders who come close but make some crucial errors that create incongruence between their actions and the leadership principles necessary for a Lean transformation to succeed. The biggest challenge that you may have in front of you is trying to get your senior leader to change, if they are not already displaying the right leadership mindset.

That likely won't be easy. One of my executive directors once told me that very few executives have the necessary self-awareness to be conscious of their own behaviours that need modification. I think this person was right. I also suspect that this person was including me within the group of leaders referenced as "executives." This is the one characteristic that I am teaching myself every day as a leader, and I assure you that it's really hard.

What makes it even harder is that so many "management best practices" that are commonplace today are wrong for the environment necessary for a Lean transformation to be possible. This creates other problems, as you may feel that you are fighting uphill in many cases to take your team away from certain familiar and comfortable "best" practices.

The questions you have before are:

1. Will my senior leader see that they can be an impediment to the success of a Lean transformation?
2. Will my senior leader be willing to undergo the significant personal transformation of themselves?
3. Can my senior leader develop a sense of self-awareness so that they can make corrections to their behaviour as they undergo their own transformation?

The answer needs to be "yes" to all three. I suppose that "maybe" is okay too. It's better than nothing.

Unfortunately, here is a stark reality with which you must come to grips if you answer a definitive "no" to any of these questions: If you are supposed to advance the organization's Lean transformation without the dedicated support of the operations executive demonstrating and living the right leadership mindset, your chances of success are very slim. You will, in most cases, be pushing a rope. Despite your desire, perseverance, Lean expertise, over-and-above effort, and dedication, you cannot make true culture change happen without visible and sincere support and engagement from the top of the organization. What the big boss supports gets done, in many cases.

The converse statement is sadly true as well. If you are some functional leader at a lower rank, or not in charge of operations in your organization, you alone do not have the clout to push this transformation by yourself. If your operations executive isn't prepared to dedicate significant time, and it will be very significant, to this endeavour, then he or she isn't serious about it. And that will be quickly visible to the staff and other leaders, who are carefully watching from the sidelines to see how this new program is going to play out.

I think that you need to have a relationship with your executive so that you can have a frank discussion with them behind closed doors, where you can speak freely. But much of how effective this relationship will be is dependent on how willing the executive is to listen to critical feedback about themselves. That's a tough pill to swallow for many of them, unfortunately. What they are about to undertake will be really hard, and will take them away from a lot of the "real" work, as they perceive it. They may have to get out of their comfort zone, and they certainly will have to get out from being safely ensconced in their private offices and go out into the sites where the real work happens. They will need to talk to front-line staff and be prepared to listen to honest criticism about practices in the organization that they themselves may have put in place.

## IF YOU ARE THE SENIOR LEADER

The problem is you. I'm sorry if this offends you, but it's very likely to be true. If you are not already the problem, you will likely become the problem at some point as you start your organization down the path of your Lean journey. I completely believe that the major root cause of failure by organizations to successfully transition into a Lean Management approach is that the leadership failed to set the stage properly for the staff to be able to trust and believe that the organization was serious about the change. I should know—I've been the problem many times myself. I have simply been fortunate enough to have had my self-awareness reckoning to realize it.

It's very easy to be the problem, and there are lots of ways to be the problem. I think that leaders typically are quick to blame the staff for failures in a Lean transformation. I don't buy the excuse that staff are to blame. The staff only really have one way to fail, and that is if they are unwilling to participate after the leadership has done everything right.

But that's the really hard part. The leadership have to try to do everything right, in order to set the stage for success. Most leaders will find this too hard, or get distracted partway through the effort, and switch to the tried-and-true formula of blaming the staff, their people.

Because that's often what we have learned over years of practice. We might not say it out loud, but we leaders, like many people, are loathe to blame ourselves for failures of major initiatives. It's so much easier to blame the people for being unwilling to make the effort to go along with our brilliantly planned and executed changes. This is selfish and short-sighted of the leadership. And it happens all the time.

Instead, what you need to do is to keep reminding yourself that, in most cases, when an organization fails to make a positive change in culture, the root cause of the failure likely rests with the behaviours of the senior leadership. The tone that you set as the senior leader, the things that you say, and how you act every day, the things that you choose to tolerate or ignore, these all work together to help to define and to reinforce cultural norms for the workplace.

You are telling people what behaviours are celebrated, what behaviours are not accepted, and what behaviours are tolerated. Unfortunately, in many instances, we as senior leaders send the wrong messages in this regard.

Most people can appreciate the problems caused when a manager talks about leadership values like "integrity" and "respect," and then demonstrates contradictory values with his or her actions towards the staff. This kind of scenario is obvious, and many of us know that we would never commit such a crime of leadership ourselves. But we still do sometimes, and we don't even know it. But just as damaging, are the many other scenarios that play out that are less obvious. They still clip our wings as we try to drive forward towards a culture shift in our organizational transformation. These situations come up and they play out in full view of our staff who talk behind our backs about how we acted. The word of our lack of congruence spreads like wildfire throughout the ranks of the organization. Trust between leadership and the staff, if it ever existed to begin with, frays and fragments further, and the progress towards a cultural shift stalls.

When this happens, the senior leadership may be confused. In many cases, they will place the blame in the wrong places. Since they will assume as a foregone conclusion that they could not have been the problem, they will blame the people. They may not say it but believing it is bad enough. This will be felt and sensed by the staff, and this will compound the problem until any hope of embedding continuous improvement into the organizational culture is lost.

It is these other scenarios that hurt us, the less obvious ones that happen all-too-frequently. And as senior leaders, we handle them wrongly all the time. And then we wonder why the culture change is so hard.

We show our staff that we tolerate workplace bullying by being silent when we see it because we don't want to initiate a confrontation, and we think to ourselves that "we will address that later."

We show our staff that we aren't serious about performance management when we allow a low-performing employee to avoid work that they don't like or struggle with—to compound the problem, we may show contempt for fairness by giving the low performer's work to a high performer, punishing them for their efficiency.

We show that we expect our people to read our minds when we say we are delegating a duty to someone, and then complain about the results that they deliver to us.

We show that we don't trust our people when we centralize decision-making within routine operational issues to ourselves, instead of letting our people handle things well within their abilities.

We show that we are aren't serious about supporting a continuous improvement transformation in the organization when we criticize someone who makes a mistake using a new procedure that resulted from a staff-led and leadership-supported continuous improvement event.

In his book entitled *It's Your Ship*, by Captain D. Michael Abrashoff, in the third chapter called "Lead by Example," Abrashoff makes a leadership statement that has stuck with me:

*"It's funny how often the problem is you."*[2]

He advocates, after situations of not getting the desired outcomes, to look inward and to ask yourself three questions:

*"Did I clearly articulate the goals? Did I give people enough time and resources to accomplish the task? Did I give them enough training? I discovered that 90 percent of the time, I was at least as much a part of the problem as my people were."*[2]

There are so many possible ways for us as senior leaders to get things wrong, and in many cases, we don't even realize it. But the most important thing is that we need to accept that we are likely to be the prime source of problems when we are trying to lead a transformation. Understanding and accepting this principle is important to be able to do something about it and to minimize or eliminate the challenges. The longer we deny the truth of the principle, the longer we will delay success.

# 8

---

*Trust Principle #3: Believe That*
*Your People Come to Work Every*
*Day Wanting to Do a Good Job*

*"Trust means 'I know that you will not—deliberately or accidentally, consciously or unconsciously—take unfair advantage of me.' It means 'I can put my situation at the moment, my status and self-esteem in the group, our relationship, my job, my career, even my life in your hands with complete confidence.'"*

**Douglas McGregor**[1]
*management professor, MIT*

Years ago, when preparing for my Project Management Professional (PMP) exam, I had to learn some of the classic theories of organizational behaviour. One that really stuck with me was McGregor's Management Theories of X and Y.[2] First developed in 1957 by Douglas McGregor at the MIT Sloan School of Management for a conference, and further developed throughout the 1960s these theories outline two competing and opposing concepts about how management can view their staff.

Theory X takes a pessimistic view and suggests that management believes that the staff can't be trusted; that they are only motivated by their paycheques; that they will avoid responsibility and only complete the minimum amount of work they can get away with; and that they have to be pushed in order to perform.

Theory Y, on the other hand, suggests that management believes that the staff are internally motivated; that the staff actually do want to come to work every day to do a good job; that they actually desire independence in their jobs; that they really do want independence in their work; that they are motivated by self-fulfillment, not necessarily by their pay; and that they will drive themselves to perform, if the environment is properly staged.

In my study of these theories, it appeared to me that the theories assumed that a leader follows more closely Theory X or Theory Y depending on their personality. But I discovered my own finding about these theories when we started our own Lean journey at Manitoba Housing: it's not based on the predisposition of an individual, it's the choice of the individual.

It's a choice that a leader can make and since it's a choice, each leader can choose to believe something different than they did previously, even if they held the other viewpoint for years. Obviously, the longer someone believes a point of view, the harder it is to change that viewpoint. But it can be done, and this is one of the most important things that the leadership needs to get right if they want the organization to succeed in its Lean journey.

I think that the hardest part for many leaders is that they are trusting their own observations of their people when they have been choosing to believe Theory X for so many years. They have observed the cynical ones, the ones who seem to have given up, or those who have "retired on the job." They have seen the people who do try to skate by with the minimum effort that they think they can provide without getting in too much trouble.

They have seen the snarky, sarcastic, self-appointed grassroots leaders who seem to want to pick apart every possible initiative that might bring hope to the organization. They have seen the people who use sick time as a bonus form of vacation leave. Possibly, they have seen situations where there was wrong-doing by staff, and it maybe seemed like, if not for the manager, everyone would be taking advantage of the company. I get it.

I was there at one point. Maybe not to such as extreme point as some leaders, but I'm ashamed to admit that I have allowed myself to drift into believing Theory X at times in my career as a leader. I maybe wasn't in this space all the time, but when challenges with the staff came up, I sometimes fell backwards into the views encapsulated in Theory X. But that was a choice that I made. The problem was, I didn't realize at the time that I was making that choice.

Your choice, and the choices of the other leaders in your organization, will influence your people more than you realize. In fact, I believe that it can completely change the tone and morale and even the *feel* of your company. If you believe the Theory X model about your people, it will affect every single thing that you say and how you behave around your people. Every situation that arises, every interaction that you have with your staff, will be affected, as you look through the tint of the Theory X lens. You simply can't help telegraphing your choice of belief through your behaviours as a leader.

The hardest part for the leadership is to take that first step of making a choice to believe Theory Y, to make themselves look through a different lens, when so much evidence before them suggests that their people really look like the model of Theory X.

This viewpoint was reinforced when I began a very extensive regimen of making regular site visits to the various Manitoba Housing offices outside of headquarters in 2015. I had to be willing to look through the right lens. When I chose to do so, I was able to see a pattern of people who obviously did come to work every day wanting to do a good job. I saw people who were trying their best but were hampered by inefficient and problematic processes.

That, of course, was what our operations excellence (OpEx) program was intended to help fix. But first, the staff needed to trust—to believe—in the operations excellence program. What I was only starting to realize, was that before they could trust in the OpEx program, they first needed to trust in me as the executive leader. In order to do that, I needed to show the staff that I was worthy of trust. I needed to set the right working environment as the leader, and in order to do that, I needed to change myself.

I met people who told me about times in the past, when they had tried to follow the rules, but then got in trouble when someone didn't like the outcome. I saw people who had tried to innovate earlier in their jobs, only to be told to follow the protocols and to get in formation like everyone else.

I saw people who, in times of crisis, would always rise to the occasion and do the right things, often without being asked. When one of our major high-rise buildings experienced a catastrophic water-supply pipe rupture in the basement that flooded and shut down the building systems, the staff were already doing all the right things to take care of the tenants, without ever being instructed to do so, before I arrived on site that evening at 8 pm.

You may need to experience your own reckoning with this model of leadership and staff behaviour. Believe that your people are trying to do the right things and believe it to the point that you show it in your behaviour to your staff, and then be patient. You will start to view problems and mistakes made by the staff differently, as well. In fact, you will need to in order to apply this principle correctly. No matter what happens, however catastrophic, you need to remind yourself that in the vast majority of cases, each of your people come to work every day wanting to do a good job. Because it's true.

But even more importantly, is that you need to realize that your choice to believe in either Theory X or Theory Y will affect your behaviour as a leader, and as a result, this will define the working environment of your staff. And this will affect the behaviour of your people. In other words, your choice will influence the behaviour of your staff.

# 9

---

*Trust Principle #4: Understand That People Become a Product of Their Environment*

---

*"Once you understand that context matters, however, that specific and relatively small elements in the environment can serve as Tipping Points, that defeatism is turned upside down."*

**Malcolm Gladwell**[1]
*author*

I think that what helped me to adjust my viewpoint, and to have the realization about the importance of the choice of the leader of how to view their people, was when I read *The Tipping Point* by Malcolm Gladwell. The ironic thing is that I never read the book for this reason at all. *The Tipping Point* is a book written to describe a model by which social pandemics race through society. I actually decided to read the book hoping for relevant insights on how to increasingly get Lean to "take off" in Manitoba Housing.

However, in this book, Gladwell spends a significant amount of time talking about the vulnerability of people to their environments. Gladwell suggests, with a significant amount of evidence to back it up, that people are very strongly influenced by their environments.[2] *The Tipping Point* points to this concept, alongside the *Broken Windows Theory*.

This theory was first formally recognized in an article called "Broken Windows" in The *Atlantic Monthly* written in 1982 by James Q. Wilson and George L. Kelling.[3] The theory suggests that, in a neighbourhood, the outlook on society by those who live there is greatly affected by whether or not the area is allowed to fall into disrepair. Broken windows, graffiti, crumbling abandoned houses, for instance, that are not fixed, indicate a complacency and an acceptance with decay. If nobody cares to fix these windows, or the other items, then it looks like nobody cares about the neighbourhood.

In the more significant situations, the people of the area start to further damage the surroundings, as though testing the authorities for a corrective response. If no response is forthcoming, then the decay begins to accelerate. Crime follows, and the neighbourhood descends into becoming a "bad" part of town.

In 1969, a Stanford psychologist named Philip Zimbardo[4] ran a field study that was referenced by Wilson and Kelling in their article. In this field study, Zimbardo arranged to have two comparable cars with license plates removed and hoods raised parked and abandoned in two very different neighbourhoods—one in the Bronx, New York, and the second in Palo Alto, California. The car in the Bronx had its battery and radiator removed within ten minutes of its abandonment by a father, mother, and their young son. Within twenty-four hours, everything of value had been removed, and then the random destruction and vandalism began; contrary to inappropriate stereotypes common at the time, most of the adult vandals were well-dressed, apparently clean-cut whites.

However, the car parked in Palo Alto sat untouched for over a week. At that point, Zimbardo smashed part of the car with a sledgehammer. After that, clean-cut, respectable-looking passers-by joined in the destruction. Within hours, the car had been overturned and destroyed. But why?

The lessons from the Broken Windows Theory suggest that repairing the neighbourhood as soon as possible shows that someone cares. It shows that decay is not accepted or condoned. Gladwell suggests that it is because the Broken Windows Theory really does capture human behaviour. He makes an incredibly convincing case for just how strongly people are influenced by their environment.

I believe that this is true—people can become a product of their environment. I can assure you that most people in operations in a social housing organization have seen first-hand some evidence that substantiates the Broken Windows Theory. However, in any workplace, this axiom holds just as true as it does in neighbourhoods. The workplace environment can very strongly influence how the staff, the people, behave. And who is responsible for the workplace environment? The leadership is.

In Chapter 8, Trust Principle #3: Believe that your people come to work every day wanting to do a good job, I refer to McGregor's Management Theories of X and Y. The simple act of a senior leader choosing to believe in McGregor's Theory Y instead of Theory X can make a big difference in that workplace environment.

Think it through. If you choose to believe the aspects of Theory X, that your staff need to be closely watched because they can't be trusted, that they need to be micro-managed because they can't do anything right, that they only come to work because of their pay, and that they would try to get away with doing as little as possible if you weren't watching, then I think it's safe to say that this will significantly influence how you behave as a leader. It makes sense, doesn't it?

If this is what you believe, then you will show the staff in various ways that you don't trust them. You will monitor their work differently if you believe they won't do anything right. You will hand out assignments and evaluate the results differently. You will treat the people differently. And it all will have a very negative feel for the people. Make no mistake, they will feel it. They will sense right away that they aren't trusted. That you think they can't do anything right. That they are only in it for the money. That you don't expect them to go above the bare minimum requirements, and this realization will affect them profoundly.

For most people, they will quickly adopt the mindset that "if that's what the boss thinks, I may as well act that way." They may not actually have that conscious thought, but trust me that will be the result. The people will become the product of their environment. Usually, the response starts as defensive. When you know you aren't trusted by your boss, but you know he or she should be trusting you, it hurts, because it's not fair. So, you become defensive to protect yourself. Over time, the defensive responses can transform into apathy or cynicism. In more extreme cases, the responses can drift towards antagonistic or insubordinate behaviours.

*The lens through which you choose to look at your organization and the team has a profound impact on how you behave as a leader.*

The big challenge for the leadership is that this is a self-fulfilling prophecy. The leaders quickly observe the very behaviours that are described in Theory X. As a result, they evaluate their decision to believe Theory X as correct, and the cycle perpetuates. In *The Fifth Discipline*, author Peter Senge references work by psychologist Robert Merton, that describes this "self-fulfilling prophesy," known as the "Pygmalion effect." This is the tendency for people to perform according to the expectations placed upon them by those in authority.[5] The hardest part for a leader is to choose to believe in Theory Y instead, despite the recent observation of some Theory X behaviours.

When you choose to believe Theory Y, and you may need to force yourself at times to continue to believe it, it will significantly change how you behave as a leader. When you choose to believe that your people come to work every day to do a good job, you can't help but treat them differently. When you choose to believe that your people really do want more, not less, responsibility in their paycheques you will treat them differently. When you choose to believe that your people are fundamentally motivated by self-fulfillment, not their paycheques, you will treat them differently. When you choose to believe that, if given the chance, your people will truly drive themselves to perform without oppressive micromanagement, you will treat them differently. And this will set up a much more positive working environment. They will sense it quite quickly. The problem will be that, at first, they won't trust that it will last.

As the leader, you will have to hang on. You'll have to hold tough through these periods of doubt, when your new, but perhaps forced, perspective of your staff doesn't quite line up with the behaviour of the staff that you are observing right then. But if you can push through and continue with your confident belief in the truth of Theory Y, you will begin to change the environment of your organization to one in which a Lean journey is truly possible.

I developed the quotation referenced in the box in this chapter after I had my own reckoning with the truth that the outlook of the leader is a personal choice, and that the leader can be the one to change others by changing their choice. When I had my reckoning, I couldn't believe it at first. How could I possibly be the cause of some of the problems?

But once I realized the strong connection between workplace behaviour and the workplace environment and culture, it started to become clearer to me the significance of the leadership approach of the executive management. It is, after all, the senior leadership that is responsible for the majority of the elements of the workplace environment.

# 10

## Trust Principle #5: Believe That You Can Change

"For a man to conquer himself is the first and noblest of all victories."

**Attributed to Plato**
*ancient Greek philosopher*

I think one of the most readily accepted concepts is that people don't really change. I may have thought this at one point, but I don't anymore. Now, there are some aspects of yourself that can never change. For instance, there are certain inherent aptitudes or talents that certain people have that greatly exceed the capabilities of many other people. I will never play golf like Tiger Woods. I'll never be an NHL star. I'll never be a world chess champion. But I think that many aspects of an individual's personality are behaviours that are learned over time to form habits. The people around us witness our habits of behaviour and judge us based on their observations. But here is what I found to be a fundamentally important point that I needed to learn before we started our Lean transformation journey at Manitoba Housing: habits can be formed. And habits can be changed by training yourself.

I think that one of the best investments that someone can make in self-study is to read *The Seven Habits of Highly Effective People* by Stephen R. Covey.[1] This timeless classic is based on the premise that people can change themselves with

"We are what we repeatedly do. Excellence then is not an act, but a habit."

**Attributed to Aristotle**
*ancient Greek philosopher*

deliberate action, by training themselves with new behaviours through repetition, until these behaviours become habits.

Another excellent book I highly recommend reading before leading an organizational transformation is *The Speed of Trust* by Stephen M.R. Covey (the son of Stephen R. Covey).[2] Ideally, read both of these books in sequence, and along the way, try to truly internalize as much as you can, and be willing to be self-critical. Assess yourself and consider that you may need to change before you can expect your people to change. But the important point to remember is that you *can* change.

As you read *The Seven Habits*, you will be encouraged to create your own personal mission statement. As senior leaders, we all have been through mission statement exercises many times in the workplace, but rarely do we think of creating and writing down our own personal mission statement that outlines the principle of how we intend to live our life. This can be a difficult exercise for many people.

There are several cognitive biases that I believe can hold leaders back on their Lean journey. One such bias is the "confirmation bias." The confirmation bias is the tendency for people to search for, interpret, and even remember information in a manner that supports their pre-existing beliefs. This bias causes people to ignore information that contradicts their beliefs, and to shine a spotlight on a scrap of information that supports their beliefs. In many cases, I believe that as leaders, we need to be aware of our own negative tendencies and biases, so that we can properly reflect and challenge ourselves when required.

I think that we all suffer from a confirmation bias about many things, and likely one of these things is thinking that we have always been following highly respectable principles as individuals living our lives. However, reading the book *The Speed of Trust* may force you to take another look at what you had created for your own mission statement—and that's a good thing. *The Speed of Trust* talks about the principles required to achieve credibility, and suggest that you ask yourself, "Are you congruent?"

Look back at the mission statement that you have written during your study of *The Seven Habits*, and then ask yourself if those around you could tell that your personal mission statement was your *centre*, that these were the principles by which you are supposedly living your life. If you cannot honestly answer "yes," then accept the fact that you might not be clearly showing the principles to which you had pledged yourself to value. The issue though, is that this mismatch between your principles and your actions will, in the view of those around you, compromise your leadership integrity, and, as a consequence, their trust of you. So, dedicate yourself to changing your behaviours, to trying to internally reinforce new habits until they no longer require reinforcement.

The challenge with committing to making such a change in yourself is sustaining the effort when nobody yet has any reason to believe that anything is different about you. Since other people have seen months or years of your previous patterns of behaviour, they believe that they have you "figured out." Saying a few things differently than you usually do is not enough for people to sit up and take notice.

It takes weeks or months of consistent behaviour and words lining up with different principles before people start to think differently about you. It's completely fair from the viewpoint of the people around you. But it is really hard when you think you are trying to change something about yourself and it seems as though no one even notices the effort. Perseverance, however, will be eventually rewarded with the trust necessary to lead your people on the cultural transformation necessary to support innovation.

# 11

## Trust Principle #6: Free Yourself from the Need for External Validation

*"By centering our lives on timeless, unchanging principles, we create a fundamental paradigm of effective living. It is the center that puts all other centers in perspective."*

**Stephen R. Covey**[1]
*leadership author*

As someone often interested in science fiction, I have been a huge Star Wars fan since I was a very young child. I remember seeing the first Star Wars movie with my parents in 1977 at a drive-in theatre wearing my pajamas. I was excited when the original series was re-released decades later, and then when other movies were produced and added to the original trilogy. With the franchise currently owned by Disney®, there seems to be about one new Star Wars movie released each year—some are fantastic, some not so much, but I insist on seeing them all. The fun part for me is that the reignition of the franchise kicked off when my son was the same age that I was when the first Star Wars movie was released. He is just as big a fan as I am.

One of the lesser-known movies in the franchise that has grown to be a favourite of both me and my son is *Rogue One: A Star Wars Story*, which leads up to *Star Wars IV: A New Hope*, and explains how the rebels gained access to the original plans for the Death Star. In this movie, we are introduced to characters known as the Guardians of the Whills, followers of the Jedi religion, who were entrusted to protect an ancient temple and its treasures and secrets. One of these Guardians, named Chirrut Imwe, although blind, demonstrates his other keen senses as a skilled combat warrior. While trapped in prison, Chirrut listens to Captain Cassian

Andor, a Rebel Alliance intelligence office, and senses the tremendous emotional pain that he is carrying. The observation of Chirrut Imwe to Captain Andor is one of the most insightful quotations that I have heard about self-constructed mental barriers:

> *"There is more than one sort of prison, Captain. I sense that you carry yours wherever you go."*[2]

Many people require constant external validation in order to sustain their sense of self-worth. Many leaders need to constantly be seen as the ones with the answers for the people on their teams, to be seen as the subject-matter experts. Sometimes, they need to be told regularly that they are good at their jobs. If they don't receive this validation frequently, they can start to question their own abilities, and descend into self-doubt.

When you as a senior leader are about to embark on leading your organization towards a culture of Lean management, you should consider attempting to sever yourself from your own need for external validation. This will take some serious introspection as you may need to learn some things about yourself which you may not have realized for your entire life. Are you a leader that believes that your value comes from having all of the answers? Or do you believe that your role is to coach those on your team towards the answers?

Do you have the need for constant validation from others that you are doing a good job? Be warned then, the journey towards organizational transformation will be fraught with challenges, and there will be push-back and complaints. You, your credibility, and your morals will all be questioned.

In the beginning, you won't hear about how great a job you are doing. In fact, you may hear the opposite. As the senior leader driving this change, you need to be prepared to stand fast despite the lack of external validation. You will need to obtain your validation from leading according to sound principles, and that validation will have to come from within, not from external sources.

The lesson from *The Seven Habits of Highly Successful People* found in Habit 2—Begin with The End in Mind can help you to focus on keeping your principles as your centre of focus.[3] It suggests that you free yourself from other distracting centres of validation. You may have to force yourself to stop worrying about what others think of you, and simply continue leading according to sound leadership principles.

Stop allowing your sense of self-worth to fluctuate, based on your perceptions of other people's reactions to what you say and do. But be warned, this habit will be difficult to form, and it will take a tremendous amount of stamina, depending if you have previously struggled with the need for external validation.

The biggest obstacle you may have to overcome if you are trying to make this sort of change with yourself may be chemical addiction. In his book *Leaders Eat Last*, Simon Sinek links brain chemistry to different types of behaviours in order to illustrate how certain types of behaviours can manifest in programmed physiological reactions in humans.[4]

Dopamine, for instance, is the brain chemical that is released when we accomplish a challenging goal, and dopamine makes you feel good. But dopamine is also very addictive. Drug addictions often are reinforced due to the brain's dependency on the associated dopamine release.

But what if, for years, your brain has been receiving dopamine rewards when you receive external validation for your accomplishments? Wouldn't this pattern your physiology into making it very difficult for you to change your behaviour in this regard? Yes, it would. But changing your behaviour is still possible.

The positive side of such a transformation is releasing yourself from dependency on forces outside of your control. Another benefit is a reduction in the negative effects of constant releases of cortisol; the chemical discharged when your body senses a threat, the fight-or-flight response. Stressful situations, such as deep worry about what others think about you, release cortisol. But continual exposure to this chemical, such as when we live in a perpetual state of anxiety, can cause us physiological harm.

Gradually, as you slowly begin to make this habit a part of your life, you should find yourself feeling freer—free from the up-and-down changes of moods that you used to ride like a roller-coaster. It is exhausting to have your sense of personal self-worth bouncing around out of your control just because you tie it to other people and your perceived (and likely incorrect) interpretations of what they think of you at that moment in time.

When you know that you are acting as a leader in complete alignment (as close as possible anyway) with solid principles, then you can be confident that you are on the right path. When a senior leader or a superior gets upset with you about some issue, you can deal with it. You are still doing the right things, and that makes you a good leader.

You can stop fussing and worrying about jockeying for position, the gamesmanship, and the rivalries that can sometimes exist at the senior level in any organization. When your team succeeds in a way that no other team can, it's impossible for you not to be recognized as a great leader. When you follow the right leadership principles, you don't need to advocate for yourself. Advocate for your team, though. Given enough time, your team and others will advocate for you as a leader.

That doesn't mean that you lay down on the road and let yourself get run over by someone who is trying to take unfair advantage of a situation. Of course not. Stand up for yourself and for your team. But you can allow yourself to let go of the *worry* and the *fear* about what other individuals think about you when one little thing or another goes wrong.

To make your organizational transformation easier, focus on the importance of following sound leadership principles, and remember that you really don't need day-to-day validation from someone above you to know that you are moving your organization in a positive direction forward. You will start to see it yourself in your people, and that is all that you really need. But first, you may need to free yourself from your own prison.

# 12

---

*Trust Principle #7: Trust That*
*Better Client Service Results from*
*Treating Your People Well*

---

"*Your people come first, and if you treat them right, they'll treat the customers right.*"

**Attributed to Herb Kelleher**
*co-founder of Southwest Airlines*

Several books on leadership, including *Start with WHY*, by Simon Sinek, refer to the story of the origins of Southwest Airlines, and one of the founders, Herb Kelleher.[1] One of the most interesting elements that I find about the Southwest story is that the company focuses on its employees before its customers, yet Southwest was known for being one of the best customer service companies in the United States.

The leadership of Southwest Airlines believed that if you focus on your employees, they will focus on your customers. I think that this relationship results from the employee engagement that comes from working for a company that the staff trust to look out for them. As Simon Sinek says in *Start with WHY*:

"*The trust between the management and the employees, not dogma, is what produces the great customer service.*"[2]

I worked in the aviation sector for fifteen years, and I believe that this type of deliberate approach to focus on employees before customers would be viewed as heresy by many companies in that industry. But it does seem to work. The problem, for the leadership teams of many

> "The way management treats associates is exactly how the associates will treat the customers."
>
> **Sam Walton**[3]
> *founder of Walmart.*

aviation companies, is that they must *trust* that good customer service will be a resultant effect from focusing their efforts somewhere else, and that can be very difficult. Perhaps this lack of trust in the staff might stem from the leadership viewing their people through the wrong lens.

It can be hard to trust that good client service will come after you invest your efforts energy on employee engagement, especially when, as a leader you might occasionally see staff demonstrating some of the wrong behaviours towards clients or customers. But what if your senior leadership behaviours might actually be leading to the poor client service behaviours about which you are so concerned? If people become a product of their environments, maybe the staff treatment of clients is a direct reflection of how they feel that they are treated in the organization.

Perhaps I was fortunate with the operations team that I inherited at Manitoba Housing. When I went out to the various site offices across the province, I found lots of people who were working hard to provide great client service. I realized that they didn't need the CEO or me to tell them to take good care of the clients because they were already doing it.

But I realized that what they really did need was to truly believe that the organization cared about them, and their ideas for improvements. Therefore, we took efforts to be clearly transparent in our approach (in keeping with the desire for congruence) and to be up-front that we were also undertaking the OpEx journey to build staff engagement. We believed that if we got the staff engagement right, by building trust between the leadership and the staff, the client service would only further improve. And I think that is exactly what we saw happen. Herb Kelleher was right.

# 13

## Trust Principle #8: Remember That Authority Matters

*"To punish me for my contempt of authority, Fate has made me an authority myself."*

**Albert Einstein[1]**
*theoretical physicist*

Many times, you seem to encounter the popular mantra in the workplace that leaders shouldn't need authority to get things done—the corollary being that they should use their charm to coax people into wanting to follow them. While being a nice person is certainly going to help win people over, pretending that authority isn't required will, in fact, make your job as a leader more difficult. The challenge, therefore, is to find that balance of exercising authority without being an authoritarian jerk. Unfortunately, for many of us leaders, this is a lot harder than it sounds.

We've all met the authoritarian jerks, of course. Those leaders who centralize every decision and action to themselves, even when it isn't necessary, even when it actually makes things visibly worse, in order to make sure that everyone knows that they are the ones in charge. Sometimes, we've accidentally behaved like them ourselves from time to time.

There are the people who wield power through intimidation. These people use their position in the organization to outright bully people into compliance. Then they discipline the people that defiantly stand up to them, despite the common knowledge that Western culture celebrates the commoner that stands up to oppressive tyranny, often becoming a leader of the revolution in the process.

Then there are the workplace psychopaths or sociopaths. These are the most insidious. These people crave power and seek advancement in the organization by any means necessary. In some cases, they are able to advance to the executive level by ensuring that they always tell the people above them what they want to hear. They can be identified by the tendency to view other people simply as obstacles or pawns to be manipulated by nefarious means in order to achieve their own personal goals. While these people can achieve business objectives, they often do so by leaving a trail of human wreckage behind them. The senior executives above a workplace psychopath may look no farther than the fact that the business objectives were achieved that quarter. But make no mistake, this type of leadership does not motivate staff, except to motivate them to move somewhere else for employment.

When so many of us have seen these stereotypical bad leaders before, it's no wonder that some new leaders are afraid to actually use their authority at all. Even worse, these new leaders want to show how different they are from the authoritarian jerks, so instead, many of them make some sort of unconscious pledge to themselves that they will only lead by being a nice person. They promise to themselves that they will lead without any reference or acknowledgement of authority.

I'm warning you right now—you will set yourself up for nothing but problems when you are trying to take the organization on a Lean transformational journey if you don't recognize the importance of authority. You, and your leadership team, need to know how to fairly, and in a respectful way, exercise your authority with your staff.

You are about to go down a transformational path of delegating authority to front-line staff to make changes to certain processes of your organization. This authority rests typically with the senior leadership. If you don't respect and acknowledge this authority, then how can you place boundaries on the delegation?

You don't want to give the message to the staff to just do whatever they want instead of following established processes, right? Of course not. That would invite chaos. I can assure you that we never took this approach in Manitoba Housing. Having Lean process improvements take place in a controlled manner is important, especially in the early stages of the Lean journey.

I don't think that we have to be ashamed to start talking about having authority as leaders. Our staff get it, perhaps more than we do as leaders. That's why the leader is often never told when their plans or ideas are stupid. The staff are afraid of the leader's authority. That's not to say that I would want staff blurting out "hey, your idea is stupid!" in a group setting. But I would want a direct-report leader to take me aside and have a respectful discussion with me privately if he or she had a concern with an approach I was taking. I suppose they could respectfully tell me that my idea was stupid.

The biggest challenge, of course, is that you, as the leader, need to be willing to listen to this feedback and be prepared to change your approach if it is truly necessary. I think the sooner that we, as leaders, stop the charade that authority doesn't exist, the better off we are, and the more honest and more sincere we will look to our staff.

When, as senior leaders, we say things like: "We are all equals here," or "Let's check our titles at the door," or, "For this exercise, don't think of me as the executive," I don't think many of the staff believe it at all. It makes us sound disingenuous. A few staff might also elect to take advantage of the invitation and ingratiate themselves with you hoping to use that relationship later.

When we pretend that we don't actually need authority, it certainly doesn't make personnel performance management any easier. I think it can cause some performance problems and amplify others. When true employee performance or behaviour problems surface, you will be fighting uphill when you attempt to bring things under control.

First, you tell everyone who will listen that authority isn't important to you, but then later you are trying to impose authority to discipline an employee who is unwilling to comply with direction. This incongruence will almost certainly work against you later.

In his training program, "The Workplace Leader," leadership consultant Linton Sellen has a great phrase about management authority within an organization. It speaks to the dichotomy that exists where so many leaders attempt to pretend that they don't need or use authority to get things done by their staff:

*"Authority only matters when we disagree."*[2]

I cannot contradict this statement at all. And since as a leader, you will eventually disagree with your staff on certain things, then it is more effective to be continually acknowledging the necessity and the importance of authority within the organization. This way, when you need to handle the disagreement, there is consistency in your approach.

# 14

## Trust Principle #9: Delegate Properly

*"Never tell people* how *to do things. Tell them* what *to do and they will surprise you with their ingenuity."*

**George S. Patton**[1]
*U.S. Army General*

I need to reference Linton Sellen, from The Workplace Leader, another time in this part of the book.[2] He has a fantastic and simple test to identify whether or not a leader is truly delegating their authority to an employee (or manager) below them. The test consists of two questions that the employee should ask the leader. The answer needs to be "yes" to each question in order for the situation to actually be a "true" delegation of authority:

1. Do I need to check back with you first?
2. Are you going to over-rule me if you disagree with me?

I think most leaders would be taken aback by these questions the first time they are asked. Unfortunately, in many cases, the leaders think that they can answer "no" to one or both questions and still be delegating authority to their employee. In these instances, however, all the leader is doing is delegating future frustration and disappointment to the employee. The employee will invest a lot of time and energy into developing something, only to have it shot down by the leader.

The employee will grumble inwardly (or possible outwardly) that he or she can't read minds, and that the leader should have just told them the "right" way to complete the task in the first place. So often as leaders we think we are being such great and benevolent entities by giving "authority" to our staff, like some sort of treat, only to reverse everything when they don't deliver something exactly the way that we wanted it done, even though we neglected to clarify our expectations up-front. How unfair.

I think the lesson for leaders to take away from this is that the standard for true delegation of authority is actually much higher than we often think. And we need to be cognizant of this. Therefore, it is better for leaders to be much more selective of delegating authority than they had been before learning of this standard.

However, when they do delegate their authority, leaders need to really mean it. And that means being prepared to accept the product that comes out of the delegation exercise. Typically, that means that the leader needs to prepare boundaries and expectations in advance of delegation, so that the "must-haves" and the "do not touch areas" are understood by everyone at the beginning, before anyone invests any effort.

One of the classic Lean texts, *The Machine That Changed the World*, written by James Womack, Daniel Jones, and Daniel Roos in 1990, is a deep study in the evolution of the auto industry from its origins of craft production, through the introduction of Henry Ford's mass production systems, and then into the introduction of Lean in Japan and then into the rest of the world. This fantastic text includes extensive examination of data and interviews with people from numerous auto manufacturing facilities around the world, and draws conclusions based on careful analysis. As the authors state in Chapter 4:

> *"Our study of plants trying to adopt Lean production reveal that workers only respond when there exists some sense of reciprocal obligation, a sense that management actually values skilled workers, will make sacrifices to retain them, and is willing to delegate responsibility to the team."*[3]

What a powerful statement, and it completely aligns with my own observations from trying to start up Lean from scratch in a public-sector organization. When I think about the message of this quotation, I think that it is another way of saying that workers only respond when there is trust between the leadership and the staff.

I can't overstate enough how important it is to understand the principles of delegation of authority when you are about to start a Lean transformation. You are going to be, in each *kaizen* or continuous improvement event, conducting an exercise of delegation of authority to the staff to change a process or procedure of how work gets done in the organization. When you do that, the staff need to feel free and clear to innovate within carefully defined boundaries that are identified and understood by everyone before they get started.

As the executive, you absolutely must not walk in at the conclusion of one of these Lean events and over-rule what they have developed as a revision to the process or procedure. You will frustrate and disappoint everyone on the *kaizen* team. You will be immediately undermining the Lean culture that you are trying to foster.

Word of your over-ruling action will spread quickly through the organization, and few people will trust in the Lean program. People will have quickly learned that, although you say you want them to innovate, you also expect them to be fortune-tellers and to come up with your preferred but unspoken answer or you will stop everything in its tracks.

However, with careful planning and forethought, you can prevent these missteps, and plan out *kaizen* events where the staff truly are empowered to fix the process within defined boundaries. When the executive comes in for the final presentation, the staff really will feel empowered when that leader says "Great job, folks! Now let's adopt what you have come up with. Thanks for the hard work!"

Typically, when the *kaizen* event is successful, you also get the benefit of the involved staff going back to their work areas afterwards and telling their colleagues that it was a great experience. This is crucial to continue to build trust in the program at the staff level. I will discuss this point about shaping *kaizen* events for success more in *The Space for Continuous Improvement*.

# 15

## Trust Principle #10: Remember That Management Still Has Rights

*"There is a difference between giving directions and giving direction."*

**Simon Sinek**[1]
*leadership author*

I think it's important to go back to the beginning, to the source of management authority over staff in an organization. Linton Sellen, in *The Workplace Leader*, does a great job of explaining the boundaries and freedom of leadership authority in an organization.[2] An important concept to remember is what a person is agreeing to when they sign an employment contract. They are, essentially, agreeing to surrender their free will to the leadership hierarchy of the organization, in exchange for pay.

There are checks on this sort of power, of course. In Canada and the United States, employers are not allowed to direct their employees to do anything that is:

1. Illegal;
2. Immoral or unethical;
3. Abusive; or
4. Dangerous.

Beyond that, the employer can technically ask the employee to do anything associated with the business that the employee is able or qualified to do. It's the concept of *residual rights*, and in most cases, those rights favour the employer. Usually, the only thing that limits the employer's authority to direct staff, beyond the four exemptions listed above, are those limitations included within the employment contract, and/or within a collective bargaining agreement.

These contracts or agreements are written not to give additional rights to management, but they instead seek to limit the already comprehensive rights of management. If you closely read a union collective bargaining agreement, it may include a clause at the beginning about "Management Rights," which typically acknowledges that management retains all rights not limited by the agreement. The caveat is that management must exercise their residual rights in a manner that would be considered reasonable and consistent with the agreement.

I'll bet that many leaders either don't know this, or they have forgotten it. I think it's really important to remember this, especially when, as a leader, you are challenged by an unwilling staff member when you give direction. I think it's important to caveat this statement with my belief that truly unwilling people are a very small minority. Some people who appear this way on the outset can change their perspective when they see the organization and the leadership going down a transformational path of culture change based on sincerity and sound principles.

But in any organization, you will have a very small number of people who truly are coming to work each day with value that are incredibly different from the vast majority of the hard-working staff. When your organizational size is beyond a few hundred people, statistically, you are certain to have several of these problem employees. But there are ways to deal with these people fairly, using the authority you naturally do have as a leader.

I have found that simply realizing how much authority I had in my role resulted in fundamentally increasing my own confidence in directing staff. To be clear, that didn't mean that I turned into an authoritarian jerk, or that I disciplined people for no reason. It also didn't mean that I did not seek the advice of human resources or labour relations consultants when personnel problems came up—in fact, I always have been quick to seek advice. But now I take this advice while carefully remembering that I am the employing authority for my division.

I see lots of leaders that seem to think that changing the job descriptions is what you need to do to effect change in the organization. If your organization decides that it now values organizational change management, or Lean, or other things, sometimes the leaders decide that you need to change the job descriptions to include statements about these things. Only then, they believe, can you direct staff to make these things part of their duties. I disagree.

I think that as leaders we often become far to hung-up on the importance of job descriptions, and we think that they limit our authority as leaders to direct staff. That's not the point of a job description. A job description can't possibly encompass every single thing that an employee might be asked to do. Therefore, it should not be considered a task listing for a particular job. But that's often what we see develop, especially in the public sector. In some cases, if the relationship that Management has with the union is combative, it can drive the problem to be worse. In some cases, the job descriptions can become entangled in the horribly restrictive practice of job control by the union.

In the classic book *The Machine That Changed the World* by James Womack, Daniel Jones, and Daniel Roos, the authors describe the challenges that had to be overcome by Toyota and General Motors in the mid-1980s in order to set up their joint venture factory in Fremont, California, known as the New United Motor Manufacturing Inc., or NUMMI. The idea was to set up a factory in the United States with GM that made no compromises on Lean practices. The senior managers were from Toyota, and they worked to implement a precise replication of the Toyota Production System. But the vast majority of the staff, about eighty percent, were former employees of the defunct GM factory at Fremont. In order to obtain the proper flexibility required for innovation through Lean, some changes to the previous labour agreements would be necessary. This required the significant cooperation from the United Automobile Workers union. As Womack, Jones and Roos state:

> "However, in place of the usual union contract with thousands of pages of fine print defining narrow job categories and other job-control issues, the NUMMI contract provided for only two categories of workers—assemblers and technicians. The union agreed as well that all its members should work in small teams to get the job done with the least effort and highest quality."[3]

By 1987, the NUMMI factory was matching a Japanese Toyota factory for quality and nearly matching it for productivity, which would have been unthinkable at the previous Fremont GM plant.

If you aren't in the position of having highly restrictive collective agreements where management has conceded to binding job-control arrangements, don't allow yourself to believe that you have to manage as though you are in that situation. We had a great end result in Manitoba Housing from changing most job descriptions in the organization from being eight-page-or-longer to-do task lists to being short, comprehensive documents based on the specific accountabilities for which the job was responsible, and the know-how required to do the job. These new job descriptions became on average about two-and-a-half pages long. That's a lot of change for a lot of people. This significant degree of change was initially met with a lot of skepticism, but in most cases, the concerns faded over a few months.

Here's the interesting thing that I realized looking back at this job description initiative later: It was an important part of the culture shift, and it helped to reinforce the importance of management authority. But I can only say that in hindsight. We only went through this initiative because we were moving towards a new job classification system, not because we wanted to change the perception of authority at Manitoba Housing. But it definitely was a useful side effect of the exercise.

Less and less did we hear "That's not in my job description," because no actual tasks were included in the job descriptions. In fact, from my perspective, the job descriptions started being referenced less and less in the day-to-day management of the staff. I think this started to become a part of the culture shift with the leadership—we were also pushing the leaders more and more to engage their staff with one-on-one discussions on a regular basis. We were advocating from the executive level that real performance management should take place every day—real performance management that addressed both the positive and the constructive types of feedback.

I hope you don't think that I'm telling you that changing the job description format alone will start a change of morale in your organization. Not at all. This book is more about the culture change that needs to start with a change to the proper leadership mindset. If that mindset change has started, then there will be a benefit to facilitating a change apart from needing each task to be written into a job description before the employee will do it. It will help to bring consistency into the way authority is handled at the organization.

I need to point out that the ninety-five re-written job descriptions were not changed again later when Manitoba Housing launched our operations excellence Lean program. We did not add the phrasing "supports operations excellence program and initiatives," or anything like this in any key accountabilities. The thing I'm somewhat embarrassed to admit is that we didn't even think about it and then have a deliberate decision and debate about it. For whatever reason, it just never came up.

But what I learned through this inaction, with the benefit of hindsight, was that we didn't need to. We didn't need to add specific phrasing to get people on board with our operations excellence program. They did it because we directed them to do so. Now, to be fair, this program had a lot of benefits for the staff in the form of empowerment and engagement, and real involvement in fixing processes that were broken. So, once we got going with OpEx, it was a pretty attractive thing for our staff and authority didn't really need to be wielded.

I am glad that we simplified our job descriptions. It was yet one more step on the complex culture transformation journey for Manitoba Housing. It helped our leadership focus, in some cases, on the real behavioural aspects of staff performance management, without the distractions of task-list job descriptions. But in order for this to happen, it needed to take place as part of a larger leadership culture overhaul within the corporation. We didn't plan it that way, so maybe we were lucky on the timing. But at any rate, it worked, and I would do it again if I could go back in time.

At one point in my career, I had a leader working for me who asked a subordinate if he might take on some additional duties so that the leader could more fairly balance the workload across the entire team. The employee answered, quite simply: "No, thank you." The leader was flabbergasted and came to me for advice on how to handle this situation.

I explained to the leader that sometimes you don't ask the employee; you tell the employee. There's no need to be a jerk about it, of course, but a better approach would be to say to that staff member: "I need your help with taking on some additional duties so that I can balance the workload across the team. Please let me know if this creates any problems with your current duties." A subtle but powerful difference.

In short, remember that management still has rights. You are only harming yourself as a leader if you forget this. Respect that you have authority, given your role in the hierarchy, and use that authority carefully and justly, in a principled manner, but without shame. When it is time to delegate authority to those at lower levels within the organizational hierarchy, do it consciously and with careful planning about boundaries.

# 16

## Trust Principle #11: Always Act with Respect for People

*"First we build people, then we build cars."*

**Attributed to Fujio Cho**
*former Chairman, Toyota Motor Company*

When I was completing my "Lean Black Belt" certification training program, one of the four modules took place in Japan. We were given the amazing opportunity to tour such state-of-the-art factories as Nissan, Mitsubishi, Yamaha, and Toyota. In these factories, we of course saw incredible technology and automation, all working together seamlessly and with symphonic precision. And yet, what caught my attention the most was that, despite the advanced technology, which might appear to be designed to reduce reliance on humans, a common theme we heard on the tours was about the corporate value of "respect for people."

In the book *The Toyota Way to Lean Leadership*, Jeffrey Liker and Gary Convis highlight the Toyota leadership *True-North Values:*[1]

1. Challenge;
2. *Kaizen* Mind;
3. Go and See;
4. Teamwork; and
5. Respect for Humanity.

The Toyota view of Respect for Humanity is quite broad in scope. It includes respect for the community, employees, customers, all business partners, and a "sincere desire to contribute to society through providing the best possible goods and services."

"When senior executives from Japan came to factories in the United States that were operating well below capacity, their first question was not about profitability, but rather 'How is the morale of the team members?'"

**Jeffrey Liker and Gary Convis[2]**
*The Toyota Way to Lean Leadership.*

During the Toyota recall crisis of 2009, in the middle of the Great Recession, Liker and Convis point out that no regular (as opposed to temporary) team members were laid off. On the contrary, Toyota made enormous investments into the development of their people, even as production slowed during the recession, and then stopped with the unavailability of certain key parts due to the 2011 Japan earthquake.

When I was in Japan, I saw for myself the common practice of some Japanese citizens wearing surgical masks out in public. The purpose for this practice, we were informed, was not to protect the mask-wearer from getting sick, which is what I had ignorantly thought when I first saw the phenomenon.

In fact, it is very likely that the one wearing the surgical mask was feeling sick, and chose to wear the mask out of respect for those around them, in an attempt to contain their illness to themselves. My uninformed assumption was not only wrong but was the complete opposite of the truth. The actual basis behind the practice was yet another example of respect for people that I would see on my study tour in Japan—the visual imagery of dozens of white surgical masks, worn out of respect, visible in a sea of pedestrians provided for me a lesson I would not forget.

But back in North America, I see, in some organizations, that it feels as though respect for people has taken a back seat to the bottom line. In fact, I believe that following this Trust Principle, to always act with respect for people, will help any organization to obtain the maximum possible efficiency out of the staff.

When people feel that they can trust their leadership to manage with respect, it is the beginning of an agreement: The management builds an environment of trust within the organization, and the employees begin to develop true engagement with their job and the organization. When this happens, performance increases, and innovation begins across the company. But I need to make one point clear—you should never adopt this principle because you are looking for the reward. You should adopt this principle because it is simply the right this to do.

Another key important factor regarding the principle of acting always with respect for people is that it often serves as a constraint against some of the other leadership principles. For instance, while you need to remember that authority matters, it is crucial that while doing so, you must act with respect for people. You need to talk openly about problems, with a focus on solutions, but when you do so you must act with respect for people. You must remember to correct workplace behaviour problems quickly, but in the process of doing this you must act with respect for people.

It is important to note that respect for people does not extend to letting problem employees do whatever they want. It does not mean that you never provide discipline; it does mean that the discipline is provided out of respect for the principles and values of the organization and that the discipline is simply intended to change the behaviour, never to inflict punishment. Respect for people also means that you need to protect those around an employee who is displaying problem behaviour.

But, on the more positive side of this principle, respect for people should remind you of the importance of developing your people, seeing this as an investment, not a cost. Invest in developing your people because it is the right thing to do, and simply know that your investment will be well repaid in loyalty, dedication, and innovation from the staff.

Sometimes you hear managers question the wisdom of investing in the cost of training staff, who might leave the organization afterwards. I think that this mindset is misguided. It presumes a combative and adversarial relationship between the leadership and the staff—ironically, sometimes these same managers also would state that their people are their most valuable asset.

If you choose to look through a different lens and to truly see your people as your most valuable assets, why, then, wouldn't you invest in developing and training your people? Look at it another way: If you never invest in or develop your people because you are afraid that they might leave, why would you want to hang onto them? They would be low-performing, poorly-trained, and ill-equipped team members.

Remember that your goal is a change in culture, and that culture must include the people knowing that you respect them and value them. Think about it from the employee perspective: If the employees know that the leadership support their staff and invest in developing them to the best ability possible, they know they have a pretty good thing going at work. An employer who is known to care about their people quickly becomes known as a choice employer, and starts to attract high-performing people, who, because they can shop around for employment, look for an organization whose culture matches their needs. A supportive employer often fits the bill. And when the employee knows that they are employed by an organization whose leaders believes in and supports their people, they can lower their natural defenses, and begin to unleash their additional potential. This latent potential is the true prize of the organizational culture change for which you are driving.

In his book *Leaders Eat Last*, Simon Sinek talks about the importance of the leadership creating a Circle of Safety for the people within an organization.[3] Inside this circle, the employees do not need to fear competitiveness, backstabbing from colleagues trying to climb over each other to get ahead, or unprincipled leadership. Sinek suggests these unfortunately common characteristics of modern workplace cultures hold employees back from true engagement, as they are in a constant state of stress—always tuned to activate the natural "fight-or-flight" defensive mechanisms.

This constant state of tension will never allow staff to truly unleash their full potential—it's not that the people are holding back, it's that the workplace culture the leadership is fostering naturally produces the wrong environment for people to completely demonstrate their full range of talents. However, if you can change the culture to one where respect for people is a critical foundational principle, things will start to change.

Free of the fears caused by the old culture, the staff are able to lower their natural defensive tendencies, which consume so much energy, and truly focus and engage as a full team member of the organization. When this happens, the output potential of the people dramatically increases. The people can "switch on" the additional potential that they have to give because they feel it is safe to do so. When, as an employee, you are treated with respect, you often feel compelled to give as much as possible to your employer out of gratitude and loyalty.

# 17

## *Trust Principle #12: Correct Workplace Behaviour Problems Quickly*

*"There comes a time when silence is betrayal."*

**Martin Luther King, Jr[1]**
*baptist minister and civil rights activist*

In just about every workplace, you will find workplace behaviour problems. These types of problems can range from an employee making disrespectful comments to colleagues or supervisors, to someone continually having workplace attendance issues, to bullying behaviour, to theft or embezzlement, to failing to declare a known conflict of interest, to someone who is struggling with job performance and as a result, the remaining staff have to pick up additional work.

In some cases, the other staff may not know that anything improper is going on with the employee. But in many cases, I assure you, the other staff do know. And they are watching the leadership very carefully to see what they do about the problem. Their respect for the leadership is often contingent on seeing decisive action and a positive change in the situation.

However, many leaders struggle with handling these situations properly. In some cases, the leader lacks enough confidence to handle the confrontation that is required, so instead, they avoid it. Either poorly handling workplace behaviour problems, or avoiding handling them, will strongly negate the positive culture change towards which you are trying to move the organization. You are trying to build the *Space of Trust*, and if the staff can't trust the leaders to handle a tough situation with one of their colleagues, then it is hard to trust that the culture is really changing.

I think many times, the leaders who struggle with these situations are thinking primarily about the stress of the upcoming confrontation with the staff member with the behaviour problems. But in the process of focusing all their thoughts on that admittedly stressful first meeting, they are completely forgetting that the rest of the staff are watching them. Not that the staff expect that what happens in private performance management discussions is ever made public, but they are certainly watching and waiting for the offending behaviour to stop.

And if the manager is aware of the problem, and the problem is allowed to continue unabated, the staff will usually blame the leader for cowardly inaction. As a leader, what behaviour do you not forbid, you have condoned. This is horribly poisonous to the workplace culture that you are trying to build, and these types of negative workplace behaviour problems need to be met head-on and in a timely manner by every leader in their own area.

I think that inaction by a leader is rarely is caused by an unwillingness by the leader. Instead, I believe that the most common cause is a lack of experience in how to handle the situation. This lack of experience leads to a lack of confidence, which leads to a fear of the confrontation. The leader isn't sure how they will handle a performance management meeting if the employee starts to challenge them or their authority.

When the leader lacks experience and confidence, it is their supervisor's job to coach them through the situation, including role-playing with them if necessary. If you are the senior leader, and you need to hold your direct-report leader's hand through such a situation, then do it. Remember, the people are watching and waiting for the problem to be addressed—if nothing changes, they will rightly hold the leader, and you, accountable for the inaction. You will have violated the *Space of Trust*. Just remember not to undermine the authority of your direct-report leaders by directly involving yourself with their staff issues—we will discuss this issue in depth in Chapter 25, Trust Principle #20: Respect the leadership chain of command.

I once had a leader who reported to me express concern about having to terminate a staff member who reported to him. The employee frequently displayed disrespectful workplace behaviour, and this behaviour persisted despite numerous attempts at progressive coaching and discipline. He was concerned that, knowing that the termination was going to happen the next day, he was behaving falsely as a leader by acting in a friendly manner towards the employee, as though nothing bad was going to happen to the staff member. He felt two-faced.

This internal conflict was causing the leader quite a bit of distress, as he felt that he was not demonstrating "congruence" with the leadership principles that we knew we were to uphold. I pointed out to him that, rather, he was in complete congruence with our principles because he had shown respect for the employee with the numerous previous coaching and disciplinary events to attempt to get him to change his behaviour. Being friendly to any employee is showing respect for people.

He was also upholding the principle of respect for people, by protecting his people by removing the disrespectful behaviour from the workplace. I pointed out to him that for some time now, the rest of the staff had been suffering, and he was showing support for them by taking this unfortunate, but necessary action. After this discussion, his outlook completely changed as he realized that his self-doubt was misplaced, and his confidence returned.

And not long after the person left the organization, the sun started to shine again in the workplace where the clouds had previously been, due to the behaviour problems. You could see the results in the staff. The smiles started again and the positive energy began to quickly return. And the performance and work output of the team ramped up as well.

*Never value a problem employee's perceived subject matter expertise over the improvements to the workplace culture and the team morale that you will obtain when the person leaves.*

Although I hold that it is truly unfortunate when someone has to leave the organization, sometimes, a person just isn't the right fit. Work with them, coach them, provide progressive discipline as appropriate, but if that doesn't change the behaviour then you unfortunately may be in the position of having to remove them from the organization. Remember to always act with respect for people through the process, but don't forget the importance of respect for the other people who may be suffering.

This sounds simple in practice because usually we think that we will have the courage to decisively act to terminate a problem employee who is deserving of this ultimate step of discipline. But in real life, there are complicating factors. What happens when that employee is the person most knowledgeable about a key part of the business, or the person who delivers the most output for the team? And what if there is a freeze on hiring or backfilling vacant positions? Now the manager may begin to lose their courage to do the right thing. As a result, the problem employee remains, and the leadership will have taught the staff that sometimes, bad behaviour is condoned. And trust in the leadership becomes seriously fractured. Here is a very important lesson that I have learned along the way when it becomes clear that a person needs to be removed from the organization: Never value a problem employee's perceived subject-matter expertise over the improvements to the workplace culture and the team morale that you will obtain when the person leaves. Usually, we fear these situations much more than we need to. Others will step up to fill the knowledge gap, and the improved team performance and team spirit will usually be noticeable shortly after the person leaves the organization.

Even if a workplace behaviour problem is unknown to the staff, such as someone failing to declare in advance a conflict of interest where they are unfairly benefiting from their position, you need to be prepared to act to uphold the principles of your company. Good leadership, I think, involves being prepared to do the right thing all the time, even when the staff might not ever know. Trust requires principled action at all times.

# 18

---

## Trust Principle #13: Talk about Problems Openly, but Focus on Solutions

*"Identify your problems, but give your power and energy to solutions."*

**Attributed to Tony Robbins**
*author of Awaken the Giant Within*

Over the span of my career, I've seen many people that know about problems, such as inefficiency in the workplace, but they often think that it is inappropriate to talk about them in a team setting. Usually, I think, the reason for this reticence is the concern about making people uncomfortable. Unfortunately, the reality is that the problems rarely solve themselves.

Therefore, an important part of the new culture has to be a willingness to talk about problems openly. But, as discussed previously, this willingness needs to be constrained and tempered with respect for people. That's why the discussion around a problem has to be focused on solutions. This means that focusing on "who is to blame" for a problem is off-limits.

One of the common refrains you hear in Lean management is that you need to be "hard on processes, but soft on people." This is another way of representing the Trust Principle that you must believe that everyone comes to work every day wanting to do a good job. When you continually remind yourself of the truth of this principle, it forces you away from the traditional management instinct of looking to lay blame, and it allows you to perform more of a root-cause analysis on a possible process challenge, not a people challenge, that allowed the problem to occur.

This part of the culture change is critically important, and very hard to get in place, especially in public service. So, often we think that problems are due to issues with individuals, and, as a result, we avoid talking about them out of deference to the accepted practice of not speaking about individual performance problems in a public forum. But that's the problem—it is occasionally due to problems caused by an individual, but most often it is not.

Most often, the problems are caused by structural barriers that the staff cannot remove themselves: poor training, poor attempts at delegation by the leadership, poor communication from the leadership, poorly designed processes, or a host of other possible causes. But note that none of these causes are the fault of the staff; rather they are solely within the influence of the leadership to solve. The concepts of the sources of employee performance problems will be discussed in more detail in Chapter 21, Trust Principle #16: Discipline only the unwilling, but know that they are few.

Unfortunately, a lack of experience with structured problem-solving among leaders often results in looking no further than a superficial glance at a problem in order to lay blame on an individual and call that the root-cause analysis. But this is short-sighted and damaging to the culture that you are trying to build. In Chapter 71, CI Principle #12: Solve the right problem, I discuss the importance of structured problem-solving in more detail.

Be willing to look beyond the symptoms of a problem, dig deeper, and ask why it happened. And then look at your answer and challenge your answer by asking why again. And then ask why again and answer again. Do it again until you arrive at the real root cause of the problem. You will need to have a culture of openness to be able to have frank discussions with your staff and leadership around problems when everyone's first instinct is to clam up and hope that no one says anything. In most cases, people don't want to talk about problems because they don't feel safe. Your job will be to make it clear that it is safe to talk about problems.

When the staff see that the leadership can consistently lead fruitful discussions with the staff about problems without jumping to the assignment of blame, they will eventually join in and support the process. But first, they need to have trust that this is truly the new way of the culture and not a one-time event. And when they begin to trust and join in, your problem-solving abilities as an organization will make leaps and bounds forward. Many of the answers to the problems will be known by the people doing the work themselves. But they need to trust completely in the leadership. They need to believe that there is a Circle of Safety around them before that will happen. And when it does, you will be shocked at how different the organization feels.

Unfortunately, this kind of cultural change cannot happen overnight, so be prepared to be patient. It may take months, or even years, depending on your organizational evolutionary starting point. But first, you may need to remember one of the first principles of this part of the book—Chapter 7, Trust Principle #2: Trust that your people are not the problem. You are. It's likely true.

# 19

## Trust Principle #14: Give Balanced Performance Feedback Regularly

*"We all need people who will give us feedback. That's how we improve."*

**Bill Gates[1]**
*founder of Microsoft*

A very poor management approach is to never give someone regular performance feedback, positive or negative. This drives employees crazy, as they crave some sort of quality check of how they are doing. And most employees really want to know if they need to do something differently so they can work on making the improvement. Deny them the opportunity to know what they are doing well and what they need to improve, and many people will fill in the blanks themselves—and they will often get things very wrong.

Some people will be far too critical of themselves, and can even drive themselves into depression, thinking the worst about themselves when they are actually doing quite well in most regards. Others who have some performance challenges and need guidance are held back by the absence of feedback. The time they could have spent growing and developing is lost forever. A few, unfortunately, who need to make significant improvements to their own performance, overestimate their own abilities tremendously, and use the silence to validate their own beliefs that they are doing just fine.

For each of these types of people, the absence of timely performance feedback penalizes them and robs them of a possible path to improvement. It also causes completely avoidable pain, if they ever do get the truth about their performance deficiencies later on. Invariably, most of them will be (in their minds) asking their leader: "Why didn't you just tell me earlier?" This would be a tough question for the leader to answer.

Telling the employee that you didn't want to hurt his or her feelings will seem quite a shallow response when the employee is sitting in front of you emotionally distraught because of your inaction. In fact, you will be viewed as either lazy or cowardly by the employee. The exception, however, is the last category of people, who would dismiss constructive feedback that contradicts their narcissistic views of their own abilities.

A slightly less poor approach, but not by very much, is to surprise employees with something in a written annual performance review. For 199 working days of the year, they get no discussions around areas of strength or weakness from their manager, but on the 200th day, the manager hands them a written performance review containing some constructive feedback that they have never heard before.

I've heard it said that "Surprises are for birthdays and Christmas, not for the workplace," and I completely agree. You should never, ever, give someone a written performance review that contains anything that you haven't already discussed with them in person previously. In fact, I think that written performance reviews should be much less of a big deal than they are often made out to be, and instead should simply be viewed as a written summary of all of the other regular performance discussions held throughout the year. A few times I've heard about the results of employees getting surprised by something in a written performance review, and it is not uncommon for these situations to involve displays of anger and frustration.

I've had this happen with only a few of the performance reviews I've delivered over the years, and in these cases, it usually involved a poor choice of wording on my part that did *Surprises are for birthdays and Christmas, not for the workplace.* not adequately match the discussions that I had previously had with those employees. In most cases, though, I am careful to ask each employee during the performance review discussion if the assessment seems consistent with all of our previous one-on-one discussions, and very frequently I would be told: "Yes, there are no surprises here." But that takes lots of work throughout the year—it's worth it, though.

Another inadequate style of performance feedback is that which is either strongly-weighted to negative, or all negative. Note that the name of this principle is *give balanced performance feedback regularly*. Balance is important if the employee is going to listen and absorb what you are trying to tell them. It's highly unlikely that the employee does nothing at all that warrants positive recognition, and he or she knows it. I once heard of a situation where an employee received a performance review where he was told that his positive strength was "good attendance." He told me, with pain in his eyes, "I've worked here for over twenty-five years, and the organization thinks that the only thing that I can do well is to show up on time for work." This was heart-breaking to hear.

If you can't recognize what they are doing well, then you will have no credibility with them when you coach them on areas for improvement. They will believe that you don't know what they do because you don't pay attention to their work, and as such, your constructive feedback will be considered uninformed. Since all you do is complain, you are written off as an overly-negative manager.

Here is the challenge for some leaders: You have to get out of your office and really watch and observe your people in order to give them good feedback on their performance. That doesn't mean you assess their performance solely based on metrics or whether or not they hit numerical targets. Yes, it's important to drive the organization towards its strategic objectives, but behaviours are important. Looking at behaviours should play a huge part in how you assess the performance of your people.

If you are a leader of leaders, you should be coaching your people on the proper leadership principles and assessing their performance against those principles. In the *Space for Change*, I talk about this concept in more detail in Chapter 50, with Change Principle #17: Value how an objective is achieved as much as the achievement itself

Once I on took on the role of COO of Manitoba Housing, I quickly found that several leaders in operations were not having regular one-on-one meetings with their staff. Without these regular individual discussions between manager and employee, I reasoned, quality performance feedback to the staff would not be possible. As a result, I took the unusual step of issuing a written mandate to my leadership team: All leaders must meet with each direct report a minimum of once per month in a one-on-one format. My written mandate included the following requirements:

- Meetings must be behind closed doors, with only the employee and the manager;
- Meetings must take place a minimum of once per month—however, for newer employees, weekly might be more appropriate for a time;

- Tell the employee what they are doing well, and give some examples of what you have seen them do recently, and thank them for their hard work;
- Talk about what they need to improve and get them involved with an improvement plan—how to get there over time. Set targets or milestones, write them down together, and follow up together at subsequent meetings;
- Think through carefully what points you want to make, and prioritize a few for a meeting, as employees would be demoralized to hear a laundry list of twenty areas for improvement all at once;
- Ask them what they need from you, and be prepared to listen and make your own commitments to them;
- Ask them what you need to do differently; and
- Most importantly, thank them for their work.

I made it clear that I expected the meetings to get started immediately, and that I would be occasionally asking employees during my site visits about their one-on-one meetings with their managers starting in a couple of months. The leaders took the mandate seriously and after only a couple of weeks I did start to hear positive feedback—ironically, it was from the leadership group. You would think they might be grumpy about having "extra work," and perhaps some of them still were unhappy about my written mandate. But I think the majority of the leadership group started to realize that following the approach gave them a good framework for effective performance management, if they had none before.

I started to hear that they were learning things about their staff that they had never known before. Performance challenges now had a venue where they could be addressed while being balanced with positive feedback. The leadership realized that, in order to tell their staff what they are doing well, they need to get out of their offices and observe the staff actually doing their work and interacting with colleagues and clients.

When this cadence of meetings started, annual performance reviews could now truly be a simple written summary of a year's worth of one-on-one balanced performance feedback discussions. But the regular feedback to the staff was the true prize, and it was certainly a tremendous benefit to the employees. People really want to know how they are doing, and silence creates a vacuum that employees will fill with over-active imaginations. So, fill that vacuum—keep it balanced, frequent, and informed by observations.

# 20

## Trust Principle #15: Thank Your Staff Personally When They Do Something Great

*"Appreciation is a wonderful thing: It makes what is excellent in others belong to us as well."*

**Attributed to Voltaire**
*eighteenth century French philosopher*

While we were beginning to measure operational metrics in Manitoba Housing, starting in 2016, we also recognized that, as valued key stakeholders, we needed to ask our staff how the organization was doing. Although the Manitoba Government does some extensive employee surveying once every two years, we elected at Manitoba Housing to do some simple surveying of our own operations staff using low-cost online survey tools. At Housing, we had been using quick survey approaches like this for a little while already. However, our experience also taught us a hard-earned lesson—never ask for staff input on something if you aren't prepared to do things differently if they request it. If you survey the staff, you need to get the results communicated back to them and tell them what you are going to do about the results.

In January of 2016, we asked the operations staff ten employee-engagement questions, with the tenth question allowing open text responses. We had a pretty good response rate, of over one-third of the staff. We learned a few things—at that time, the areas for improvement that the staff raised to our attention were about leadership communication, and employee recognition.

In June of 2016, we went back to the operations staff with a follow-up survey of four questions, designed to dig deeper to find out what we could do differently about those leadership aspects. Again, we had a great response rate of over one-third of the staff. A few key findings about employee recognition jumped out at me from the responses:

- eighty-five percent of respondents felt strongly, or very strongly, that it was important to them to feel that their work was valued and appreciated.
- sixty-five percent of respondents felt strongly, or very strongly, that it was important to them to get a verbal thank you for a job well done.
- fourteen percent of respondents felt strongly, or very strongly, that it was important to them to be recognized in the awards program.

At that time, we had a very professionally-produced Manitoba Housing annual awards program. Yet, what was kind of amazing to me was that over four-and-a-half times as many people simply wanted a "thank you" (likely from their direct supervisor) when they did a good job, compared to being nominated in a formal awards luncheon. Guess which one was free? Yet the feedback from the staff suggested that they most valued the simplest form of positive recognition from their own managers.

I get it. I've been guilty of getting wrong the ratio of constructive-to-positive feedback when I'm leading staff. When you get busy, it can happen very easily. What this did reinforce for me, with data from my own division, was that our people need us as leaders to make this a high priority. They deserve to hear their boss recognize that they finished the project early, or under budget, or that they exceeded expectations on their assignment. It's hard for anyone to keep putting in additional effort every day when you don't think that the leadership even notices, or cares. Remember, the best benefits of practicing this principle come when every leader personally and privately thanks each staff member for a job well done. It's okay if senior leadership thanks front-line staff, but that cannot replace the obligations of the front-line managers to recognize the accomplishments of their own people.

I think that once you commit to *choosing* to believe McGregor's Theory Y model of staff motivation, that your people generally all come to work every day wanting to do a great job, then it isn't too much of a stretch to make it a habit to thank people for doing a great job. When you are consciously on the lookout for great work, you will find it happening all over the place. The lens through which you choose to look at your people really does affect how you behave as a leader. Look through the correct lens, and catch your people doing great things all the time. And tell them "thank you."

# 21

## Trust Principle #16: Discipline Only the Unwilling, but Know That They Are Few

*"When people make mistakes, the last thing they need is discipline. It's time for encouragement and confidence building. The job at this point is to restore self-confidence. I think 'piling on' when someone is down is one of the worst things any of us can do."*

**Jack Welch[1]**
*former CEO of General Electric*

I think that one of the biggest challenges for leaders when trying to change their own perspective of how they view their staff is handling situations of poor performance by staff. As leaders, we can be incredibly quick to jump to the wrong conclusions. Linton Sellen, in his training program "The Workplace Leader" has developed a unique framework for leaders to apply when faced with a problem of staff performance.[2] Sellen identifies four major root causes of performance problems:

1. A lack of *understanding*. The staff member doesn't adequately understand what is expected or required of them. The request or assignment may not have been clearly worded or explained by the issuing manager.

2. A lack of *capability*. The staff member may not have the skills or knowledge to complete the assignment. This root cause can be subdivided into those situations where training can improve the staff member's ability to perform the task, and those situations where the staff member lacks the inherent aptitude required; training cannot compensate for a serious deficit of aptitude.

3. *Obstacles.* The staff member may be prevented from successfully completing the assignment because obstacles block or slow the way forward. These obstacles may take the form of inefficient or inadequate processes that they are required to follow, inadequate authority, or a lack of supporting resources. Lean is definitely able to help in many of these situations.

4. A lack of *willingness.* The staff member may be unwilling to follow the instructions or to complete the assignment at all. This inherently involves some form of insubordination to management direction, either overt or passive-aggressive.

While this list of four major root causes is useful in itself, Sellen provides a very insightful assessment of how these four root causes are often handled in the real world of management: very poorly. If you carefully review the first three root causes, you begin to see that none of these items can be the fault of the staff member. They are, in fact, only within the control of the leader.

For number 1, if the staff member lacks the proper *understanding* of the assignment, that is usually because the leader did not do a proper job of explaining what was required or checking throughout the progress to make sure questions were answered as needed.

For number 2, if the staff member lacks *capability*, then either the leader failed to properly ensure that their staff received sufficient training for the assignment, or the leader failed in their selection of a staff member without the necessary aptitude for the assignment. Getting upset at a staff member who lacks the necessary aptitude to complete a job that you assigned them is like asking someone who needs glasses to just "try harder" when trying to read an eye-testing chart across the room.

For number 3, if *obstacles* block or impede the progress, this problem is also the responsibility of the leader to remedy. The staff do not usually have the inherent authority to change processes of an organization; that authority rests with the leadership, unless it is consciously and explicitly delegated to the staff.

Only number 4, the lack of *willingness* of the staff member, could be considered to be the fault of the employee if they choose not to do what is required of them.

But more often than not, you find that the root cause of a performance problem is actually one of the first three categories. And these three categories are under the control of the leadership, not the staff—yet, many times we see the leadership criticizing the staff for problems over which they have no control (Category 1, 2, or 3). Sellen continues to argue that, since most leaders fall prey to the confirmation bias of believing that one's own leadership approaches are sound, they often overlook the first three categories and they then incorrectly jump to the assumption that the problem is caused by Category 4, a lack of *willingness* by the staff.

There are a few common misconceptions that give leaders a push in the wrong direction when trying to diagnose the cause of performance problems. For one, a memory problem, or simply forgetting to do something using a new method, for instance, is a capability issue. Very often, we as leaders jump to the assumption that, since someone didn't do something that they were directed to do by their leader, that staff member is showing defiance—but this is often wrong.

One of the justifications for this incorrect assumption that I've heard is that: "We gave this guy training. He sat in the training class, and I have his name here on the attendance sheet. He just clearly doesn't want to do as he was instructed." I realized from Sellen that I, like many other leaders, have often fallen prey to a poor assumption: that a single session of instruction is all that is needed for "training."

I've come to believe that proper training involves repetition and practicing the "new way." A single instruction session is communication, not training. In order for a staff member to learn a new way of doing things, they need practice and repetition, sometimes with a supervisor watching over them to coach them as they work, and to correct mistakes as, or before, they happen. Habits can be formed, and changed, but only with practice. Being told to change once is rarely enough to change a person's work habits when they have been doing it a different way for months or even years. This concept is further discussed in Chapter 43, Change Principle #10: Remember that we learn by doing.

The other corollary with the four categories is something very similar to what I had said earlier in Chapter 9, Trust Principle #4: Understand that people become a product of their environment. Regarding McGregor's Theory X: If someone does not have a lack of *willingness*, but you treat them like they do, they will quickly develop a lack of *willingness*. They will start to reflect back to you the very lack of *willingness* that you had assessed them to have. As I have previously stated, the people will become a product of their environment, and that environment is shaped and maintained by the leader.

In his book *It's Your Ship*, Captain D. Michael Abrashoff includes a chapter entitled "Create a Climate of Trust."[3] In this chapter, he has several sections in which he speaks to things a leader should consider when trying to build or improve the trust relationships between the leadership and the staff. Although the tone of the naval officer author is quite blunt and might be offensive to some people, a few of the section headings really spoke to me, as the lessons in each of these sections are valid in any organization:

- Even the worst screwup may be redeemable;
- Welcome the bad-news messenger; and
- Protect your people from lunatic bosses.

In the three sections I have highlighted, there are some great teachings that I have found also apply in non-military organizations. For instance, sometimes, you find a staff member or a leader that is simply in the wrong job for them. I will admit that moving someone, especially a leader, into another job is much easier said than done. In most cases, it will take a lot of work with Human Resources, and the leader in charge must really understand the skills and abilities of the person being moved. As well, when moving someone, you need to have good trust relationships with other senior leaders in the organization.

The receiving leader needs to trust that you are not simply moving your problem into his or her area. You must be able to convince yourself before you can convince your colleague that the individual you want to move can actually be successful in a different role in a new area, when they have struggled before. Rarely do you find a situation where the person is completely beyond redemption and cannot be moved into another job where they can use their skills and abilities to great success. It may not be at the same pay-grade though, and that in itself can be a tremendous barrier for the affected individual to overcome in their own mind.

Notice I said "rarely" and not "never." It can happen, and sometimes you will run into that individual that just really doesn't want to be in the organization but doesn't have the courage to leave. This type of person is usually taking out their own frustrations about their "lack of fit" on the people around them, or on their own leader, creating a toxic environment for all. When the behaviour challenges are pointed out to this type of individual, that person then has a choice to make about what path their journey forward is going to take. In some cases, when the spotlight and the pressure is put on them, they self-select out of the organization. In other cases, they internalize the feedback and make a complete turnaround in behaviour. In the remaining cases, they dig in their heels, refuse to change their behaviour, and the leader must apply more and more progressive discipline until either the behaviour is changed, or they are terminated from the organization, usually to the relief of many.

If your organization has previously had leaders who wielded their authority through a pattern of punishment for errors, then you have a tough job ahead of you. People will be afraid to come forward to admit that something went wrong, or that something is about to go wrong. They will be afraid, at first, to trust that you, as the leader, will be any different than your predecessors. You need to build the climate of trust within the staff so that they understand that when mistakes are made in good faith, then what they can expect from management will be questions about how we can improve the processes to prevent the mistake from happening again.

Since you are beginning a Lean transformation in the organization, you are going to be asking your people to innovate, to try new things. When people try to do things differently, they will make mistakes. Therefore, you will need to work hard to create that environment of trust within the leadership that mistakes made in good faith are not met with anger or punishment. You will have to work even harder to teach the staff that you *want* them to come forward with bad news, and as early as possible so that the impact of the situation might be reduced. A few times I've found myself thanking my staff for coming forward with poor business performance metrics or bad news about a pilot project. I recognized that, because of my executive title, they were often afraid of the consequences of being the messenger of bad news, so I needed to positively reinforce the right behaviour.

I have used the term "good-faith error" a few times. This is to distinguish these situations from the more ominous kind that require a completely different method of handling. A good-faith error is one where, upon close inspection, you can determine that a lack of *willingness* was not the reason for the mistake. Instead, you find that one or more of the other three root causes for performance problems (*understanding, capability, or obstacles*) were involved.

However, you will occasionally run into a situation when the mistake was not made in good faith, and a lack of *willingness* to do the right thing really was the root cause. In these cases, the progressive discipline of the individual, assessed with the advice of human resources, is necessary. In severe cases, such as theft or fraud, don't be afraid to jump right to the last step of discipline and terminate the individual outright. These people are poisonous, and they need to be removed from the organization immediately.

But these are the very rare and extreme cases. Remember the principle: Discipline only the unwilling, but know that they are few.

# 22

## Trust Principle #17: Protect Your People

*"A good leader should take a little more than their share of the blame, a little less than their share of the credit."*

**Attributed to Arnold Glasow**
*American humorist and businessman*

Sometimes, you will need to protect your people from those above you. A few times over my career, I've been asked by my senior leader who was responsible for a particular problem, which was caused by a good-faith error by one of my staff. I didn't always do the right thing, and sometimes I identified the individual. But since realizing the importance of my behaviour as a leader shaping the culture of the organization, I think I've handled such situations differently.

Once, a senior leader asked me who was the cause of a communications mix-up that was simply an innocent case of misunderstood expectations—I replied that I wasn't going to throw my staff member under the bus. The error came from my part of the organization, and I would take responsibility for that error. I would, however, work with my team to make sure this type of mistake didn't happen again. The person who asked me for the name of the staff member who made the mistake didn't know where to take the issue after that.

When you support your people in this way after they make mistakes, they won't always find out. But they will be looking for evidence that you don't support your people when they make an "oops." And if you don't show support for them in those situations, word of your disloyal leadership behaviour will spread quickly throughout the ranks. But if you support them when the situation requires it, eventually, someone will find out. Someone will see, or hear about, how you took the blame for someone on your team, and that's usually too good a story to keep to themselves.

In this case, the organizational grapevine will work in your favour. But this isn't why you should protect your people. You should do it because it is the right thing to do. It is critical that you remain consistent in your support for your team members.

Remember, a part of the culture is innovation, and you can't innovate without trying new things. Trying new things means that mistakes will be made in good faith as people experiment with new approaches, or as they struggle to get used to a new way of doing a process after ten years of doing it the old way. If you want innovation, you need to be able to protect your people when mistakes happen as a consequence. If you punish for the mistakes that result from trying new things, your innovation culture will die before it can flourish.

A few times, when coaching my leaders about the importance of protecting their people, I've even told them that I expect them to protect their people even from me, if necessary—however, I did pledge to do my best to make sure that would never happen!

> "When the people have to manage dangers from inside the organization, the organization itself becomes less able to face the dangers from outside."
> **Simon Sinek**[1]
> *Leaders Eat Last.*

In Chapter 16, Trust Principle #11: Always act with respect for people, I reference the concept of the "Circle of Safety" as described in the book *Leaders Eat Last* by Simon Sinek. Knowing that the leadership and the organization will protect you from harm, even if you make a mistake in good faith, offers a tremendous sense of relief to most workers. When their minds are freed from the distractions of defensively watching for the next attack, they can redistribute that previously-wasted energy towards their work, and this is where innovation can flourish.

This is a variation of Maslow's Hierarchy of Needs, first proposed in the 1943 paper in the *Psychological Review* entitled "A Theory of Human Motivation," by Abraham Maslow.[2] His theory was more fully expressed in Maslow's 1954 book *Motivation and Personality*.[3] The theory suggests that human needs are ranked by a natural priority and that people will not strive for higher-level needs until the lower and more fundamental needs have been satisfied. This theory commonly ranks the priority of needs as follows, from lowest (and most fundamental) to highest:

1. Physiological (air, water, food, sleep, shelter, etc.);
2. Safety (personal security, economic security, health, etc.);

3. Love (affection, belongingness, friendship);
4. Esteem (recognition, status, importance, respect from others); and
5. Self-actualization (to become everything that one is capable of becoming).

Simon Sinek's model is to ensure that the lower-level needs of an organization's people are satisfied, in order to free the workers to drive towards achieving their full potential. This implies a significant role of the leadership in creating that protective working environment, where safety is felt, and negative workplace behaviours are prevented from entering, or quickly removed once detected.

I once heard the word *courage* defined as being willing to undertake an action despite the likelihood of harm to oneself. In some cases, it will take moral courage to protect your people, because, depending on to whom you are reporting, there may be negative consequences for yourself. But this is what is required to build trust with your staff. If you don't have the courage to protect them when they need it the most, you don't deserve to lead them anyway.

# 23

## Trust Principle #18: Show Loyalty to Leadership above You

*"Leadership... It is a two-way street, loyalty up and loyalty down. Respect for your superior... and take care of your crew."*

**Grace Murray Hopper**[1]
*Rear Admiral, U.S. Navy*

The 1998 wartime drama movie *Saving Private Ryan* has a great scene where the lead character, Captain Miller (played by Tom Hanks), is explaining to one of his soldiers why he doesn't gripe in front of them about their assigned mission to go into enemy territory to save a single soldier, Private Ryan:[2]

*Captain Miller: I don't gripe to you, Reiben. I'm a captain. There's a chain of command. Gripes go up, not down. Always up. You gripe to me, I gripe to my superior officer, so on, so on, and so on. I don't gripe to you. I don't gripe in front of you. You should know that as a Ranger.*

*Private Reiben: I'm sorry, sir, but uh... let's say you weren't a captain, or maybe I was a major. What would you say then?*

*Captain Miller: Well, in that case... I'd say, "This is an excellent mission, sir, with an extremely valuable objective, sir, worthy of my best efforts, sir. Moreover... I feel heartfelt sorrow for the mother of Private James Ryan and am willing to lay down my life and the lives of my men—especially you, Reiben—to ease her suffering."*

*Private Mellish: [chuckles] He's good.*

*Private Caparzo: I love him.*

In this example, Captain Miller jokes about his own fear of backlash from telling the truth to his superiors. You will have to set up a different environment. I have had to, a few times, tell my leadership team to ensure that their managers understand that complaints should go up, and not down. You absolutely cannot have a leader griping or complaining to the staff about the time a *kaizen* takes away from the "real work," or about how inconvenient it is that a staff member has to leave their job for a couple of days to facilitate a Lean event. If that leader has a legitimate concern, then that leader needs to tell their supervisor in private, and that supervisor needs to address the concern if it is warranted.

If a staff member asks you if you agree with your own boss's direction about something, think very carefully before you answer. The easiest thing to say is: "That's the boss's call, and we are going to make it happen." If someone continues to press you about your opinion about whether you like the direction, you need to make it clear that you aren't going to offer an opinion about your boss's direction: "I talk to my boss all the time and him (or her) my opinions when appropriate. But it's never appropriate for me to give you my opinion about the boss's direction." So, you need to ensure that your leadership team understands the balance that is crucial to the culture change. Yes, we want people to speak their minds, but they must show respect for people when doing so. When it comes to leaders, they must never disagree with a superior's direction in front of the staff. They need to feel free, however, to disagree with the superior behind closed doors, and to be able to speak truth to power, without fear of retribution. The same as it would be with staff, though, respect for people needs to remain fundamental throughout the process.

If you violate this principle of showing loyalty to leadership above you, you will fracture trust within the organization. People will see you acting disloyally to your boss, and they will know you then act one way to someone's face, and a different way behind their back. They won't trust that you will not do the same thing to them in another situation. It's hard to trust someone who can't show loyalty when they should.

This won't always be easy, depending on your boss. But it is the right thing to do, and it is very important to follow this principle in order to develop and maintain the *Space of Trust.*

# 24

## Trust Principle #19: Go and See to Truly Understand

*"When you go out into the workplace, you should be looking for things that you can do for your people there. You've got no business being in the workplace if you are just there to be there. You've got to be looking for changes you can make for the benefit of the people who are working there."*

**Taiichi Ohno**[1]
*Japanese industrial engineer,*
*and founder of the Toyota Production System*

In January of 2015, I made a commitment to getting out into the field on a regular basis to meet the staff and to see operations at work. A regular *gemba* (meaning "the real place" in Japanese) walk, so to speak. There were a few reasons why I wanted to do this. First of all, I was still fairly new to operations, and I needed to learn how the program really worked at the front-line level. Second, I needed to build relationships with the staff. Third, I needed to get the word out to the staff about Lean. As the Lean Champion for Manitoba Housing, I knew that the staff needed to see me supporting Lean and endorsing it.

The time commitment I made for the entire year 2015 was tremendous. I asked my executive assistant to block out three half days per week for site visits for me—I couldn't always do all of them, but we tried our best to make the time commitment in advance whenever possible. At first, the visits weren't announced. I talked to the senior leadership of property services and told them that I would be making pop-in visits to the field offices to talk to staff. This new approach presented its own challenges and created a few problems of its own, as discussed in Chapter 25 called Trust Principle #20: Respect the leadership chain of command.

I got tremendous benefit from leaving my office in the headquarters building and getting out into the field as often as I did. According to my schedule records, I made over 100 visits to site offices in 2015. I really kept the staff on their toes at first. When I walked in unannounced, the look of shock on the faces of the clerical staff was obvious. They weren't really used to the executive visiting like this unless something was wrong. But I stuck to my plan: I made the effort to go meet each staff member at their own desk, introduce myself, ask them to tell me about themselves, how long they had been with Manitoba Housing, where they used to work before, and what their biggest challenges were. Then I would ask them if they knew about operations excellence, or what a *kaizen* was.

Early on, I got the expected looks of confusion, as the concept was still quite new to our people. I told them, in as plain and simple language as I could, what operations excellence was, and why it was different from other approaches to improving efficiency that they may have seen in the past. The typical script went something like this: "The traditional way to make improvements to a particular process is for the senior leader to tell the staff how the process will be improved, using their experience as in the area. But with operations excellence, we believe that the staff, the people doing the work with the process every day, have better ideas about how to fix things that we do as leaders. So, we get a group of front-line subject-matter experts into a room for a two- or three-day *kaizen* event, where another staff member trained in *kaizen* facilitation leads the group through some exercises to map the process, the staff identify areas for improvement, and they come up with some ways to fix the problems. And then we, as the senior leaders, support the staff in putting these changes into practice as our new way of running that process."

In most cases, the staff would look slightly skeptical, but admitted that the idea sounded pretty good. They were going to adopt a "wait and see if it's true" approach, which was fine with me.

In these site visits, I would do my best to talk individually with each and every staff member that I could find in each office. This included property managers, clerical staff, tenant service coordinators, building superintendents, district managers, and regional directors.

I would assume that in many organizations, the traditional approach for executives to take during a regional office visit would be to visit the most senior leader in the office, and then to leave without talking with the other staff members. From what I gathered at Manitoba Housing, previously, it was highly unusual for the operations executive to visit the site offices at all, never mind on a regular basis. When I started talking with the frontline staff one-on-one, it must have been mind-blowing to these people who remembered the old way.

But I felt that what I was trying to accomplish was just and principled, and I did need to learn more about the organization, so I decided to persevere. I'm glad that I did. What I started to see, over time, was less and less fear from the staff when I showed up. I started to see smiles and recognition when I would pop in. Faces had become familiar to me, and people started saying they were glad that I had come, that it had been a little while and they were wondering when I was going to come back. It felt good when I started to hear people say to me: "You know, a few years ago, I never knew who the COO was in this organization. It's really great that you take the time to go out and talk to staff like this."

If you are an operations executive in an organization, I think that your personal office in the headquarters building has the potential to be poisonous, not necessarily because of you, but because of what issues come to you. As a senior leader, the issues brought to your attention are not usually routine ones—those routine issues are usually handled by leaders below you in the organization. And as you might expect, the higher up your rank is in the organization, the more critical the issues which are brought to your attention. Therefore, it seems that the only issues that come to your attention often involve some implication that your staff did something wrong. If this is all that you see, after a while, it can start to influence how you see your team.

It's easy to start to develop a very negative perspective on the capabilities and the motivation and dedication of your team members. This is what I mean when I say that your office can be poisonous. It's very easy to stay in the headquarters building all day, every day of each week. You will be busy, as there are always things on which to work. But your environment is potentially unhealthy for you, and you may develop a skewed and unfair view of your people.

Getting out of your office and going out to where the real work is being done, and most importantly, to meet and get to know the people doing the work is healthy and is a part of being a good leader. This approach helps to break the cycle of abstraction, which can easily develop when your organization starts adopting the use of performance metrics. Managing solely by report is an extremely short-sighted and dangerous way to lead. But it happens all the time in the modern business world.

In 1961, Yale psychologist Stanley Milgram set up an experiment to attempt to prove whether or not Adoph Eichmann and his Nazi accomplices were truly "just following orders" when they carried out their atrocities during World War II.[2] In this experiment, a volunteer (given the role of the teacher) was told that they had to ask another volunteer (given the role of the student) a series of questions, and if a question was answered incorrectly, the "teacher" had to flip a switch on a console and administer a fifteen-volt electric shock to the "student."

The next time a wrong answer was delivered, the "teacher" was instructed to flip the next switch on the console, which was labelled with a higher voltage. In fact, the console had thirty switches, each labelled with higher and higher voltages, right up to 450 volts, and clearly labelled to indicate that death would be the outcome from shocking the person with this switch.

The experiment created a few variations, such as having the teacher beside the student and having to place the student's hand on the electric plate to receive the shock or having the teacher simply in the same room as the student. Another variation involved having the teacher separated by the student by walls, so that the teacher could not see the student, but could hear them through the walls, and another variation had the teacher and student separated by walls so that the teacher could not hear the student speaking or shouting but banging on the walls could be heard.

Whenever the shocks were administered, the students would react as expected, and as the console voltage increased, expressed more and more pain, begging the teacher to stop. But if the teacher volunteer turned to the scientist conducting the experiment to ask about stopping, the scientist calmly stated that "the experiment requires that you continue," or a few variations on that theme.

In reality, the "students" were all scientists cooperating with the experiment. No actual electric shocks were ever administered, and the reactions were all acted out by the "students." The intent of the experiment was to see how far ordinary people would progress, given only minimal encouragement to do so, despite the knowledge of the pain that their actions were causing to others. As you might expect, the more separated the teacher was from the student, the more likely the teacher was to progress farther with the electric shocks

The experiment was criticized for being very unethical, although Milgram defensively claimed that his critics were more frightened by what the results suggested about human nature. Out of 160 volunteer "teachers,"

*"Just like the conditions Milgram set in his experiment, the physical separation between us and those on the receiving end of our decisions can have a dramatic impact on lives... the lives of people who cannot be seen or heard. The more abstract people become, the more capable we are of doing them harm."*

**Simon Sinek**[3]

*Leaders Eat Last.*

almost half progressed all the way through electric shock progression to the point where the "students" were made to appear as though they had been killed by the shock. As a result, nearly eighty ordinary people learned that they had the capacity to kill someone. In his own reference to the Milgram experiment, Simon Sinek draws a very important conclusion—abstraction by the leadership in an organization can be absolutely poisonous to the culture.[4]

When you combine this principle of "go and see" with the other leadership principles such as described in Chapter 8, Trust Principle #3: Believe that your people come to work every day wanting to do a good job, and Chapter 9, Trust Principle #4: Understand that people become a product of their environment, you can really learn a lot and help your people. However, I think that by far, this principle appears to be one of the easiest to understand, and yet the hardest one to get right in practice.

Since many of the methodologies of continuous improvement and Lean management have origins from the Toyota Production System developed in Japan, it is common to find many Japanese words as a part of the Lean lexicon. To the uninitiated, these foreign words can be daunting and sometimes off-putting, and as a result, I believe that when first introducing Lean management concepts to an organization, you should avoid most of the Japanese words and find common English equivalents where possible. It is for that reason that almost every chapter heading in this book is free from jargon and uses plain everyday language—the intent is to allow the reader to more easily remember the leadership principles of the Three Spaces of Lean.

However, I find that to learn more deeply about each principle, there are benefits to understanding the origins of the terms and concepts. In my studies, I have discovered that the principle of "go and see" is something with which even senior leaders at Toyota can struggle. The book *The Toyota Way to Lean Leadership* by Jeffrey Liker and Gary Convis offers some excellent insight into the true intent of the practice of "go and see" as a leadership principle.[5]

"Genchi genbutsu [go and see the actual situation] means imagining what you are observing is your own job, rather than somebody else's problem, and making efforts to improve it. Job titles are unimportant. In the end, the people who know the gemba [where the actual work is done] are the most respected."

**Akio Toyoda**[6]
*president, Toyota Motor Corporation, 2009.*

While going to out to where the work is done, to where the actual situation is, sounds simple enough, the correct approach is much more complicated than it sounds. Your role when you are on a *gemba* walk is not to go out to solve the problems for your staff. Your role is to ask the proper questions to coach them to solve the problems themselves. This is extremely difficult, and I continue to struggle with this ideal form of coaching. Most leaders find this very hard to get right as well.

If you are an executive, you need to be aware of the potential negative side effects from a *gemba* walk by such a senior leader out on the operations floor—it can actually distract the staff so much that it causes its own problems.

At a Lean conference in 2018, I had the benefit of hearing presentations from Mike Rother, the author of Toyota Kata.[7] Mike said that he once had warned a company vice-president on a *gemba* walk within the operations of his factory to stop pointing at things and asking why this-or-that was happening. Mike said that he told the vice-president that every time you point at something, you start a project, even if you don't intend to. Mike is right—authority does matter on a *gemba* walk.

This caution is appropriate when your leaders understand the new culture, including structured problem-solving and coaching through questioning. However, at first, you will need to be a little more involved until your leadership team understands their roles. But it is important to understand that you want to minimize the side effects of your own *gemba* presence.

This principle needs to be very closely matched with many other principles, in order to not produce a conflict within the culture. In fact, I believe that the principle of "go and see to truly understand" requires coordination with the most other principles compared to any individual leadership principle described in this book. Some of the other principles with which you must coordinate when practicing this one are as follows:

- Trust Principle #2: Trust that your people are not the problem. You are (Chapter 7);
- Trust Principle #3: Believe that your people come to work every day wanting to do a good job (Chapter 8);
- Trust Principle #4: Understand that people become a product of their environment (Chapter 9);
- Trust Principle #8: Remember that authority matters (Chapter 13);
- Trust Principle #11: Always act with respect for people (Chapter 16);
- Trust Principle #13: Talk about problems openly, but focus on solutions (Chapter 18);
- Trust Principle #18: Show loyalty to leadership above you (Chapter 23);
- Trust Principle #21: Listen effectively (Chapter 26);
- Trust Principle #23: Be a coach, not a judge (Chapter 28);
- Trust Principle #24: Coach with questions, not answers (Chapter 29);
- Change Principle #7: Challenge the status quo continuously (Chapter 40);
- Change Principle #12: Ask them to show you, not tell you (Chapter 45);
- Change Principle #13: Use visual metrics regularly to teach and reveal, never to assign blame (Chapter 46);
- Change Principle #21: Celebrate team accomplishments, large and small (Chapter 54);
- Change Principle #23: Teach your leaders to operate in the gray (Chapter 56);
- CI Principle #1: Defend Continuous Improvement as an investment, not a cost (Chapter 60);
- CI Principle #12: Solve the right problem (Chapter 71);
- CI Principle #14: Share widely best practices (Chapter 73);
- CI Principle #17: Drive towards effective daily *kaizen* (Chapter 76); and
- CI Principle #19: Reflect and improve (Chapter 78).

This is a huge list. As a result, this principle will be the most difficult one to master. But work at it, because it will be crucial to the development of the new culture.

# 25

## Trust Principle #20: Respect the Leadership Chain of Command

*"Leaders must be close enough to relate, but far enough ahead to motivate them."*

**John C. Maxwell**[1]
*author, speaker, and pastor*

Linton Sellen, in the Workplace Leader, spends a lot of time discussing the importance of following the leadership chain of command.[2] I've come to realize that this is an important principle when leading a Lean culture change. Ask yourself this: Is it possible to undermine a leader that reports to you by agreeing with her? The first time someone hears this question, it really makes them think. And they usually ask for clarification. Let me give some clarification. Imagine that an employee is told by their manager to use Procedure 1 instead of Procedure 2 to handle a certain situation. The employee disagrees and tells the manager. The manager listens to the concern but reiterates that Procedure 1 is the correct one to use for that situation. The manager may supply the rationale for that decision to explain why they arrived at that decision if they so choose. But the employee still disagrees with the direction.

Later, they approach you, the branch director, and tell you that their manager, your direct report, has directed them to use Procedure 1 instead of Procedure 2, but they believe that the direction is misguided and that Procedure 2 is the better one. They tell you the manager's rationale around selecting Procedure 1, but then supply their own rationale as to why Procedure 2 would be a better choice. You listen to the employee and then tell them that you agree with the manager's choice and that they need to take their direction from their manager.

You have just undermined your manager.

For many people, this is hard to believe, but it's true. Even though you were supportive of your manager and told the employee that they need to take direction from their manager, the mistake that you made was when you stated that you agreed with your manager's decision. This implies that you evaluated the judgement of your direct report right in front of that manager's staff member. Because they heard this, it suggests that you are, in fact, the "court of appeal" with decisions that employee doesn't like from their manager.

Although you supported the manager today, the implication is that tomorrow you might not. On a different issue, maybe you will disagree with the manager and support the employee's recommendation. You made it sound as though you were telling the employee that they need to take direction from their manager *because you agree with the manager in this instance*, not because they have the delegated authority to direct their staff. This scenario is the mildest form of undermining that can occur in a leadership hierarchy. Most of the other scenarios are much more obvious and hurtful to the manager than this case.

I'm sure many managers have experienced being undermined by their senior leaders in front of their staff. I'm ashamed to admit that I've done it myself, although in most cases I just didn't realize it at the time. However, I believe that this is one of the easier types of things to change about yourself as a senior leader about to take your organization through a Lean transformation. You just need to develop that sense of self-awareness about these situations and think through very carefully what you are about to do before you act. Whenever you are about to talk to staff that don't report directly to you, you should always be on your guard.

When a staff member approaches me and says they need to talk to me about something, I'm always ready to listen. You do need to listen long enough to ensure that they aren't coming to you with a cry for help about wrong-doing or ill-treatment by their manager—in those rare instances, you need to be prepared to step in and conduct an investigation if the story appears to have some substance to it. In these situations, I usually start with a call to Human Resources for some guidance about how to proceed appropriately, and then I either conduct the investigation myself with human resources or, if it makes sense, my executive director for the area handles the investigation.

A more common situation is what I call the "Hail Mary" pass. An employee sees you walking around and approaches you to complain how their manager is holding them accountable for something, or carefully managing their attendance, or the like. You should quickly be able to sense that this is something that you know is within the manager's authority to handle.

When a staff member corners the senior leader and challenges a workplace decision that their manager has made around something well within his or her authority. The safest answer to give in either situation like this is: "Have you spoken to your manager about your concerns?" If they answer no, then it is easy to direct them back to their manager and end the conversation right there without passing any judgement on the action of your manager.

If they answer yes, but state that the manager is being unfair, you can simply indicate that *it is the manager's decision, not yours.* If they press you and ask if you are going to look into the situation and talk to your manager about it, you can say that you talk to your managers all the time, but what is discussed with them doesn't get discussed with the staff. At that point, I would end the conversation. Now, you can go talk to the manager privately about the situation if you are a little concerned about how it is being handled and get the context around the problem. I would then ask the manager for their rationale and approach for the issue.

You may be coaching the manager on improving his or her performance management or decision-making methods, so maybe this is another part of the coaching regimen. But give the manager suggestions about how to go back to the situation so that it doesn't appear that you over-ruled them—you need to let that manager keep their authority intact with the staff, and you don't need that staff member telling their friends that if you complain to the big boss, he will make the manager reverse course. You should never pass judgement on the authority decisions of your leadership team in front of their staff.

After a few exchanges like this, I found that the staff stopped attempting to get me to over-rule my leaders. They quickly learned that the approach isn't effective, and they stop trying. When they approach a very senior leader, they do feel quite exposed, and not getting a warm reception to an approach that they know shows disloyalty to their manager is not something that they are willing to repeat if it isn't effective.

> *You should never pass judgement on the authority decisions of your leadership team in front of their staff.*

Respecting the leadership chain of command is very important to remember as you are working to develop the *Space of Trust*. If you, as the senior leader, start walking around and talking to front-line staff, you will need to be very careful about what discussion topics you are willing to entertain with the staff.

The best guidance that I can give is to stick to topics that are appropriate from your level on the organizational chart. Do the staff know about some of the major strategic initiatives that are underway? If not, explain what they mean in simple terms. If you are starting a Lean journey for your organization, that's a safe place to start for discussion topics. Do the staff members know what operations excellence means? Do they know what a *kaizen* is? You need to be prepared to talk to any staff member, at any level in the organization, in plain, non-technical language, about what operations excellence will look like to that employee in the future.

Be prepared for staff to approach you with other concerns or problems. If they are bringing to your attention a process problem that might be a candidate for a future *kaizen* event, that's fair game. But if they start complaining about a decision their supervisor made, be aware that you are instantly walking on thin ice. You've got to be on your guard to ensure that you avoid the easy temptation to step into a decision made by one of your leaders and undermine their authority in the process. A simple response to remember is: "That's your supervisor's call."

If you keep focused on discussing topics that are appropriate for your level in the organization, such as operations excellence improvement ideas, and refuse to engage in issues that could undermine the authority of your manager, the staff will learn and respect the rules of engagement with your visits.

# 26

## *Trust Principle #21: Listen Effectively*

*"The most important thing in communication is to hear what isn't being said."*

**Peter Drucker[1]**
*management author*

I think that many leaders struggle with the challenge of truly listening when their staff speak. I know that I struggle with this skill myself. Likely, this is because for so many years of my life, I had felt that my purpose was to be a guy who had all the answers. All throughout my engineering education, I was told that I was learning to be a problem solver, so that compounded the issue. As a result, I struggled to believe that I needed to hear what others had to say, since I believed it was my job to have the answers. To be fair to myself, I never actually had these thoughts inside my head, and I would have probably denied it if anyone had challenged me with this observation. But in retrospect, with the benefit of years of hindsight, I can see it now myself.

When someone would be talking to me about a problem with which they were struggling, I would sometimes be just waiting for them to take a breath so that I could jump in and solve their problem for them with my knowledge. It was almost as though I thought I was in some sort of gameshow, with a buzzer to press to be allowed to answer first and claim the prize. Ridiculous, isn't it? But when you feel that your role is to give out answers to problems, then you inherently want to improve your efficiency at that task. And listening to other people talk just gets in the way of giving out answers. It must have been so frustrating for people to experience this when dealing with me years ago, and I deeply regret my past behaviour.

Two books, *The Seven Habits of Highly Successful People* by Stephen Covey,[2] as well as *The Leadership Challenge* by James Kouzes and Barry Posner,[3] speak to the importance of the leader listening intently to their people. In *The Seven Habits of Highly Effective People*, Stephen Covey names Habit 5 as "Seek First to Understand, Then to be Understood." One of the subsections in this Habit is entitled "Diagnose Before You Prescribe."

The Leadership Challenge has a section called "Listen Deeply to Others," under the practice of "Inspire a Shared Vision." I found that both of these books, along with others, were tremendously helpful to me as I set out to learn how, as a leader, I could best set the stage for Manitoba Housing's Lean transformational journey.

When you make the commitment to reinvent and redefine your role as a leader to that of a coach for those working for you, you will have no choice but to change your approach with which you listen to others. It will come out of necessity. When you use the approach of coaching through questioning, you need to decide in advance that you aren't going to just provide the answer to the staff member coming to you with a problem. Therefore, you should have nothing to preoccupy your mind, except to totally focus and listen as the person across from you shares with you what they are thinking.

I have found helpful active listening phrases such as "I'm hearing you say that…" and "What I understand from you is…" I use these phrases to ensure that I really understood the concern from the employee's point of view, before I started guiding them towards a new direction with a line of questions. When I needed more information to understand the issue at hand, I used exploratory phrases such as: "Do you have any idea what might be the cause of this?" and my favourite: "Really! Tell me more about that." But this type of approach has to become and feel natural, and a part of who you are. You need to use words that feel normal to you. It can't come off sounding like a forced tactic, or it will appear dishonest to the other person.

The change in the feel of the leadership dynamic between yourself and your subordinates should become quickly apparent. It might be a little embarrassing to think that one of your staff might talk to one of their colleagues and say: "Hey, guess what? I had my meeting with the boss today, and it was so weird. It seemed like he/she was actually listening to me!" But keep going. It may very well be that you will start to enjoy the new style of your one-on-one discussions with your staff as a side effect of adopting this principle. It's also very likely that your staff will appreciate your leadership so much more than they did before.

If you believe today that you are the "expert" leader, that your role is to have the answers, then you need to be prepared to consider some changes for yourself if you are going to succeed as a Lean champion. If you typically give out the answers rather than listen to those in your organization, you need to consider a different approach. The hardest thing for a senior leader, though may be to admit that they need to change something about themselves. However, change is possible, and becoming a leader-coach is one of the best changes you can possibly make for yourself. Your people will greatly appreciate you for it, and your Lean journey will be much more likely to succeed.

# 27

## Trust Principle #22: Understand the True Source of Your Value as a Leader

*"Leaders accept and act on the paradox of power: You become more powerful when you give your own power away."*

**James Kouzes and Barry Posner**[1]
*leadership authors*

When you go through years of your career thinking that your value results from your subject-matter expertise, it can be very difficult to adopt a different view when you are to take on the role of a leader in an organization trying to develop a continuous improvement culture. Part of this may result from your inherent need for external validation, where people acknowledge the value of your knowledge and thank you for your expertise. But I believe that leadership requires more than simply being the most experienced or knowledgeable person in a given working group. But what is the "more" that is required?

Leaders who believe that their value comes from their subject-matter expertise often allow this belief to manifest itself in their leadership behaviours:[2]

1. They control information, insisting that they are the central focal point through which all information within the team must flow;
2. Information is only given out to team members on a strictly need-to-know basis, as determined by the leader, and it is frequently determined that many people do not need to know;
3. They centralize all decision-making within the team through themselves, as the final arbiter of all choices;

4. They establish themselves as the quality-control inspector for all work within the group, the person whose approval must be received before any deliverables leave the boundaries of the group; and

5. They make decisions based on the desire to preserve their place of primacy in the organization, and not necessarily based on what is best for the organization.

These behaviours set up a culture within the team of complete and total dependence on the leader. There is no innovation, and why would there be, in this type of environment? If any innovation occurs, I would say that it happened *despite* the best efforts of the leader to create an environment to discourage it.

Where someone has created a culture of dependence on themselves as a leader, why would that be? I believe that in many cases it is because they cannot see the role as a leader beyond that with which they are most familiar, that of the subject-matter expert. They have simply taken their promotion to leadership to mean that they are now a subject-matter expert with supervisory authority. But by neglecting to realize that their role needs to substantially change upon becoming a leader, to that of a coach for their people, they are failing in their new role.

The irony is that, by giving more authority away to your people, with proper training and a supportive delegation system, the more power that you will actually have to change the culture of your team, and your organization. But you will feel vulnerable at first—if your people are coached enough and grow more independent in their own roles, won't the organization at some point decide that they don't need you? I wonder if this is central to the challenges some leaders have with the idea of abandoning their role as an expert.

I have seen many people struggle with the transition from expert to leader. I have struggled with it myself. I encourage you to deeply study, understand, and apply CI Principle #19: Reflect and improve (described in Chapter 78), based on the Japanese concept of *hansei*. Apply the fundamental principles of structured problem-solving to understand why you may struggle with the transition. Use the 5-Whys approach, or whatever approach that works, but you need to understand yourself before you can change yourself.

Ask yourself this question: "If your value as a leader does not come from your subject-matter expertise, then from where does it come?" For a long time, I was conflicted with this question during my own self-reflection.

When I took on the role of COO of Manitoba Housing, it was my first professional job that didn't require an engineering degree as a prerequisite. This job covered many disparate areas of subject-matter, and my inherent knowledge didn't seem to count for much when I started in the role. This prompted the question that I posed at the beginning of this paragraph. And I struggled to answer my own question for a long time. This journey of self-discovery, I think, is valuable for any leader to travel. This doesn't mean that the leaders are not supposed to develop expertise in other areas of course. In fact, with enough time, it would be hard not to develop experience in areas you manage outside of your primary area of expertise.

What you need to learn, however, is how to use your subject-matter expertise as a coach, without using it primarily to be the answer-provider for your team. The true value of a leader is to assume the role of a coach. To follow the sports metaphor, the players play the game, but the coach does not. The coach's role is to guide and to improve the players and to equip them for the game. Stop trying to play the game and assume your rightful role as a coach.

# 28

## Trust Principle #23: Be a Coach, Not a Judge

*"A leader is a coach, not a judge."*

**W. Edwards Deming**[1]
*management consultant and pioneer of the
modern quality system*

Moving from the role of a subject-matter expert into that of a leader can be very difficult for many people. It can be surprising for many people to accept that the best leader may not be the most experienced, most knowledgeable, or most senior person in a working group. In fact, leadership skills are very different and distinct from those skills that make someone so proficient at their job as a member of a team.

Many times, over my career, I have encountered leaders who seem to spend a lot of time evaluating their people, and passing judgement on them, but not helping them. At one point, I was even among the ranks of these leaders, unfortunately. When your focus is on judging the performance of others, I believe that you are committing two crimes as a leader:

1. You are incorrectly assuming that people "are who they are" forever and that no one can change; and
2. You are abdicating your role as a coach for your people.

When you look at your staff performing their duties, you need to move away from evaluating them and grading them, as to whether or not they "have what it takes." The reason I say this is that it is your job to help them, so they do "have what it takes." That needs to be your focus. Yes, look for performance challenges with each person on your team, but make sure you understand that it is your responsibility to get them to where they need to be with their performance.

In Chapter 9, Trust Principle #4: Understand that people become a product of their environment, we learned that people are incredibly perceptive to their environment, and that the environment plays a very strong role in how people behave. Therefore, assume that your employees can read your thoughts about them. If you think that your employee doesn't know what they are doing, there is a good chance that the employee will be able to sense your disappointment in them through your behaviour. Instead, talk with them openly, but respectfully, in your regular one-on-one performance feedback discussions about their challenges, and engage them and work with them collaboratively on a step-by-step plan to help them improve.

Your role of a coach is likely to be very different and it may feel very foreign to you, compared to whatever you felt that your role was before in the organization. Kouzes and Posner, in *The Leadership Challenge*, have a great way of defining the concept:[2]

> *"Leaders significantly increase people's belief in their own ability to make a difference. They move from being in control to giving over control to others and becoming their coach. They help others learn new skills, develop existing talents, and provide institutional supports required for ongoing growth and change. In the final analysis, leaders turn their constituents into leaders."*

When I really began internally self-identifying myself as a leader-coach for my team instead of an expert, it forced me to think about many things very differently. It also resulted in me acting very differently as a leader, which was good. One of my goals was to make the leaders that reported to me better in their jobs as leaders. This meant, I believed, that I needed to get them to learn how to handle situations independently without me being there to "give them the answer." As such, I started asking a lot of questions when my leaders would come to me with problems. I would try to walk the person through the thought process themselves without giving them the answer if possible. Someday, I reasoned, I will not be around, and they need to become prepared for that eventuality.

Embrace your role as a coach to help your team members become the most that each of them can be. Help them achieve the best that they can be. Get them to the point where their reliance on you disappears. Recognize that your fear of this point is natural, and understand it, embrace it, and then free yourself of it. When you become a great coach for your people, you will be in demand forever, even after you run out of things to teach your people. Your staff will be grateful for your leadership. Trust that your organization will see the value in what you have accomplished and will want you to improve another team, and perhaps even give you a leadership role with larger responsibility.

Stop seeing your people as a collection of problems, and start seeing them as unique individuals, each with potential that lies within that needs nurturing. Remember the metaphor that I included at the beginning of this book, about the Angel in the Marble. In every organization, I believe that you have amazing potential within the people, hidden from the superficial view. It is your job to develop a view beyond the superficial. Get to know your people, and you will find hidden talents and skills that can result in so much more performance, provided that these talents and skills are properly nurtured and encouraged—and that is your job.

Remember that there is an angel within the block of marble that is your team. It is your job to free it by removing the stone that obscures it, holds it back, and hides it from view. Free that which is hidden within.

# 29

---

## Trust Principle #24: Coach with Questions, Not Answers

*"Coaching will become the model for leaders in the future... I am certain that leadership can be learned and that terrific coaches... facilitate learning."*

**Attributed to Warren G. Bennis**
*founder of Leadership Institute, University of Southern California*

Since I adopted my leadership role as a coach, when someone would tell me about a problem that arose with a project, I might ask them: "Really! Tell me why you think that might have happened?" and listen. I would then take the time necessary to guide them with more questions until they might arrive at the answer. This was sometimes incredibly hard for me because I might have known the answer outright, and I could have ended the discussion right there very quickly. But then the person would have left without understanding how to arrive at the answer themselves.

The technical term for this type of coaching or training through the use of questioning is sometimes called the Socratic Method, although this terminology historically referred to something different, known as Socratic debate. Socratic debate is a form of cooperative debate between individuals, asking and answering questions, to brainstorm ideas and review the underpinning assumptions. In order to avoid confusion, I prefer the more self-explanatory term "coaching through questioning."

Sometimes, during my coaching sessions, it didn't seem appropriate, given the situation, for me to ask questions, or maybe the person seemed stuck and was unable to answer the questions. The closest that I would ever come to giving the answers to someone would be to share my complete thought process with them, regarding how I would reason my way through this type of problem. I would tell them I what I was doing from the beginning, too.

I can't count how many times my leaders have each individually heard me say: "I'm going to share my thought process with you, not because my way of doing it is necessarily the best way, but because I want you to understand how I would deal with this situation." It felt different than my old way of just jumping to the solution. It felt better, and my leaders seemed to appreciate the new approach. But still, the preferred approach is always coaching through questioning. As you start down your own Lean Management journey, you will need to think very carefully about your own leadership style, and whether or not it is suitable for the direction in which you are taking your organization.

You are about to start getting staff team members involved and engaged in solving some of your organization's process problems. Let's be fair; the team members probably will have some better answers to the process problems than their leaders, because they are involved with these processes hands-on every workday, and the leadership is not. The staff need to believe that their ideas matter. Once you delegate authority to your staff, within the boundaries defined before the *kaizen* event, you need to be able to trust that the staff will make some good improvements to the processes.

I understand that this kind of trust can be hard when you have thought for many years that if you are the leader, your role is to be the super-expert on the processes. But having gone through this experience myself, I can promise you that in some cases, they will come up with some of the same improvement ideas you would have

> *When the staff help develop something, they don't want to see it fail.*

yourself, but many times they will come up with different ideas. Some will sound okay to you, and some will sound questionable. You will have to be prepared to accept them all, since you delegated your authority to them at the start of the *kaizen* event.

But be prepared, there will be some improvement ideas that catch you by surprise, and these ideas may be much better than anything you could have thought of yourself. Make sure that you tell the team that when it happens—they'll love you for it.

When there are decisions to be made on your Lean journey, think about using the model of coaching through questioning to have your staff or your leaders come up with the answers. Use questions to try to lead them through their own discovery processes to arrive at the solutions. It's not too much of a stretch to believe that staff will more easily accept and adopt into practice process changes into which they had input, as opposed to changes that were developed by the senior leader and transmitted down from on high. When the staff help develop something, they don't want to see it fail. Their emotional investment in the changes they helped to create will often result in over-and-above efforts on the implementation side. There is no emotional investment in the staff when the senior leader dictates a new way.

This is not to say that a coaching leadership style prevents the senior leader from giving direction when the situation calls for it. I would argue that a coaching leadership style involves knowing when giving direction is required, and when to engage the staff to arrive at solutions. Sometimes, the coach just has to tell the team: "Folks, we're all turning left now." Don't let anyone tell you that a coaching style means that the staff are allowed to debate all decisions and that they get to vote on everything. The hierarchy of the organization means that it is not a democracy. Remember, authority matters. But when you delegate authority, make sure you mean it, and use coaching through questioning if at all possible. The hardest part for me, when asking questions, was to sit still and listen.

In the Toyota Way to Lean Leadership, Jeffrey Liker and Gary Convis refer to the Japanese principle of the *Shu-Ha-Ri* style of mentorship, which is based on a very traditional style of training involving an apprentice and a *sensei*, or teacher.[1] This approach is also similar to the method used to train martial arts students. In most cases, the *sensei* is expected to be a master of the subject-matter, with the typical guideline being a minimum of 10,000 hours of experience within a subject area to be considered a master.

In the *Shu* (meaning "to protect") stage, the *sensei* breaks down the work into manageable pieces, performs each piece, and requires the apprentice to mimic what they do. Soon after, the *sensei* adds with each demonstration an explanation of why each step is done the way that it is. Gradually over time, the student learns the steps that are required to complete all of the tasks in the job.

In the *Ha* (meaning "to break away") stage of mentorship, the *sensei* allows the apprentice more freedom to perform the work on their own, but the *sensei* still takes accountability for the end results and is available to support the student when challenges arise. The student is able to perform most of the tasks without even thinking.

In the *Ri* (meaning "freedom to create") stage of mentorship, the *sensei* recognizes that the student has become a master in their own right. It is considered at this stage of development that the apprentice is able to properly innovate to improve the processes. The student is now able to become a *sensei* to other apprentices.

When studying the *Shu-Ha-Ri* apprenticeship model used within Toyota, I found the most striking point is the concept that no answers are to come from the *sensei*. I am certain that many North American leaders would struggle with this concept—I know that I continue to feel painfully constrained by the idea. But the concept of "no answers" is a fantastic ideal to remember to reinforce the principles of becoming an effective coach.

A key element of being a leader-coach is to free your people from being dependent on you when they perform their jobs. Answer their questions when they come to you for help, and you will reinforce to them that they must come to you for answers. Instead, teach them with questions, and they will grow in their abilities and skills. They will learn how to answer their own questions and free themselves from dependence on you as a leader. This will free more of your time to plan strategically, and you will be able to set your planning time-horizon farther and farther into the future.

Coach with questions, not answers, and watch your people become more than they are today and watch your power as a leader increase beyond what you had previously thought was possible.

# 30

## Trust Principle #25: Eliminate Competition in Favour of Teamwork

*"The best competition I have is against myself to become better."*

**John Wooden**[1]
*UCLA basketball coach, 1948–1975*

What if we say that we value teamwork, but then the boss publicly recognizes an individual's accomplishments in the workplace? If we value teamwork, why are we celebrating individual achievement? Maybe the organization has an employee-engagement program with annual awards for certain individuals: employee of the year, best innovator, top performer. You probably have seen something like this at one time in your career. But how congruent are these things if you as the leader say that your organization values teamwork and collaboration? Your message conflicts with the behaviour of the organization, which comes from your direction as the senior leader. In order to win one of these awards, that implies that the others must lose. A true culture of teamwork values everyone.

It started to become clear to me that I had to be on the lookout for these incongruences in elements of our organizational culture, and that I had to work to remove them whenever possible. We did value teamwork and collaboration—both items are crucial to a successful Lean journey. Competitiveness in a *kaizen* event is not going to achieve anything close to what cohesive teamwork can achieve in the same setting.

A key activity that contributed towards our trademark Manitoba Housing culture was our housing leadership team (HLT) monthly presentations, which I will discuss more in Chapter 38, Change Principle #5: Communicate everything you can. Part of my monthly presentation to the entire organizational leadership team, which would eventually make its way to all staff, was a slide that I called my "One More Thing" piece.

I lifted this phrase from Steve Jobs, the late CEO of Apple. It was one of his trademark phrases in his keynote addresses he used to give during product announcements. He often would give his presentation, and then take a step away from the podium as though he were finished. He would then turn, grin mischievously, and say, with the words echoing him up on the screen, "Oh wait, there's ...*One More Thing.*"

I have been a huge Apple fan for many years now, and I love the culture of innovation from that organization. I guess I hoped that by copying a piece of Steve Jobs' showmanship it might help me appear less boring as a public speaker. The jury is still out on that question. But the point of the One More Thing piece in my presentations was different—I would use this small segment to recognize examples of over-and-above staff effort, as nominated to me by my leadership team. It sounded great in concept, and it certainly had a positive feel to it. I recognized property managers, building superintendents, project managers, security personnel, and so on, all individually, for their hard work. But gradually I started to sense a problem with an incongruence in my behaviour.

I knew that we wanted teamwork and collaboration from our operations staff. But I started to wonder, what would the quiet staff member think of my One More Thing selections? Maybe that quiet person works just as hard as the extroverted staff member but just doesn't get noticed by the boss as often. Does that mean the quiet person wasn't worth recognizing? Of course not. But what would that person think? Or the many different people throughout the organization?

Would they be thinking something like "Oh, so nice to see Bill's name up there on the screen. The big boss doesn't know that Bill really isn't the fastest at that task. I am, but I just don't brag about it like he does. I guess you only get recognized if you push your accomplishments in your boss's face." Might I have been possibly creating something negative when I was trying to be positive and celebrate achievements? I became conflicted.

One month, I changed my One More Thing message. I said that I was taking a different approach to the recognition. I used that month's One More Thing piece to thank the staff who were taking on extra duties so that their colleagues could work on the project team developing the new corporate IT system, or the project team updating the policies and procedures. I thanked those people filling in with extra work while we struggled to hire a replacement for someone who had left. I thanked everyone who came to work every day, did their best, and wondered if the senior leadership even noticed. I assured them that they were just as important as everyone on those project teams.

That day, and the next day, I was surprised to have several staff see me in the hallways and thank me for the message in my presentation. It had resonated with people. Soon after, I decided to permanently switch the flavour of my message to celebrate some excellent examples of teamwork, instead of individual accomplishment, in the organization.

I think that every senior leader needs to ask themselves if they do anything within the organization currently that fosters competition. If so, you need to realize that this is in conflict with a goal of teamwork. In the next chapter, I review one of the most important principles of the *Space of Trust*, Trust Principle #26: Be congruent. In that chapter, I outline the importance of your message as a leader matching your actions at all times.

You absolutely cannot say that your organizational culture values teamwork while at the same time having the culture recognizing individual achievements—this is showing that you value competition. If you want teamwork, then you must, as the senior leaders, remove all promotion of competition from your organizational culture. Remove the conflict. I believe that it is an oxymoron to say, "There is nothing wrong with a little healthy competition in the workplace." I disagree—I think there is a lot wrong with it.

I believe that a competitive environment inherently supports selfish behaviour. It suggests that employees should each think about "me before we," and that teams within the organization should think about "us before them." There is no benefit to this type of selfish thinking. If we really want teamwork, that requires unselfish behaviour. It means that we want employees to think about each other before themselves, and it means that we never want one team to attempt to "win" at the expense of another team.

> *I believe that it is an oxymoron to say, "There is nothing wrong with a little healthy competition in the workplace." I disagree—I think there is a lot wrong with it.*

But furthermore, I think that it is important to recognize that teams are made of individuals, and not faceless masses. This means that to help the team improve its performance, you need to begin by supporting the performance development of every individual on the team, using the approaches described in Chapter 19, Trust Principle #14: Give balanced performance feedback regularly. Since every team member is a unique individual, their own performance feedback should be specifically tailored to them. This takes a lot of work, but if you undertake this approach as the leader of a team, you will build a stronger team. A strong team comes from strong individuals.

A corollary of this concept is that group proclamations about the behaviour of people on the team are rarely helpful. Behavioural issues on a team rarely come from everyone, but rather, from a few people on the team—therefore, deal with those few people privately as individuals about their own specific behavioural challenges. If you make a blanket statement about negative conduct by some within the team, you will confuse and frighten the innocent, while the guilty may become emboldened by mistakenly believing that their own behaviours are more commonplace than they had thought.

And you need to be continually reinforcing the proper approaches that support teamwork. You need to consistently show that unselfish behaviour between team members is the goal—everyone should first think about "we" before "me." As Linton Sellon suggests in The Workplace Leader, cliquing, rankings, and internal status between team members must be eliminated, as these run contrary to the collaborative team environment which you are trying to foster.[2] If you see cliques forming, shake things up and change the seating plan if you must to break those harmful sub-groups. Make sure that every team member understands the value of each other's role on the team. There should never be the perception that some people on the team are more "elite" than others. If the team manager doesn't see the harmful destructive back-biting but you know it is going on, then move the team manager right in the middle of the group to more closely observe, to direct the proper behaviour, and to model the way.

Having a good leader in place to support a team is crucial. I think that the idea of self-directed teams is misguided. In the absence of a formalized leader, a new one will emerge from the ranks. And it may not be the leader that you would want. Leave a team unattended without a leader for too long, and eventually an alpha team member will step up to fill that vacuum, and it may take you a while to figure out what has happened. By the time you realize that a self-appointed leader has stepped into the role, it may become difficult for you to replace that "leader" with a legitimate replacement, without having the new leader's authority being constantly challenged by the alpha and his or her supporters.

Oh, and by the way, hoping that employees who are in conflict with each other over some issues can just "sort things out for themselves like grownups" is a pipedream. Even directing them to do so may not help. The leader may have to get involved personally to work things out. Don't get the employees together at first, that rarely accomplishes anything productive. Linton Sellon advises to deal with each person separately, learn about the concerns, dig in deeper for more facts if you must, and then advocate for one employee to the other; make sure they each understand the value that the other brings to the team and the purpose of their role on the team. When the leader does this, it doesn't sound self-serving, which it would if you make each employee advocate for themselves to their colleague. In the course of resolving the conflict, if there are behavioural changes that one or more employees must make, don't be afraid to direct that change of behaviour, and monitor for compliance with your direction. Just don't make up a behaviour directive for an innocent employee just to appear even-handed, as sometimes a problem is one-sided.

Competition takes many forms within organizations, and in many cases, it can appear very harmless and even positive. Many companies have some sort of workplace awards program in an attempt to boost employee engagement by recognizing outstanding achievements. They are recognized as a "management best practice" by many leaders simply due to their prevalence. But that doesn't mean that they are right for your workplace. Manitoba Housing was no different.

Our awards luncheon was a top-notch event from start to finish. Staff nominations were submitted to an official evaluation committee to select the best nomination using a carefully developed evaluation matrix. All nominees and nominators were invited to the luncheon, where the executives would take turns announcing the various award winners, who would in turn go up to the podium to accept their trophies. The event had a professionalism to it that was quite impressive. There were both individual and team awards, with names like the Spirit of a Community Builder Award, the Spirit of a Rising Star Award, the Spirit of a Leader Award, and so on.

The problem for me came shortly after the awards ceremony in mid-2016. I started to question the congruence of the program with our values. We valued teamwork, but we were picking winners from our team. Even more ironic, was the fact that we had an award for the Spirit of Excellence (Team) Award. Not only were we naming winners (and by corollary, losers) from our organizational team, we were even ranking our small teams within our large team into winners and losers. I became even more conflicted now.

My concern grew as I spent more time looking for areas of incongruence in my own management style, and in our organization over which I had influence. When we as an executive team met to discuss the next year's award luncheon, I finally admitted my concerns to the other executives. Since I had previously advocated strongly for this awards program, I was now making a significant about-face. One of the other executives looked at me and said, "I thought it was just me. I've felt the same way for a while too." We agreed that we would gradually shift the awards program to equally recognize all who were nominated in a slightly different program, instead of one that separated "winners" from the team.

I wouldn't stop thanking people for their hard work when I was visiting site offices and meeting staff, but I needed to be consistent with the message of leadership culture that we were trying to foster—we were all a part of the same team. I began to realize that the right place for individual recognition was in private, one-on-one, and that the best person to give regular recognition to an employee was their own manager. It's become very trendy in the leadership literature to suggest that leaders need to understand each individual employee's desires for "how" they want to be recognized, and then to recognize them the way that they want. I've come to conclude that this is an extremely risky move.

You will make a mistake trying to keep the likes and dislikes of eight, ten, or twelve different people separate and remembered in real-time as you walk around trying to lead your team. And when you make a mistake about this type of thing, it can spectacularly backfire on you. Recognize someone publicly when they only like private recognition, and they can react very angrily and even make a scene. But I've never heard of some getting angry that their direct supervisor privately thanked them sincerely for something that they did well at work. You cannot go wrong that way. But you can easily go wrong with any attempt to customize public recognition, and the backlash from those mistakes will cost you dearly in terms of trust with your team. And, I believe, the people who dearly desire public recognition likely struggle with their own need for external validation—why should the leader make it their duty to set up a show when they can thank them one-on-one for a job well done?

If you want teamwork, and I believe that it is essential for a continuous improvement culture, then you need to be on the lookout for any type of competition that your leadership approach may inadvertently foster, and work to eliminate it. Unselfish behaviour among team members is critical. Build your team by building the individuals that comprise that team. And remember, you want every team member to think first about "we" before "me."

# 31

## Trust Principle #26: Be Congruent

*"The conviction of your message must be apparent in your words and in your life."*

**John C. Maxwell**[1]
*author, speaker, and pastor*

Your people will place a tremendous amount of importance on the alignment of their leaders' behaviour with their messages—this is sometimes known by the word "congruence." In simple terms, it means "walking the talk." When you are shaping and developing the *Space of Trust*, this principle of congruency is absolutely critical. Kouzes and Posner, in *The Leadership Challenge*, identify five key leadership practices.[2] Practice 1 is "Model the Way," and they suggest further that the leader needs to "set the example." I really believe that this is important when building trust relationships between staff and the senior leadership.

As Stephen M.R. Covey proposes in *The Speed of Trust*, credibility is the important foundation on which trust relationships can be built.[3] Covey identifies the Four Cores of Credibility as follows:

1. Integrity,
2. Intent,
3. Capabilities, and
4. Results.

The first two Cores refer to an individual's character, and the last two Cores refer to an individual's competence. All four, however, are necessary for trust. The first Core, Integrity, might mean different things to different people. I'll define it simply to mean that, as a leader, your behaviours need to match your messages, all the time—congruence.

If you want all of your staff to start doing things a new way, you need to demonstrate that you are willing to be the first patient to try out the new surgery. At the end of 2015, we were approaching the time in our Lean journey to add the 5S principles to our organizational culture at Manitoba Housing. The Lean concept of 5S, which is described in more detail in Chapter 48, Change Principle #15: Realize that in an office, 5S doesn't just mean cleaning off your desk, involves applying a structured process to optimize the processes and workflow around everyone's workstation.

In a factory, the benefits of this approach are somewhat more intuitive— carefully organizing the equipment and supplies at a manufacturing workstation will obviously improve the efficiency at that workstation. However, the CEO and I knew that this would be a tough sell for many of our folks who worked in office environments. Therefore, the CEO and I knew that we had to set the examples. As a result, we were the first people in the company to ask for our offices to go through the 5S transformation procedure.

When we were actually holding the 5S transformation, we put signs on the outside of our office walls saying "5S Event in Progress," and the CEO and I made sure that we were active participants in the process for our own workspaces—it would be terrible form to delegate this to an administrative assistant to manage. The signs had the desired effect. People walking by would stop and peer in and ask what the commotion was. This gave me an opportunity to explain to people, one-on-one what 5S meant, and why it was important.

When the event was complete, we posted an "audit tracker" on the outside walls of our offices. The tracker would be a sheet of paper with a colour photo of the office taken right after the 5S event, and beside the photo was an explanation of what 5S meant, in simple terms. Underneath the photo were two side-by-side coloured rectangles: one was green, one was red. There was a sticker on the green rectangle. We told the staff, in public presentations, that we wanted them to hold us accountable by moving the sticker from green to red if they didn't think that our offices matched the picture in the audit sheet.

This did present a bit of a novel challenge to some of the staff (and leaders) in the headquarters building. A couple times I found the sticker on the red rectangle and for the life of me, I couldn't figure out why someone was calling me out—I thought the desk looked perfect. Later, someone finally owned up to it, that they had tagged me for having my reading glasses at a slightly different angle than in the photo. We were okay with the fact that some people were having a little fun with us as the senior executives. That was part of building trust with the staff. A few times, some anonymous people did catch me (fairly) letting a couple of unnecessary things sit on my desk. So, I put the files back where they belonged, took out a cleaning wipe, cleaned off the desk surface, and then I moved the sticker back to green. Eventually, it did become a habit for me to keep my desk the way it looked the day that my office 5S was completed.

The CEO and I knew that if we were to expect our staff to adopt a new, and initially baffling, concept such as 5S redesign of their workspaces, but not be willing to do it ourselves, we would damage our leadership integrity. And that would impede our ability to build trust with our staff, because our message would be incongruent with our actions. As they say, talk is cheap, but action is real.

The idea of the importance of congruency of behaviour with actions is not new. Many well-known leaders have spoken in favour of this principle. Mahatma Gandhi once said:[4]

*"My life is my message."*

I think that this quotation speaks to the importance of modelling the way as a leader. It's very easy to give mixed messages as a leader without even intending to. It happens all the time in organizations in seemingly innocuous ways that appear to follow common management practices, assumed to be best practices. I believe that practicing the leadership principle of congruence is one of the most important principles within the *Space of Trust*. You have to keep remembering that you are trying to build trust relationships between the staff and the leadership. In order to trust, they need to see the leadership walking the talk, all the time. Stephen M.R. Covey says in *The Speed of Trust:*[5]

*"A person has integrity when there is no gap between intent and behaviour... when he or she is whole, seamless, the same—inside and out. I call this 'congruence.' And it is congruence—not compliance—that will ultimately create credibility and trust."*

The hardest part about practicing this leadership principle is that you, as a leader, are always being observed—so you need to be always

*It's very easy to give mixed messages as a leader without even intending to.*

"on." The principle of congruence means that as the senior leader, you need to be always modelling the way of every leadership principle in this book. While it seems like a lot of separate principles to remember, I have tried to break them up into small, easily-understood pieces. And most of them have a common-sense feel to them, anyway. The value in this book, I believe, is the assembly of the set of these principles and the way that they are arranged, for a senior leader guiding their organization through the beginning of a continuous improvement and Lean Management culture change.

The principle of leadership congruence cannot be an act that you switch on when you enter your office, and then switch it off when you leave. In fact, I believe that a leader's congruence needs to become such a crucial part of who they are, that it needs to follow them home as well. You should be consistent in following the same principles outside of work as well as at work. Otherwise, you are inconsistent.

In a way, I think that the principle of being congruent is physiologically healthier for people—I believe that trying to remember different ways of behaving in different environments, in different company, among different people, between home and work, is mentally stressful and exhausting. Get rid of that stress and do yourself a favour—be congruent. Always.

# 32

## The Space of Trust—Concluding Thoughts

*"If something is important enough, even if the odds are against you, you should still do it."*

**Elon Musk**[1]
*engineer, entrepreneur, founder of SpaceX and Tesla, Inc.*

When I think through the personal leadership transformation journey on which I have been for several years, I have a new appreciation for the truly great leaders out there. As Manitoba Housing began to build for itself an increasingly positive reputation with the obvious success of its operations excellence Lean program, the CEO and I started getting frequently asked to meet with different organizations from within Manitoba, and even internationally, looking for advice on how to get started with their own Lean programs.

I have to say that occasionally I wondered if the all of executives with whom we met would really have the internal fortitude to change themselves, if necessary, before they started taking their organization down the Lean path. I now realize that some leaders may have no idea what they are really in for, and that some may not be prepared to make the necessary personal sacrifices to develop and shape the culture necessary in order for Lean and continuous improvement to become a part of the fabric of the organization. But those of you who are already there, those of you who have already embraced as leaders the lessons which I have assembled in this part of the book, you are in a great position to start your Lean journey.

For those of you who are not already there, but are willing to commit: Hang on tight, you've got a tough road ahead, but I promise that you'll be better at the end of the ride for having made the effort.

The approach I've described in this part of the book about adjusting the leadership environment to properly shape the *Space of Trust* involves giving great respect to the leadership/staff trust relationships. Take those relationships for granted, and your *Space of Trust* will suffer a tremendous setback, and so will your entire Lean journey.

Whenever you are making a key decision that will affect your people, you need to also weigh the impact on the *Space of Trust* before you act. That's not to say that you should never do anything that people won't like because it might negatively impact the *Space of Trust*—sometimes you won't have a choice. But you can think about changing your approach to one more in keeping with valuing the trust with your staff.

If you think that you will apply some of the approaches that I'm describing here as tactics, or techniques that you will switch on when you walk into your office and switch off when you leave, you're making a huge mistake. You really have to be all-in when you go down this path. If you give the appearance of wanting to develop trust with the staff, but you are not sincere in your approach, you might deceive your people for a while, but when they detect that you are pretending, you will be finished. The staff will not deeply engage in the manner that is necessary for the improvements to be developed or implemented. People will avoid your Lean events. Your whole Lean management transformation will be poisoned, and you will make it difficult for your organization to attempt a Lean management approach after you are gone, as the institutional memory of your deceptive approach will be associated with the very word "Lean," and it will last a long time. If you're not prepared to change yourself as the senior leader, and to go all-in, then you shouldn't even try. You would be doing your staff a disservice if you did proceed.

The former CEO of the aerospace organization where I used to work was a true Lean champion, and he preached the value of the approach personally wherever he went. When he would walk the shop floor, he would know many of the technicians by name and would call out to them with a wave as he passed by. Many people in the company greatly appreciated his leadership style. After he left that organization, he was hired on as the CEO of another major manufacturing organization headquartered in Manitoba. He often put one of his quotations in presentations when he would talk about the importance of leaders being completely congruent in both behaviours and values:[2]

*"You can fool the fans, but you can't fool the players."*

I completely agree. A leader putting on a good show might fool the board, the vice-president, or the other senior executives, or the senior bureaucrats, or the elected officials, but if the leader isn't sincere, he or she can never fool their staff for long. They will always see right through the smoke and mirrors.

The CEO of Manitoba Housing and I were once asked by a very senior leader in another organization how we "handled" the union regarding the start of our Lean journey. We were surprised by the question because we never considered "handling" the union at all. We informed the union at our earliest opportunity about the upcoming Lean management approaches that we would use. There was nothing at all that would upset the union: Management would involve front-line staff to determine changes to improve the efficiency of processes, and management would listen to the staff and implement their ideas.

The only "handling" that happened was when the CEO and I realized that we needed to change ourselves as leaders and that we needed to try our best to be congruent at all times. When we lived the message, we didn't need to "handle" anyone.

# Part III

# Understanding the Space for Change

# 33

## The Space for Change Explained

*"The secret of change is to focus all of your energy, not on fighting the old, but on building the new."*

**Dan Millman**[1]
*author*

Within the larger *Space of Trust* exists the smaller *Space for Change*. During normal operations in an organization, only some things are in the *Space for Change*. Much of the day-to-day business that occurs is routine, and status quo. But when the leadership is deliberately working to change the status quo, those efforts take place within the *Space for Change*. This is where organizational change is focused, and the leadership needs to carefully define and shape this space, and then maintain it once it is defined. You will be needing it forever.

By its very definition, a Lean program is about continuous improvement, and improvement means change. People cringe when you talk about change, and it seems that they cringe even more in the workplace. But there are ways to make change more palatable.

Studying and following organizational change management principles of leadership is one way to minimize the negative impact of change. Establishing multiple communication streams from the senior leadership to the staff in an organization, and across levels as well, is another key approach to minimize the pain of change. It's important to work with people to explain the leadership culture change every step of the way, as the organization begins new approaches like huddle board meetings and regular reviews of team performance metrics.

Eventually, you aren't so much focusing only on trying to minimize the negative aspects to change, but you will be focusing on trying to make the change as successful as possible to help the team. And when you get the *Space for Change* working properly, your team will feel it. They will feel supported by the leadership, and it will make a big difference in the morale of the team as they go through these changes.

But again, I maintain that it is very likely that in your organization, the biggest change may first need to take place within the senior leadership team, as they work to adopt a new philosophy in dealing with the staff. If the senior leaders can adopt that new outlook, then the *Space for Change* will develop as it should.

# 34

## Change Principle #1: Recognize That Sometimes Terminology Does Matter

*"The art of communication is the language of leadership."*

**James Humes[1]**
*American author and presidential speechwriter*

If your organization is completely foreign to the concepts within Lean management, then, yes, terminology does matter. Announcing that you are going down this path to your staff will invoke a lot of fears in your people. Some will be wary that this is just another management fad that will pass in time, only to be replaced by something completely different.

In the public sector, some may be concerned that this involves making public servants follow an approach that only works in the industrial world. Many will be fearful of drastic measures that might follow, like layoffs. A very typical fear of people when a program like this is initiated is that it is a veiled move to trim staff. Some people may have even heard of organizations where Lean was actually used for this purpose. I cringe when I hear these stories where the solid principles of Lean management were misunderstood and weaponized against the very staff that Lean management is intended to support and engage.

One of the worst situations I heard of involving the misapplication of Lean management principles was from a private sector company. This company started a Lean program, but the expertise and toolkit were highly centralized to a few secretive highly-placed people. When a *kaizen* event was held, the senior leaders would not involve any front-line staff at all. They would hold the event with the senior leadership only and then invite the manager in to review the flow chart. The manager would be instructed to identify areas for improvement and wasteful steps that could be eliminated. The manager was then sent out of the room, and the optimized process was then finalized, and some staff were labelled surplus as a result of the *kaizen*—they were terminated shortly afterwards.

As you can imagine, word of this approach spread like wildfire through the organization, and the Lean office quickly developed a dangerous reputation with the staff. No one would willingly offer information any more about processes that would be necessary for *kaizen* events to be successful, so these activities quickly stalled out. Over time, the program lost its effectiveness, and it was soon discontinued.

This example illustrates a company applying the complete opposite of every principle of Lean management. The worst part is that legends like this spread to people working in other organizations, and these people may now be working for you. Now you are battling uphill against unfair prejudices against Lean management principles that, if applied correctly, will be tremendously beneficial to your staff and the morale of the organization.

Because Manitoba Housing was one of the first departments in the Manitoba Government to begin applying Lean management principles in earnest, we asked our consultant to help us with branding and terminology. He suggested initially using the name operations excellence in place of Lean, as it is an industry-recognized term that includes the use of both Lean and sometimes Six-Sigma methodologies.

Imagine you are a front-line staff member in an organization and the executive announces that they are going to start applying "Lean management" approaches. If you have never heard of Lean management, the term might invoke thoughts of a butcher trimming fat from meat. That image immediately brings to mind cuts and negative impacts on staff. As a result, you might be already apprehensive of the idea, and the organization hasn't even begun to adopt the approach yet. This makes the upcoming organizational change management so much more difficult.

In the public sector, you need to be very careful about referring to the citizens who are receiving the services of government as "customers." Early on in the Manitoba Housing Lean journey, I was yelled at in a conference panel forum discussion on transformational leadership by an audience member who was apparently quite upset over the Lean language I was using. While I believe that his reaction was heavy-handed, I did adjust my terminology after that.

Although people in the private sector might see the words "customer" and "clients" as interchangeable, I do think that there is a crucial difference in perception within the public sector that deserves respect. From my perspective, customers usually have choices as to where they shop for services or products, but clients of a government service may have no other options beyond the service that the government is offering. For example, Manitoba Housing provided subsidized housing options, either directly or through partners, to low-to-moderate-income people across Manitoba. We were the primary provider in the province for this service. If our clients were unhappy with our service, there might have been nowhere else for them to go. The same could be said for many other government departments and the services that they provide. There is no point in using wording that evokes negative reactions in people when you are trying to get them to realize the benefits of the Lean management approach.

Another key challenge I find with the definition of a customer for government services is that you often hear the customer described as "the person who pays for the services or product." In most cases of government services, the client either pays indirectly for the service through taxes, or he or she may not pay at all. Further to that point is the difference between the taxpayer and the citizen. Nearly everyone is a citizen, but not everyone is a taxpayer (at least in the once-a-year tax return sense). As a result, I found that the term "customer" in government often had to be replaced by a stakeholder group, usually consisting of both citizens and clients. That's not to say that we forgot about the client-focus because it seemed inconvenient. Not at all. We always worked to ensure that the client was a focus of every improvement that we made to our processes at Manitoba Housing.

Although in this book I have included many descriptions of the Japanese lexicon to further explain the origins behind some of the principles, I have been very careful to ensure that each leadership principle is worded in simple English terms. Many Lean practitioners love to use the Japanese terms, sometimes, it appears, for no other reason than to demonstrate their worldly knowledge to those around them. But I've come to realize that there is absolutely no value to using terminology that makes it more difficult for you to achieve your goal.

If your goal is a transformational culture change in your organization, then be prepared to adapt your terminology to achieve that goal. Go easy on the Japanese words, if they are going to make Lean seem foreign, strange, and off-putting to your staff. Don't make your own job harder than it needs to be. You need to ask yourself: are you trying to get your staff to incorporate the new approaches into how they work or are you trying to impress them with your subject-matter knowledge?

At Manitoba Housing, we used only a few Japanese Lean terms during our Lean journey, such as *kaizen*, and *gemba* walk. But instead of using the many other Japanese terms, I found it much easier to get people to understand what I was talking about when I used the plain-language terminology that I have adopted into the leadership principles of the Three Spaces model used in many of the chapter headings in this book.

Our consultant was very careful to go out and to talk to staff in the field in his first few months working with us. He learned some of the terminology that they used out in the field, and then used what he had learned to shape Operations Excellence training to suit the language that would be more familiar to the staff. In some cases, this was an iterative process, but I know from our experience that it was worth the effort.

Sometimes, semantics aren't worth fighting over when you are trying to win people over to a new way of thinking. It pays off to be willing to adapt your language to suit what works for your organization. Make your work easier, not harder, by choosing your terminology thoughtfully.

# 35

## Change Principle #2: Explain WHY Many Times

*"The very essence of leadership is that you have a vision. It's got to be a vision you articulate clearly and forcefully on every occasion. You can't blow an uncertain trumpet."*

**Rev. Theodore Hesburgh[1]**
*President of Notre-Dame University*

Why are we doing this? What was wrong with the way we were doing things for the past ten years? Why do we have to learn about this operations excellence stuff at all? Why indeed? When you ask some leaders, who have been told that they need to develop Lean management programs in their departments, why they think Lean is important, you will get a variety of answers. You might be told that Lean will bring cost savings. Or that Lean will bring efficiency or a better use of taxpayer dollars. Or that it will bring better client- or customer service. Or better outcomes for citizens. The problem is that these are all hard to truly address in practice early on in a Lean journey.

In his book, *Start with WHY*, Simon Sinek outlines a naturally-occurring pattern which he names the *Golden Circle*.[2] He outlines a graphic, similar in construct to the Three Spaces model to which I refer in this book, a set of three concentric circles: the outermost circle is labelled "WHAT," the middle circle is labelled "HOW," and the innermost circle is labelled "WHY."

He suggests that it is best to communicate from inside the Golden Circle first and then move to the outer circles for your organization to be more compelling. In other words, *Start with WHY*. Don't first tell people what you do, or how. Telling them WHY you exist, WHY you are doing what you do. Start with the more intrinsic motivational aspect and allow that to engage people on a more fundamental level. As Sinek says:[3]

*"To inspire starts with the clarity of WHY."*

Only after you understand yourself WHY you are taking your organization down a Lean transformational journey can you properly explain it to your team. And you need to get this part right. *Start with WHY* is a thought-provoking book that encourages the reader to contemplate the source of true engagement.

Our official message of WHY we were undertaking our Manitoba Housing operations excellence program was as follows:

- To improve program and service delivery to our clients;
- To develop and maintain efficient processes;
- To evolve our organizational culture by engaging and empowering *all* employees; and
- To help involve staff in decision-making.

Ensuring that the customer or client remains the primary focus of Lean efforts is quite fundamental to the methodology of Lean. You can see that the first element of our WHY-factors spoke directly to this fact. The last two factors spoke to our people. Some people might argue that the first bullet should be the only WHY statement, and that the last three bullets support the HOW. I might agree with them on an academic level, but we were truly trying to achieve something additional through our Lean journey—true employee engagement.

For an organization just getting going with its Lean journey, I have come to believe that the answer is against what the traditional Lean dogma would tell you. At first, just understand that you are doing it for your staff, for your people. When you keep that foremost in your mind as the senior leader in charge of the program, I don't think you can go wrong. As we discussed in Chapter 12, Trust Principle #7: Trust that better client service results from treating your people well, treat your people well and they will take care of the customer or client.

Focus on making it work and having it be a tremendously positive experience for your staff. Show them that you trust them to improve the processes by delegating some of your authority to them during a *kaizen* event. Show that you appreciate their input by accepting the process improvements that they develop in the *kaizen* events and put them into practice right away.

Do it for your people and start your organization down the path of a culture change, the likes of which many of them will never have experienced. That culture change is what you are going after. When the culture changes in the right way, you will start to achieve all the other desirable goals without difficulty at all: better client- and customer service, more efficient processes, more effective programs, better uses of taxpayer or corporate expense dollars, more profitability, and, in government, better outcomes for citizens.

But you will need to communicate the WHY to your people with simplicity and clarity. Your message will have to be in words that feel comfortable to you, or it will sound forced and insincere to your staff. You will find that you will have to explain the WHY more than once—many times, in fact. It may start to feel frustrating at times, to be repeating the same message over and over again, but that is part of what is required to build trust. This journey on which you are beginning with your organization is so different from what is "normal" for them, that they are skeptical, and they need to see that the leadership is committed to the cause. To build that credibility required for true trust takes some evidence, and that evidence is often a consistent pattern of behaviour from the senior leadership—that means you have to keep giving the same positive message repeatedly for months to show that this is really how management is behaving now. Consistency demonstrates congruence, and congruence, along with competence, demonstrates integrity.

So, when people ask, "why are we doing this Lean stuff?" make sure you have the right answer at your disposal. And be prepared to give that answer many times in the months ahead. Don't look at it as a waste of your time, but instead, look at it as an investment in the culture change that you desire.

# 36

## Change Principle #3: Be Wary of a Goal of Quick Cash Savings

*"Lean is about being an athlete, not a skeleton."*

**Sami Niemela**[1]
*designer and co-founder of Nordkapp, in Finland*

I'm always so hesitant to mention the topic of cost savings from Lean because many leaders jump right in and make it the prime focus of the transformation. This is tremendously risky, and it is a terrible mistake to make. In fact, I believe that you need to be on guard constantly to fend off demands to quantify the cost saving of a Lean journey in the early stages.

The risk is that many of the cash savings in the first year or so of your Lean program won't be easily quantifiable, or will be small, such as reduced paper savings costs in an office environment. Here are the two key danger areas when discussing cost savings in the early stages of a new Lean program:

1. Some critics will not like the unquantifiable savings and suggest that the program be scrapped as an ineffective investment; and
2. Some critics will look at process improvements that save staff time as opportunities to reduce staff.

The second one will be the end of your Lean management initiative, and it will poison the psyche of your staff with regards to Lean for years to come if you allow it to happen.

Staff know that management loves things that save money, so often when they quantify the results of a *kaizen* event for the final presentation, they

*165*

will look for the items with dollar signs in front of them. Sometimes, they will think that saving 1,000 sheets of paper monthly from reduced filing activities, at a very minimal reduction in office supplies costs, is the true benefit of the exercise.

At Manitoba Housing, I know that my staff were surprised when I told them that, while the few hundred dollars of cost savings around reduced paper and file archiving was nice, the real savings in which I was interested was the staff time. Because, to me, their time was valuable, and I didn't want to have them wasting their time on non-value-added activities.

But eventually, your team will develop a *kaizen* so amazing that the staff time savings will be huge. One of ours at Manitoba Housing resulted in over 160 hours per month of reduced clerical work by eliminating non-value-added steps in the processes. At 7.25 hours per day, 5 days a week, and 4 weeks per month, a single clerk works approximately 145 hours. That means that this *kaizen* resulted in savings of more than one clerical staffing position.

I was very careful in how I handled the messaging back to the staff of my acknowledgement of the savings. I said that: "This is an extra 160 hours of clerical time that you can now use to focus on the more important parts of the job to support our clients." On another occasion, I told the staff: "This is like finding an additional clerk to help with the value-added tasks."

The danger of going down the path of looking for staffing reduction opportunities from your Lean program is that you will be violating the trust covenant between the leadership and the staff that you will be working to build in the *Space of Trust*. If you engage front-line staff in *kaizen* events, and then delegate to them the authority to make changes to a business process, how do you think they will feel if you take the results of their efforts and eliminate a staff position on their team? They will feel betrayed and used. They will immediately revoke their trust in the Lean program, and word will get out quickly that the Lean initiative is a Trojan horse, an initiative that is actually intended to cut staff but is disguised as something to engage staff.

Sometimes the staff will try to be helpful in outlining cost savings associated with staff time, by multiplying the staff fully-burdened labour rate against the monthly staff hour savings and add this number to the monthly material cost savings, to produce a total monthly cost savings resulting from a process change. This is truly a common approach that you find in many different organizations, in both the public and private sectors. Unfortunately, this is built on a completely false economy, as the staff savings won't show up anywhere unless you eliminate a job and send an employee home.

Instead of looking at this as savings, you need to redirect the "saved" staff hours towards something else that is causing the organization a problem right now. In the example I gave with the clerical staff time savings, this particular team had been struggling with service-delivery effectiveness, so it happened to be quite simple to redirect that "found time" back to focusing on other aspects of client service where we needed more time anyway.

You must be constantly vigilant as the senior leader driving this type of transformation—you may need to be prepared to handle this type of questioning from your CEO, your board, the executives to whom you report, or senior government officials. It's not that these people are necessarily against Lean when they question you, but it's more likely that they don't understand completely how it works and what it can do. For most people, it is not apparent at first how important the focus on culture change over costs needs to be when implementing Lean.

In *The Toyota Way to Lean Leadership*, Jeffrey Liker and Gary Convis have a section entitled "Why a Short-Term Focus on Cost Reduction Will Kill Real Lean Transformation."[2] In this section, they suggest that doing Lean properly and saving money are not opposites at all, but that driving your Lean transformation from the singular viewpoint of using it as a tool to save money is very dangerous:

> *"...we have emphasized the challenge and resources required to create a true culture of continuous improvement. Commands from the top for quick cost savings generally kill this investment in the culture for the future and ruin employee trust, and Lean becomes a tool-based program to cut costs."*

In Lean management, when you are starting from the very beginning, your true cost savings will be further down the road. You won't see very much in actual dollar savings at first. And the staff-times savings, of course, cannot be realized on the expense statement unless you send someone home. This you absolutely cannot do in any manner that is associated with your Lean program.

In most cases, the opportunities for actual cash savings are to be found in an organization's supply chain. This is where supply-chain process improvements, partnering with suppliers, consolidating contracts, asking for early-payment discounts, reducing inventory with approaches such as

*Kanban* or supplier-based inventory, can really help to provide visible cash savings to the organization. But when other elements of your business environment have created permanent short-staffing situations where a business unit is struggling to keep up with the pace, then Lean can help to streamline the work so that they can truly do "more with less," or the more likely situation requiring you to do "the same with less."

Trust me, you will get cost savings eventually, when the staff engagement switches on. And when that time comes, make sure you trumpet those savings to the right stakeholders—just make sure that the savings are real, and demonstrable on subsequent financial expense statements, or you will lose credibility quickly.

# 37

## Change Principle #4: Appreciate the Value of Change Management

*"The leader must make personal changes before asking others to change."*

**John C. Maxwell[1]**
*author, speaker, and pastor*

Don't underestimate the fact that change is hard for people. We as leaders can mandate a change using our authority, but that certainly doesn't make it easy for people to absorb it into their work behaviours or their thinking patterns. Properly implementing a change with the staff takes quite a bit of planning and effort during execution, and even afterwards. If you think this is a waste of time, you are greatly mistaken. This is an investment that you need to be prepared to make if you want your organizational transformation to really work and to last.

The CEO of Manitoba Housing had a great way of asking people to consider the importance of change management. He would ask you to think back in your own career to a time when a decision to change how you did a part of your job was made for you. How did that make you feel? Did anyone explain to you why it was necessary? Did anyone explain to you the benefits of the new approach? Did you receive adequate training or instruction on how to follow the new method? Did you have a chance to practice the new way in a safe environment where mistakes were not punished? Did management provide positive reinforcement afterwards to make sure the changes were supported long after the training had occurred? If you answered "no" to one or more of these questions, I'll bet that you didn't remember this experience fondly. You probably were thinking "that could have been handled so much better." And you were right.

Organizational change management, or OCM, is a field of study that I had heard about when I was working in the private sector, but I had never had the opportunity to learn about until I joined Manitoba Housing. The Manitoba Government had embraced OCM training, and in particular, had selected the Prosci® ADKAR® model as the methodology of choice. ADKAR is actually an acronym that is designed to help you remember the elements of the framework for Change Management:[2]

- Facilitate the *Awareness* of the need for change;
- Build the *Desire* to support the change;
- Educate them with *Knowledge* of how to change;
- Provide the *Ability* to demonstrate new skills and behaviours; and
- Ensure that leadership provides the appropriate *Reinforcement* to make the change stick.

I have to admit that, when I first was signed up for an introductory OCM training session, I was very skeptical. But I quickly appreciated the teachings as I started to study the assigned ADKAR book I was provided as pre-reading for the class. I immediately saw a rationale for why I had seen some organizational changes in my career work well, while others failed. The changes that had worked well were ones where the leaders had, either intentionally or by coincidence, applied the principles of OCM when rolling out the changes.

If you haven't studied this field yet, I highly recommend that you invest time in either reading about it or in taking a class before you start your organizational transformation journey. It can greatly help you to avoid making many preventable mistakes along the way.

One of the most common phrases you hear in the field of change management is "what's in it for me," or WIIFM. This should always be a part of your change planning, to help the staff to be able to interpret some aspect of the change in a manner that offers them a better future vision of their work, or the culture. After explaining WHY (see Chapter 35, Change Principle #2: Explain WHY. Many times) at Manitoba Housing we were taking the organization down the path of operations excellence, we then had to get into the HOW we were going to do it. That involved providing an introduction to operations excellence, prepared and delivered by our consultant, to staff through an all-hands presentation that was broadcast to all staff.

We then committed to delivering a basic half-day training program about operations excellence, to every one of our staff. Although our consultant helped to develop this presentation and provide the initial delivery sessions, we quickly developed in-house staff Lean practitioners who were able to take over the delivery themselves. At three-and-a-half years into our journey, we had delivered this training to approximately 450 people out of our total of over 700 staff.

In Chapter 34, Change Principle #1: Recognize that sometimes terminology does matter, I talked about the often-negative connotations that people have with the term Lean in the initial stages of an organization's cultural transformation. An interesting side note is that, after we moved people past the initial fearful stage early in our journey, we were able to call these training sessions "Lean 101" without any negative repercussions.

When your organizational leadership decides that you are going to start a Lean transformational journey, you should be prepared for skepticism and cynicism from the staff. It's not your people's fault; it's just that if they have been around for a while, then they have likely seen management fads come and go. And to make matters more challenging, these people may believe that they can "wait you out," because they've seen that approach work before. Even more likely, these people either have experienced, or may be currently experiencing, bad leadership that doesn't line up with the principles of Lean management. It's also possible that the bad leadership may include you. Don't worry though, that doesn't mean you can't change.

You need to be prepared to stand strong through some negativity from your own people. Don't despair; it may not last that long depending on how long it takes you to really show some progress in the form of Lean 101 training for the staff, or your organization's first *kaizen* event.

> *"Stamping out fires is a lot of fun, but it is only putting things back the way they were."*
> **W. Edwards Deming**[3]

Over the course of my career, I've many times seen Lean management being introduced into organizations that have never seen it or heard about it before. Sometimes, people will say that they have been doing Lean for years already, but that the only difference was the terminology that you are now bringing in. I remember hearing some people say that while Lean may work in the private sector, this is the public sector and things work differently here. "You just don't understand public sector enough." However, I was not ignorant of the fact that the Lean management approach with which I was most familiar, from the aerospace industrial sector, would have to be adapted to suit a public-sector application.

I remember hearing people say, "You know, this isn't the private sector; we don't make widgets here." I agreed with them. However, I somewhat took offense from the widgets comment, because I felt that this was a crack about the aerospace organization at which I worked previously. We didn't make widgets there either.

A gas-turbine engine has thousands of complex components, exquisitely engineered to incredibly fine tolerances; rotor bearings, for instance, can have manufacturing tolerances on the order of a few ten-thousandths of an inch or less. The assembly of these complex machines into a working unit fit for flight propulsion is a very technical undertaking that takes dozens of technicians and specialists, each with countless hours of training, both in the classroom and on the job. Equating this business to the manufacturing of widgets, like simple plastic toys, was a little hurtful to me. I was proud of where I came from, and I wasn't ashamed of my career experience. But I realized that the staff were uncomfortable with the idea of yet another drastic change coming their way, and they were simply voicing their concerns in different ways. It was understandable.

I have heard many times people say that their team was very special. Things were too "fluid" or "dynamic" here to even think about creating metrics for business unit performance measurement. In my experience, the "unique" theme is a very common one that people use to push back against a Lean program. That's entirely understandable too. Everyone wants to believe that their field of expertise is special and unique. They want to believe that everything they have learned over their years in their roles can't possibly be understood by some outsider who is going to tell them how to fix their procedures. It's a classic defensive response to feeling threatened in their area of speciality.

But what they don't realize at first is that the "outsiders" aren't going to tell them how to fix their procedures. The staff working in these areas every day are going to help to inform the leadership with ideas to fix the procedures. The outsiders are simply going to set up the environment and the structured approach to allow this to happen in the Lean way. But the staff don't know this at first, so they are simply jumping to conclusions because they don't yet understand how the Lean program will work.

Although this concern, and each type of concern that I have mentioned in this section, needs to be treated gently by the Lean executive, I can assure you that no area is so "unique" that correctly-applied Lean management principles cannot help. I had even heard the "unique" comments from engineering and technical personnel back in the aerospace sector a few times, and that was within an organization that had started its Lean journey before I had even started working there. I believe that this concern is a common fear from people regardless of where they work, in the public or the private sector.

I think that people tend to believe that they each bring an element of artistry to their field, and it troubles them to imagine what they do every day being reduced to a process map of sticky notes on a wall. Such a mechanical and standardized methodology appears to strip away that perceived artistry that they learned from years of experience. But I still believe that every process, even in the public sector, can be improved to some extent using the Lean approach. Many public-sector procedures involve information flow, whether by paper or electronic means, and Lean processes, guided by the expert knowledge of the staff, are perfectly capable of optimizing these.

I think that the simple way to handle these initial concerns is to listen and show respect for the worries of the staff. I wouldn't criticize them or tell them that their fears are irrational. I would listen, but then I would tell them that the people who were going to improve the procedures of the organization were the staff who are involved with them every day, the real subject-matter experts, not the leadership blindly imposing uninformed solutions from above.

The other thing I would do is tell them that our goal was to provide training about what Lean is, the "Lean 101" training, to the staff and that I hoped that they would be among the first to take the training and maybe even participate in one of the earliest *kaizen* events. What they really needed to address their apprehensions was a combination of education and hands-on experience with what Lean really was all about. And they also needed to see the leadership environment change from the top down as well. The first two items were much easier to deliver than the last one. If you can get the staff to adopt a "Well, I'll wait and see" approach, take it and be happy. For them, seeing it for themselves will help them to believe.

Study carefully the science of OCM. Everything about your cultural transformation is going to involve lots of change for your team, so you owe it to your organization to learn how to handle change correctly.

# 38

## *Change Principle #5: Communicate Everything You Can*

*"The great enemy of communication is the illusion of it."*

**William Whyte[1]**
*author, urbanist, and journalist*

You probably guessed that a key element of success involves communication, right? One of the critical factors necessary to define the *Space for Change* is setting up the channels of communication between the senior leadership and the rest of the organization. And a single communication vehicle is not sufficient. At Manitoba Housing, we used just about every option that we had available to us:

- Town hall meetings;
- Presentations;
- Email messages;
- Newsletters;
- Intranet sites;
- Leadership meetings;
- Branch team meetings, and more.

The in-person delivery method of communication about key organizational issues from senior leadership at director or manager meetings is very important to convey the priority. In order to maintain the *Space of Trust*, however, the senior leadership needs to set and establish a pattern of being open and forthright when communicating with staff.

I think another lens that the senior leadership needs to choose to look through when viewing their team is how much they trust them with information about what is going on in the organization. At Manitoba Housing, the CEO and I deliberately chose to *communicate almost everything, unless we had a compelling reason not to do so.* I believe that the leadership of any organization taking on this cultural transformation needs to adopt this philosophy towards communicating with their staff. I cannot state enough how critical I believe that adopting this approach is going to be in your journey.

> *At Manitoba Housing, the CEO and I deliberately chose to communicate almost everything, unless we had a compelling reason not to do so.*

This doesn't mean that we passed along inappropriate information in public forums, of course. Performance observations of an individual team member, union negotiation material, or confidential government budget information, are obvious examples of what would not be communicated with this mindset.

However, the old way of the organization was *not to communicate any information beyond the minimum required unless it was absolutely necessary.* I'll bet many people have worked in organizations that operated with the latter approach, but this is no way to build trust between staff and the senior leadership. I think that in order to earn trust, you need to demonstrate it with your team.

One of our most successful communication channels that we set up at Manitoba Housing followed a format that we lifted from our former aerospace employer—it was the brainchild of the CEO at the time. In that organization, it was called senior management group, or SMG. At Manitoba Housing, we called it the housing leadership team, or HLT. This monthly meeting was a critical part of the culture change that the CEO and I had envisioned for our organization, and it was a huge contributor to developing the *Space for Change* in the organization. It also enhanced the *Space of Trust* as well.

In December of 2014, we held our first HLT meeting. The scheduling pattern was established to be consistent and reliable. Every third Wednesday of every month, from 10 am until 11 am, every manager, director, and senior leader would gather in our largest boardroom at the head office. The leaders in other towns and cities across the province would join in remotely using Skype®, where they could see the presenters, hear the audio, and see the presentation as well.

Usually, the site offices around the province would set up their boardrooms for the leadership to view and hear the HLT presentation together on the big monitor on the wall. Each executive (the CEO, the COO, the CFO, and the assistant deputy minister) would, in sequence, give a short presentation relevant to their segments of the organization. The topics would usually focus around updates on major initiatives or an introduction to new things that were relevant to our organization. Major program transformations, reorganizations, new policies, federal-provincial-territorial consultations, budget speech impact analyses, government directives, fiscal performance updates, we shared everything that we could. In most cases, this information was technically available publicly, although almost certainly our staff would never be able to easily find it themselves.

When the presentation was over, the electronic file was posted on our intranet site, along with the video recordings of each executive presenting. The leadership team was instructed to re-present the HLT presentation to their own staff teams within two weeks of the HLT date. We were very aware that cascading the message from the executives to the executive directors, then to the directors, then to the managers, and finally to the staff would likely produce transcription errors, like the "telephone game" that children sometimes play. Using our approach, we would reach the entire population of Manitoba Housing staff, with only one handoff in the message between the executives and the front-line staff. In many cases, the branch director would present to multiple teams at once in the branch staff meetings, so that three managers didn't have to arrange their own individual presentations, which was fine with us.

The consistency of the schedule was incredibly important. When we first advocated for doing this, I'll admit there was a little skepticism that we had to overcome. Would we actually have things to talk about every month? Maybe quarterly would be a better place to start? We stood firm on the monthly cadence—when you think about it, if you have an organization with over 700 staff and you can't think of something to tell them every month, there is something wrong. There are always things to discuss monthly in an organization that size, and especially for an organization that is going through a major transformation. To top it off, we had several strategic initiatives on the go at the same time: a major revamping of our Social Housing Rental Program policy and procedure manual, the development of a new IT system for social housing, as well as our new Lean management methodologies. Even the normal course of the annual government budgeting cycle involved a lot of activity across the organization.

I think that one of the most important things that helped us to define the culture change in the organization came when we began sharing financial information with the staff through HLT. The first time at an HLT meeting when the leadership group presented on a single slide the revenue and expense statement for the corporation, I think the jaws dropped for many of the leaders in the audience. Sharing this type of financial information, including the amount of revenue and all major categories of corporate expenses, had never been done before in Manitoba Housing. It was likely assumed previously by many team members that this information was secret, and that the staff weren't allowed to see it. But we shared it with them all.

The information was not confidential, of course, but it would have likely been impossible for the average staff member to be able to find the financial reports themselves. And the interpretive explanation that was provided along with the numbers was crucial to support the understanding of the information. After the first time, this type of financial update was provided in HLT, I had several leaders stop me after the meeting to express their gratitude that we shared the information with them. I could see on their faces that the implicit message of trust from the senior leadership had started to register.

The first time we held the HLT meeting, we told the leaders that they would be responsible for re-broadcasting the presentation themselves to their staff. That day, I remember seeing only one leader taking notes on a clipboard while we were speaking. I was certain the other leaders would struggle, when their times came, to try to remember what we had said during each PowerPoint slide when presenting it to their staff days later. Sure enough, the next month, well over half of the leaders showed up at HLT prepared to take notes. Part of the intent behind the exercise was to ensure that each leader was conversant in the material that we were presenting—having to present it yourself later is one way to ensure the leader pays attention in HLT. Another key element of the HLT initiative was to ensure that the leaders had a focal point for monthly staff meetings, in case they were not occurring already.

When we first started HLT, we also warned the leaders that after a month, we would be auditing the front-line staff during site visits to ask if they had been receiving the HLT presentations from their leaders. For at least the first year, it took a while for the pattern of leaders re-broadcasting the HLT material to become a habit. There were a few times that CEO or I would find out that some staff hadn't been getting the presentations, and when we would privately question the leaders about it, we would usually get a sheepish response about being very busy, but *they would get right on it!* After a few of these cases, I think we made it clear that we were serious about the HLT expectations, and that it wasn't a fad about which we would get bored after a while.

A question that we heard a few times in the first year was whether or not leaders had to present the material to all staff, or just to some of them. Sometimes I was asked if it made sense to present the material to staff that didn't need it to do their jobs. We stood firm with our direction that *all* staff were expected to receive the HLT presentations from their leaders. We believed that all employees were valuable, and as such they all deserved equal access to the information about what was going on in the corporation. If a few people didn't want to listen, then fine, but that was their choice. We promised that we would share everything that we could with them because that was the culture we were forming at Manitoba Housing—there would be no "second-class employees." Maybe a clerk or a building superintendent wanted to be promoted someday to a property manager job. In that case, they would need to understand how to read a financial statement, so seeing some of the financial statements from the corporation would be just one more way that we could help prepare the staff for bigger jobs if they were interested.

When I occasionally was told that a particular employee was too valuable or busy to sit in a meeting to hear the HLT presentation, I might remind the leader that "1.5 hours out of approximately 160 working hours per month is only 0.9 percent of their time. We can spare 0.9 percent of their time to hear about what is going on in our organization." Gradually, these types of concerns stopped, as the people realized that we were steadfast in our commitment to the communication protocol.

This HLT system eventually did become an organizational habit, and it became accepted as a part of our organizational culture. In the second year, after a year of non-stop consistency, when discussing a new initiative, leaders started asking, "Hey, should we have this presented at HLT next month?" It did become known as an effective communication channel for the organization. The CEO and I spoke about this HLT approach when speaking about the Manitoba Housing operations excellence program at a government Lean conference in October of 2016 and the audience was blown away by it. Most of the questions that we received were focused solely on HLT, and how it worked. This type of regular communication with all staff, not just selective team members, was considered at the time very unique within the Manitoba Government.

It was very hard work though. It took a lot of energy to organize and to plan it every month, and the logistics around it were very time-consuming. The technical challenges were significant. In the beginning, we spent a little bit of precious discretionary funding on proper lapel microphones and a video camera, so that the staff in the field could hear and see us properly, instead of us shouting into a laptop.

Getting the software to sync up with the microphones and the video didn't always work on cue either. After two years, I think that we could have assembled an entire full-length DVD of all the HLT bloopers where the technology didn't work when we started the presentation—the poor CEO was always the first presenter, so it always happened to him. We found that the IT staff had to start setting up the room an hour beforehand, just to make sure the kinks were worked out before we started the presentation. Gradually, as everyone gained some practice and experience, the tech problems faded away, and it started to work more often than it didn't work.

When I started to roll out this system to another division within the Department of Families, we started to get complaints that the presentations were not engaging to staff out in the field offices. After digging in, I realized that this division had placed far too much emphasis on the video recording of the presentation, instead of the presentation itself. Some leaders were playing the video for their teams instead of actually re-presenting the material and having a conversation with their teams to connect the staff with the content in a relevant way. I agree, just watching the video would be boring, if I couldn't see what they were talking about. We had to make a significant correction with the leaders that the expectation was for them to give the *presentation*, to their people in a regular monthly staff meeting, and that they were only to use the video to *supplement* the presentation if required.

I remember the month before we started the HLT program in Manitoba Housing in 2014, we told the union about it in our regular labour management meeting. We told them that we were setting up a system where we would present important information about what was happening in the organization, and then the branch leaders would share everything with all staff. We said that we didn't want the staff to feel like mushrooms any more: kept in the dark and fed manure. We trusted our staff and wanted them to know everything that was going on in the corporation. We warned the union that some staff might complain about getting *too much communication* from us, but we preferred that to the alternative.

As you can imagine, the announcement was met with a pretty positive response from the union.

In early 2017, our CEO was out meeting a group of staff in a regional office, and he cooked breakfast for the whole office—this was something that he liked to do to show his appreciation for the team. The staff always appreciated it when the CEO showed up, and if he wanted to prepare breakfast for them too, well, that was a huge bonus. The CEO also took the time to answer questions from the staff about major changes in the corporation. He ended with asking the office staff if they felt that they knew what was going on in Manitoba Housing. They all answered affirmatively—yes, they all felt that they understood the big strategic initiatives that were moving forward in the organization, and the challenges the corporation was facing. This really resonated with the CEO, because three years earlier, he was told at the same office location that the staff felt like mushrooms—what a change in only three years.

# 39

## Change Principle #6: Find Your Voice

*"Find your voice, and inspire others to find theirs."*

**Stephen R. Covey[1]**
*leadership author*

In *The Leadership Challenge*, by James Kouzes and Barry Posner, it has a very profound statement in "Practice 1: Model the Way," where it suggests that if you are going to truly lead, you need to find your voice. You can't simply repeat words that I have used myself, or words that you have read in books, and expect people to take you seriously. If it doesn't sound like you, it sounds fake and forced, and you won't be able to build that *Space of Trust*, or *The Space for Change*.

*"If the words you speak are not your words but someone else's, you will not, in the long-term, be able to be consistent in word and deed. You will not have the integrity to lead."*

**James Kouzes and Barry Posner[2]**
*The Leadership Challenge.*

In other words, you need to be able to absorb the lessons of how to build the Three Spaces yourself, so that you can talk in your own words to your leadership team and your staff about where you are taking the organization.

I think that one of the more interesting historical anecdotes that I have read about a well-known event pertains to the Rev. Dr. Martin Luther King, Jr. Although many people have heard of the "I Have a Dream" speech that he gave on August 28, 1963, at the March on Washington, few people likely realize that this was not the original title of his speech. In fact, the working title of his speech was called "Normalcy, Never Again."[3] Even more surprising to many people is that the written text of the speech did not include any of the best-known material from the "I have a dream" section at the end of the speech. He improvised all of the best material in his speech.

You can prove it to yourself, by watching a video replay of the speech. The speech is about fifteen minutes long, and usually the online video recordings of it available on YouTube include a couple minutes at the beginning of scenes from the March on Washington, before it shows the speech. For the first two-thirds of the speech, he is clearly reading from his prepared notes on the lectern. But then he says:[4]

> *"I say to you today, my friends, so even though we face the difficulties of today and tomorrow, I still have a dream. It is a dream deeply rooted in the American dream."*

And he stops looking down at his notes on the podium. From that point on, he never looks down again and ignores what he had written. And from that point on, the crowd response to his words is remarkably different.

According to some of the historical literature about this famous speech, Martin Luther King was told the night before by his advisor, Wyatt Walker, not to use the lines about "I have a dream," as he had in some previous speeches to smaller crowds, as Wyatt felt the words were clichéd.[5] But partway through the speech, Mahalia Jackson, King's favourite gospel singer, who was sitting behind him, called out "Tell 'em about the dream, Martin." And he went with it. He improved the remainder of his speech, drawing on phrases he had used comfortably in the past, inserting pieces here and there, and finished his speech in a such a momentous manner that his words have been accorded a special place in history. When he spoke from the heart, in his own words at that moment, free of written notes, he found his voice, and the difference helped to change the world.

I found that my own public-speaking abilities drastically improved when I threw away my own speaking notes. This was truly terrifying for me because, like many people, I had for many years an almost-crippling fear of public speaking. I was always so afraid that I would stumble, stammer, or forget what I was going to say, and as a result I would write carefully scripted speaking notes capturing word-for-word my message. But the problem was that when I read from my notes, it felt and sounded like I was reading from notes, and, while the content was sincere, it just wasn't very engaging, and it didn't sound nearly as genuine to the listeners.

Finally, I decided to work without a net, and I stopped using speaking notes for the most part—my only exception would often be a page or two of bullet point notes if I was speaking to a PowerPoint slide about some specific business metrics with key trends and numbers that I wanted to point out. But aside from that, I started just improvising my speaking, often just by glancing at a slide during at a presentation. I believe that there are a few aspects that you need to remember at a formal public-speaking engagement in order to effectively speak without notes:

1. You must really know your material. This means that you can't delegate making the slides to someone else. When you make the slides, you know what you are thinking, and what you will say when it's time to present it. This aspect is quite simple to get right—just prepare it yourself and know your stuff!

2. Don't clutter your slides with too much text, or you will automatically jump to reading the text from the slides—this is no different than reading from printed speaking notes. Instead, put the theme of the slide at the top, put a few key bullets on the side or the bottom, and let a graphic that captures the message be the focal point for the audience. This is easy to say, but hard to do at first, if you are used to speaking from written notes.

3. Scale your presentation material and the level of detail appropriately for the amount of time that you are allotted. I usually budget an average of one minute per slide for uninterrupted presentation, and two minutes per slide if the audience can stop the presentation partway through. Therefore, simply take the speaking time you are allotted, and divide it by either one or two minutes per slide in order to calculate how many slides you should have in your presentation. Then build your presentation appropriately. If you don't follow this rule, you will find yourself having to talk like an auctioneer in order to finish on time.

4. You need to be able to pace yourself carefully and be able to glance at the clock to seamlessly be able to adjust your cadence to match the time allotment that you have. This aspect takes some practice so that changing your pace doesn't seem abrupt to your audience. You need to know how much time you have in advance, and before you start speaking, quickly calculate your target finish time. And you need to have some way to keep track of the time that isn't distracting to the audience. Raising your wrist to look at your watch while you are speaking is obviously not a good idea. Either bring a watch with you to put on the podium or check out the room beforehand to find out if there is a wall-mounted clock that you can see from where you are speaking.

As the senior leader starting on a Lean journey, it will be natural at first to feel some discomfort and unfamiliarity with the subject-matter. Read, study, and get familiar with the material. But don't be afraid to tell your people that you are learning some things too. Do feel confident in where you are taking them. Find your voice and speak to them in your own words when asked: "why are we doing this." It has to be your voice, and no one else's, if you are to get your people to believe, and to trust.

# 40

## Change Principle #7: Challenge the Status Quo Continuously

*"Progress cannot be generated when we are satisfied with existing situations."*

**Taiichi Ohno[1]**
*industrial engineer, and founder of the Toyota Production System*

In organizations that have just begun to adopt a culture of continuous improvement, there is often a legacy within the existing culture of assuming that the current method of doing things is just fine. In some cases, I believe that this results from some of the people in the organization who are most experienced in key areas.

They have worked their way up to a level of mastery with the current ways of doing things through years of trial and error. As a result, they have cultivated an aura of respect from those around them, and they are often in demand for their knowledge and expertise. Threatening their places of primacy in the organization is usually not an attractive proposition to many of these people, so in some cases, they will respond by attempting to undermine the Lean program or the culture that you are trying to build.

But if you stay persistent and continue to follow the principles that I outline in the Three Spaces, these concerns will eventually fade away. It is my experience that it is usually not the new people who struggle the most with new ways of working, but rather, it is the more senior staff who do. I think that the best way to get the more senior people engaged with this way of thinking is to recognize their significant experience by asking for their advice on the process improvements. Just be prepared to gently challenge them to look at the status quo differently than they have before.

It will take time to get your people used to questioning themselves if the way they normally do things is really the best way. And you will need to start them on this path by modelling the way yourself. When you are told that "we've been doing it that way for years!" you need to be prepared to gently question the team to think about whether a better way exists that we haven't yet tried.

Think about it this way: If the company started up today from nothing, is the current process the one that everyone would design from a blank slate? In many cases, people would answer "No, we would do things differently." This is where you can then ask them to write down the way they would have designed the process in the first place.

Often, unnecessary steps creep into work processes over the years. They may have made sense at the time that they were added to the process flow, but years later, many steps eventually become superfluous and add no value at all. Sometimes this happens when a process is designed, and then a re-organization takes place, but the process is not updated to correct for the change in reporting structure. As a result, approval steps remain programmed

> *Think about it this way: if the company started up today from nothing, is the current process the one that everyone would design from a blank slate? In many cases, people would answer "No, we would do things differently."*

into the process, but they no longer match up with the current organizational structure. Sometimes, manual or paper-based steps remain in a process long after technology allows these steps to be either eliminated or to be replaced with a faster electronic step.

Resistance to changing these steps can often appear strange to someone coming in from the outside—it might appear obvious that a step is unnecessary, or that an approval could be handled electronically instead of passing a piece of paper around for signatures, but yet, some people will adamantly insist that these steps cannot possibly be changed.

In government work, a favourite defense of paper-based approval processes is that you "might get audited someday and you need a paper trail," or that "auditors often ask to see this paper form." My response to these types of concerns is to remind the staff that auditors don't usually tell you *how* to do something, but rather they want to ensure that you are following a well-defined process and that proper approvals are in place. How you obtain and record those approvals is usually defined by the organization, not the auditors. The auditors asked to see your approval paper forms the last time because that was all you had to show them. If you said you had an electronic-form approval and tracking system, the auditors would ask to see that instead.

The second key point is to question whether or not the approvals are required at all in the first place—does each and every approval actually add value to the process? It is hard to convince the staff by simply *telling* *them* that they need to question the necessity of approval steps in the process. Instead, this is usually best left as a journey of discovery for the staff through the course of a process-mapping exercise within a *kaizen* event.

*Remember, it's called "continuous improve- ment," not "final improvement."*

Usually, when the approval steps (and resulting typical waiting times of each) are posted up on the wall sequentially, and a trained facilitator encourages people to look for waste within the process that can be removed, these approval steps should be challenged. When someone insists that the approvals are necessary, it is fair game to get them to answer the question of "why?" They may have a compelling reason, but in many cases, they might struggle to answer why the approval steps are as critical as they believe.

Sometimes, the people to best challenge the status quo are those individuals who are "outsiders." People foreign to the process will see everything as new for the first time, and they will be quick to ask "why" many times. Don't pour cold water on these people and their questions, and don't let your senior subject-matter experts shut them down either— make sure they are respected if they are respectfully challenging the current way of doing things in the spirit of continuous improvement. I discuss this concept in more detail in Chapter 65, CI Principle #6: Choose the right people for an event.

If you are truly going to develop a culture of continuous improvement within your organization, you need to get everyone to believe that every process should be looked at as something that can be improved. No organization with significant experience in continuous improvement believes that once it optimizes a process, that process doesn't need to be looked at again. Sometimes you find the need to look at the process again after only one year—after gaining experience with the revised approach, you will see things differently, and you may find new types of waste in the process that can be removed. Remember, it's called "continuous improvement," not "final improvement."

# 41

## Change Principle #8: Respect the Current State of Evolutionary Growth

*"Culture does not change because we desire it to change. Culture changes when the organization is transformed; the culture reflects the realities of people working together every day."*

**Frances Hesselbein[1]**
*former CEO of Girl Scouts of America*

### UNDERSTANDING ORGANIZATIONAL CHANGE EVOLUTION

Anyone who comes from a company that has made significant progress down its Lean journey and moves to an organization that is new to the continuous improvement culture knows what it feels like when you walk in. You move from a place where people know how to just "do" certain things without debating it, or without having to have it explained why it's the right thing to do. Depending on how far the gap is between the old company and the new organization, it can be very disconcerting for a leader joining the new organization with a mandate to effect positive change. Sometimes, the fundamentals that you need in place before you can effect that change are beyond the current capabilities of the team that you inherited. None of this means that the team is incompetent, or unwilling to do the new things, but in some cases, they just aren't ready for them yet.

I think that the concept of organizational change evolution is important to understand and accept if you are going to be attempting to make significant change in a team. Organizations, large and small, have a pace of evolution that they can undertake. It is my experience that you can increase the pace of that somewhat as the leader, but the fundamental rule that I have learned is that you cannot leapfrog major steps of evolution.

Consider this analogy: In the year 2018, most people are familiar with smartphones, such as the Apple iPhone™. Online banking, ordering a pizza, scanning digital copies of documents, recording and editing digital videos are all examples of tasks that can be commonly done on such devices. However, imagine if you took your current smartphone, and the knowledge of how to use it, and went back in time to visit yourself in the year 1998. You hand the 1998 version of yourself the 2018 iPhone and tell yourself to order a pizza online with it.

The 1998 version of yourself wouldn't even know where to begin. Since the iPhone wasn't even first invented until the year 2007, the 1998 version of yourself might view the device itself as a strange piece of witchcraft, with a touchscreen and a biometric thumbprint or FaceID™ scanner to unlock it. The onboard digital camera would be unlike anything that was seen in the year 1998, as film cameras were still in common use. Cellular phones at that time might have looked like the Motorola StarTAC™ flip phone, or one of the competing Nokia models.

To be fair, there have been annual incremental advances in the Apple iPhone since it first debuted in 2007, so we have had the benefit of gradually watching the technology advance over more than ten years to 2018. It's perhaps not that surprising that the 1998 version of yourself would have no idea what the 2018 piece of technology could do, much less how to use it to its full capabilities.

So, does that mean that there is anything wrong with the 1998 version of yourself? I don't think so. It just wouldn't be fair to push the 1998 version of you past the normal steps in your own necessary evolution towards understanding the elements of the new technology. If someone took the time to explain piece-by-piece how the device worked, and what you could accomplish with it, and let you practice along each step of your learning journey, the 1998 version of you would get there, and I suspect, much more quickly than the ten years it took the technological world to develop the 2018 device.

Why would it be any different when talking about organizational evolution? You can't hand someone from 1998 a 2018 model iPhone, give them a one-hour PowerPoint presentation to "train" them on how to use it and expect them to be fully up to speed. Similarly, you can't jump key steps in an organizational evolution, or people will get left behind on the journey. You may find that people get stuck at one point on your change path, and then you will realize that you need to establish comfort with a fundamental concept first before you can move forward to the next milestone.

I've discovered that this is normal, and as the leader you must be okay with this natural limitation to the pace of change in a team. As the leader, you should be prepared to push the evolution along as much as you safely can, but there are limits to how fast you can push. There are steps that your team members will need to take, sometimes in a proper sequence, before you can get the team to the desired end state of organizational maturity.

As I've learned, sometimes the problem isn't that the people aren't learning fast enough, but rather that the leader is moving along too fast for the team to follow along. Again, it can come down to the leader being the problem, not the people.

## KNOWING WHERE YOUR ORGANIZATION IS IN ITS EVOLUTION

At times, it isn't always apparent why the team isn't advancing the way that you think it should be able to. Sometimes, the evolutionary limitations are only apparent in hindsight. As a result, it can be very difficult to map out in advance the stages of evolution that you need to complete along your transformational journey. But with time, and experience with managing the change of your people, you will get better at making these predictions.

The first time we started using metrics or key performance indicators (KPIs) at Manitoba Housing, it took a while just for the leadership in operations to get used to the concept. My experience is that many leaders in this situation may be very fearful at first of how KPIs are going to be used in practice. Sometimes, leaders new to KPIs can be so concerned about the concept of "keeping score" that they may initially overlook the true value of learning by measuring.

At Manitoba Housing, we took over twelve months just to allow people to build trust with how the executives used the metrics. We got our first set of metrics up on the wall outside my office, updated them each month, and then we paused in the evolution there for a whole year, while the leaders acclimatized to this major change in culture. When the results of a metric one month looked surprising, it would prompt questions from the executives, but the questions were always around the theme of "what might have caused this to happen, and what can we do to help?"

---

## THE DANGERS OF TRYING TO LEAPFROG

In my example of introducing the leadership to KPIs, I could have jumped right to Six-Sigma statistical analysis of some of the metrics that we were doing, with upper and lower control limits. But would that add value at that stage in the growth of the team? Not at all. They would be lost because I would have gone too far too fast. And jumping steps in the evolution, I believe, will cost you time in the long run. You will break trust with your team, and they will retreat defensively into their own individual safety zones because you have made them feel inadequate.

Remember, there is a reason that it is so often called a Lean journey instead of a Lean race. You don't get points for finishing first, and there is no benefit to the Lean champion getting to the finish line without any of the team arriving at the same time. I'll discuss the Manitoba Housing experience with starting to use measurements and KPIs in much more detail in Chapter 46, Change Principle #13: Use visual metrics regularly to teach and reveal, never to assign blame.

Although the concept of 5S (set in order, Sort, Shine, Standardize, and Sustain) is very fundamental to the Lean methodology, and is considered foundational, we actually didn't introduce it to our people in Manitoba Housing until later on in our operations excellence journey. We got them to understand the concepts of Lean, and to see the staff engagement benefits of *kaizens* to help improve everyday processes first. Once we had gained some traction and positive energy around our OpEx program, then we moved into the other concepts like 5S and metrics.

*Remember, there is a reason that it is so often called a Lean journey instead of a Lean race. You don't get points for finishing first, and there is no benefit to the Lean Champion getting to the finish line without any of the team arriving at the same time.*

I realized that if we had introduced office 5S too early, it would have been seen cynically as "a crazy idea that cleaning your desk can make things better," and the idea would never have been taken seriously by the staff. We started by getting them familiar and comfortable with some positive Lean concepts, such as having staff participate in some *kaizen* events, and having people take "Lean 101" awareness training.

I think the most important part of this step was to have front-line staff experience the benefits of process-mapping, and then to have the staff see what happens to the process flow when non-value-added steps are eliminated. Once we got some traction with these milestones first, then the concepts of the Lean methodology were de-mystified enough that 5S could be finally introduced.

At this point, there was a better chance that the staff would view the concept of 5S in an office space as something more than "cleaning your desk," but rather a process that involves changing your workflow patterns to prevent the pile of paper from accumulating on your desk in the first place. Although we still had resistance in various areas to the concept, overall, the audience was much more receptive. Still, the CEO and I made sure that we were the first guinea pigs for this "experiment" at Manitoba Housing. The trust element of this approach was critical and was explained in more detail in Chapter 31, Trust Principle #26: Be congruent.

It is very important to remember not to get too far ahead of your people. If they seem to be stuck on an upward climb, unable to push over the summit and move onto the next challenge, don't be quick to blame the people. It's very likely that you are pushing them too fast, or that you haven't properly explained or reinforced something much more fundamental to your team so that they can stand on that foundation to reach the next step.

You may need to probe some of your leaders that you trust to be open and honest with you about your approach with leading the changes, and you will need to be prepared to listen and accept what you hear. Be ready to pause your journey and hover where you are, until the staff get comfortable with the new approach. If it's a big change for your people, you may even have to back up a step or two to build for them that evolutionary foundation.

A senior leader who used to report to me used to say that it can take up to seven times of being told about a new way of doing something for the message to sink in to a team. There will be times that you feel like this is what you are doing, and it may feel frustrating to you as the Lean champion. Perseverance will be essential. But if you aren't prepared to be patient and work with your people through these changes at the correct pace of evolutionary change, then *you* will be the barrier to your team's success. The problem will be you.

## THE RIGHT SEQUENCE OF STEPS FOR YOUR LEAN JOURNEY

While I have outlined the order of some steps that Manitoba Housing took, I don't necessarily believe that this sequence is a one-size-fits-all recipe for success for every organization. We didn't have every single step that we would take mapped out in advance. In many cases, the next step was only obvious after we had taken a few steps already. We needed to see how the leadership and the staff would react to certain activities before we would know the best way to continue our journey. It will be the same for you and your organization. Understand the fundamentals of building the Three Spaces of Lean in your organization, but make sure you select the sequence of steps to fit the needs of your own team.

Try to understand at which stage of the evolution of organizational maturity your team is before trying to push them to another stage—be wary of trying to force your team to leapfrog too far in their own evolution. Many people read books like The Toyota Way by Jeffrey Liker and try to quickly move their organizations to be where Toyota is, or at least was in 2003 when the book was first published.[2]

But they forget that Toyota really began its Lean journey in earnest after World War II, under the guidance of people such as Taiichi Ohno. Toyota has had well over sixty years of evolution, including many steps of trial and error, to arrive at where it is today. It is very unrealistic to take an organization that has had no exposure to any of the Lean tools and expect it to jump to any significant level of Lean maturity in only a short time. It may not take sixty years to reach a high level of organizational maturity because you can learn from the successes and challenges of other teams. But be prepared for a journey of years, not months.

Depending on the starting point of your team, it could very likely take close to a decade to really show a difference that outsiders would notice. But once the difference is truly visible, then I believe that the transformational changes can accelerate at a rapid pace. Just remember that, as you steer the evolution of your team, you must establish and maintain trust between the staff and the senior leadership. Otherwise, you aren't going anywhere in your quest to develop the *Space for Change.*

# 42

## Change Principle #9: Start with the Willing, Convince the Skeptical, Then Deal with the Resisters

*"People aren't your problem. Your problem is that your work systems and processes don't allow people to shine."*

**Karen Martin[1]**
*author and leadership consultant*

Many leaders when taking over a new group of team members wonder about whether or not the combined skill set of their people is up to the challenges ahead. I fully admit that I have, at times, fallen prey to the negative mindset of wondering if I have the right people to take the team to the next level. But I have learned a lot in this regard, and much of what I have learned came from the OpEx journey at Manitoba Housing.

While you may need to bring a few new people onto your team to obtain a very specific set of skills, like a Lean practitioner, you also need to realize that you can train for knowledge gaps. The soft skills, however, are much harder to fix with classroom training. Before you start your transformation, you need to accept that what you see today as the abilities of your people will likely not match your viewpoint of the same people months down the road. In fact, if things go well, you will find that your people can do more than you ever expected.

A "switched-on," engaged workforce has the ability to unlock latent potential and capacity that has been lying dormant and unseen within a team. It's not that the people have been deliberately or selfishly holding back, but when a team member really *believes* in the organization for which they work, they often have trouble holding back the desire to take the initiative in areas where they might not have felt comfortable before. This untapped potential is the reward for the organization to go down this Lean Management path in exchange for the investment in their people.

This additional potential will benefit the organization in several ways:

1. It will improve customer/client service;
2. It will improve your organizational reputation;
3. It will improve operational efficiency;
4. It will improve program effectiveness;
5. It will improve morale;
6. It will improve your employee retention; and
7. It will save money.

Note that the last one I listed was that it will save you money. In Chapter 36, Change Principle #3: Be wary of a goal of quick cash savings, I speak to this issue in more depth.

It's an exciting time when the team starts to "switch on." Once the people start to believe that this new approach is sincere, you start to learn things that your people can do that will surprise you. You will find people that are fantastic and confident public speakers on the front lines of the organization. You will find people that are great staff facilitators. You will find people that come up with great improvement ideas that you would never have thought of yourself.

You will find people with a knack for handling, manipulating, and analyzing data using software like Microsoft Excel, even though it might not be a part of their regular job—hang on to these people for dear life when they surface, as this skill set will become incredibly useful when you start business measurements and developing key performance indicators. Obviously, the more people you have in your organization, the more you are statistically likely to find surprising unknown abilities within your team.

In Manitoba Housing, once people realized that we were serious about Lean, we gradually started to find people with some knowledge that could further help us out on the front lines. Once, I was talking to a front-desk clerk in a regional office and discovered that this individual had a Lean Green Belt certification from a previous employer. In subsequent months, my leadership team found a maintenance tradesperson that had Lean Yellow Belt training, and they also found a building superintendent, sometimes called a caretaker in other organizations, that was an overseas-trained engineer with a Lean-Six-Sigma background. We tried our best not to squander these opportunities to demonstrate our commitment to engaging our people and where it made sense, we worked to get these people involved with our culture change efforts.

I highly encourage you to set aside your current doubts that you have the right people to get the job done when you launch your Lean management transformation—you likely do have the right people. You just might not be able to tell at first, given how things are operating today. Before you get going, you will likely have staff and leaders in the following categories:

1. Those who are enthusiastic about trying the new way—the early adopters;
2. Those who are willing but cautious about trying the new way;
3. Those who are suspicious of this program, and need to see it work first before they trust that the Senior Leadership is serious about the approach;
4. Those who add value to the organization, but are in the wrong roles, including leadership roles;
5. Those leaders who will give lip-service to the new way, but won't follow through in practice; and
6. Those who are thoroughly poisoned in their mindset and will never accept the new way.

You will have a few of the Category 1 people. Bring them in as soon as you identify them and get them directly involved. These people will be your champions to other members of the staff, and they will help to convince those in Categories 2 and 3.

Category 2 people likely are just cautious because they are unfamiliar with what Lean is. That's okay. Try to address their unfamiliarity with education and information. Show them what Lean means, and if you are the senior leader or the Lean champion, be prepared to tell them in person using plain language.

Category 3 will likely be the largest portion of your staff. These people may have had bad experiences in the past. Likely they have seen other management fads come and go, with no staying power, and they are wary of getting their hopes up only to have them dashed later. They may also have experienced senior management in the past displaying behaviour contrary to what is required for proper Lean management. They may have had previous senior leaders who ruled by fear or publicly berated the staff when they made errors. They may have a manager who doesn't model the proper behaviour right now.

However, if your staff demonstrate unacceptable behaviour, don't let them get away with it—you should be prepared to address as quickly as possible any disrespectful or insubordinate behaviour from staff in the proper manner, as discussed in Chapter 17, Trust Principle #12: Correct workplace behaviour problems quickly. However, many Category 3 people will convert when they see the new way happening in practice, and when they see the senior leadership modelling the new way in their behaviours. They will convert when they feel the organizational culture above them begin to change. And when they convert, these people will help to take the culture change even farther. They will make those in Category 6 seem less influential.

The people in Category 4 are ones you need to treat carefully and with respect. Unless you determine through observational evidence and first-hand one-on-one conversations that someone is a member of Category 6, it is possible that they are just in the wrong role. Sometimes, these will be people in leadership roles. You need all of your leaders to eventually get on the same page and to be willing to model the way of the Lean management leadership behaviours. If leaders continue to display the wrong behaviours, then it may be possible that they are in the wrong roles. Work to respectfully transition them into roles that better fit them and their skills. This is easier said than done, I fully realize, but it is a worthwhile change that may be necessary to make the culture change happen in the organization.

The leaders in Category 5 may be doing fine in many respects, but they aren't living the message about Lean management when you aren't around. You may hear them say the right things when you are with them, but eventually you may get clues that they are not consistent with their leadership approach.

You may have a few of these leaders, and unfortunately, due to the covert nature of their behaviour, it will take a while to detect them. In my experience, simply holding them accountable in private one-on-one respectful conversations with clearly laid out expectations and follow up is often all that is needed. It may not be an unwillingness to follow the new way, but rather, a simple lack of follow through.

Category 6 people are, and likely for some time have been, a poison to the workforce around them. Thankfully, there aren't many of them. These people are truly unwilling to follow direction and may be working hard to undermine anything that the leadership brings forward. It is possible that leaders may be included in this category. Be careful not to put people into this category prematurely—they may simply be Category 4 types, and they might just be more outspoken than others.

Give them the benefit of the doubt and invest in them with opportunities and training but hold them accountable to the proper standards of behaviour like everyone else. Call them on behavioural outbursts as soon as possible, and don't let them get away with trying to poison a continuous improvement event for others. If necessary, use progressive discipline to attempt to change the bad behaviour, and if nothing changes, continue to the point of termination.

My key point is that while you may not at first be seeing many of the behaviours that you would expect in an organization you are trying to take down a continuous improvement transformation path, don't write off your people yet. When the culture change starts to take effect, your people will come alive and surprise you with their engagement levels, and their hidden talents.

Remember, in many cases, these people have never been asked or allowed to show initiative before, and they have never been asked about their other skills and abilities beyond what they normally do in their current jobs. As I mentioned in the Introduction, think of your staff as that unhewn block of marble, and know that there is a beautiful angel statue within that block of stone. You aren't trying to change your people; rather, you are simply trying to free what is hidden within. But to do that, you will need to work to change the leadership culture within the organization.

# 43

## Change Principle #10: Remember That We Learn by Doing

*"For the things we have to learn before doing them, we learn by doing them."*

**Aristotle[1]**
*ancient Greek Philosopher*

I have come to realize that learning by doing is quite fundamental to the necessary organizational cultural change. Often over my career, I have encountered staff and leaders who appear to believe that doing something more than once is a fate worse than death. I call it the "fear of the do-over."

How many times have you seen a major change that everyone knew needed to happen be put on hold in order to wait for information from some other decision that turned out in the end to be irrelevant? To be fair, there are crucial prerequisite steps that need to happen before we proceed with a project or a change. But I think that many times we delay action due to an unnecessary fear of the do-over.

In many situations, I think that we are afraid of committing our time to something and then later having to change the product into which we have invested so much of our time. We convince ourselves to wait, to hold out, until we have in our possession every single piece of information, so that there is no chance that we will ever have to redo something on which we worked.

But this mindset can more often than not lead to an unfortunate paralysis of the organization that is trying to develop a *Space for Change*. Therefore, you need to recognize that if you have to do something a second time, then you will understand it even better at the end because *we learn by doing*.

Don't get me wrong; I'm not suggesting that organizations should give up on planning and sequencing activities in an order that makes sense. What

I am saying is that you cannot let the fear of having to redo something paralyze you from undertaking a change that is important to the team or the organization as a whole. Just get started, and let the learning begin.

In a way, the fear of the do-over is strange because we accept without question the principle of learning by doing for developing so many new skills. For instance, few people would suggest that someone could learn to swim simply by reading a book about how to swim. Of course not! Practice would be required for the new swimmer to properly develop the skill. Learning a new language requires oral practice in order to get the correct pronunciation, cadence, and syllable emphasis. Learning to play a musical instrument requires practice to develop the proper motor skills in order to produce the correct sounds. Learning to drive a car requires practice so that the driver can understand the sensitivity of the controls of the car, and the physics of how the car accelerates, turns, swerves, and decelerates. Therefore, why cannot we extend this principle of the necessity of learning by doing to situations of implementing a new or changed process in the workplace? Practice will be required to make it "stick" and truly become a part of the new way of doing things.

When you are confronted with a situation where, as the senior leader, you know that a change has to be implemented, but you are told that "we need to wait for _____ before we proceed," stop and ask yourself: "What is truly the risk of proceeding with the change?" There will certainly be many situations where waiting for the suggested preceding step is the right thing to do.

But you will also encounter many cases where the risk of proceeding with the change without waiting is quite low. Appreciate that the do-over simply might give the people of the organization some more opportunities for practice with the new change. Your response to this situation could simply be "That's okay, in this organization, we learn by doing."

The principle of learning by doing is crucial when developing training for your staff about changes to work processes, and this forms the basis of Change Principle #11: Understand that a presentation does not equal training (described in Chapter 44).

# 44

---

## Change Principle #11: Understand That a Presentation Does Not Equal Training

*"I never teach my pupils. I only provide the conditions in which they can learn."*

**Attributed to Albert Einstein**
*theoretical physicist*

In the previous chapter about Change Principle #10: Remember that we learn by doing, I discuss the importance of practice for people to learn a new skill, and also to learn new or different processes at work. In *The Toyota Way to Lean Leadership*, the authors Liker and Convis do a fantastic job of explaining the Toyota approach to leadership development (although this applies to staff as well), which involves learning by doing with a coach (called the *sensei*, which means both teacher and master).[1]

> *"Unfortunately, Western education has largely abandoned this method in favour of a lecture-oriented model, in which 'teaching' is defined as showing or telling the student what to think or do, then providing shortcuts that will speed up the pupil's route to proficiency." Jeffrey Liker and Gary Convis.*

*We learn by doing, not by watching.*
It is often appreciated that significant practice and experience are required in order to learn a new set of skills. There are various suggestions on the length of time that it would take to develop expertise at something new, but a common standard is 10,000 hours of practice.

People can debate the number of 10,000 hours if they wish, but I think it is hard to argue with the concept that practice, and repetition is required in order for people to really begin to absorb new methods of working into their daily business. Why, then, do we in the workplace often give our staff a single presentation on a new work process and call it "training?" The presentation can have some value in outlining the reasons why we are bringing in the new process, and it can help to identify for people the steps. But practice by the staff will be required for the new process to really be understood and to become part of how the staff does their work. We learn by doing, not by watching.

And the practice needs to be in the workplace, doing the new process, under the watch of their supervisor, who is there to coach using questions to guide them. As discussed in Chapter 28, Trust Principle #23: Be a coach, not a judge, it is so important for the organizational culture change for the leaders to remember their proper roles as coaches for their team members.

The coaching needs to follow the basic methodology that one might use when learning to play a musical instrument. Start by playing slowly, and then even more slowly, and don't worry about if the tune is recognizable— what is important is whether or not the notes are being played correctly. Break the music into small pieces for easier learning, and then assemble the pieces together later for a complete package. Look for and listen for errors, and then use them to navigate towards the correct notes.

Look again at how you are training your people and consider doing it differently. When you hear about staff not following a new process the way that they are supposed to, look to see if they were simply provided with a presentation as the sole means of training. Look to see how much coaching-supported practice they have had. I'll bet that in many cases, you will find that the training was simply a classroom presentation without the opportunity for true practice.

One corollary of this training approach is that you will need to really invest in your supervisors to show them how to be coaches because that is a true skill that needs training in its own right. At Manitoba Housing, we realized that we had for years followed the "a presentation equals training" approach in many areas, and then questioned why people struggled to follow the new processes. It led us to begin our journey that was within our culture journey that consisted of transforming our leaders into coaches to better support our staff.

Training might begin with a presentation, but rarely can it end there. Repetition and practice in the real world, using the new process in the everyday course of doing business, with the support of a coach, is how the real training will take place. The presentation is simply the initial instruction.

# 45

## Change Principle #12: Ask Them to Show You, Not Tell You

*"Trust, but verify."*

**Russian proverb**
*often quoted by former U.S. President Ronald Reagan*[1]

A simple, but important, thing to remember for leader coaches is the concept of "show me." Many times, when supervisors are attempting to train their staff on something new, they will arrive at a point where they need to assess whether or not the employee (the student) understands the new concept. Early in my leadership career, I many times made the mistake of simply asking my employee if they understand. When I received a nod from the employee to indicate "yes," I moved on. But so often, when I used this approach, I later saw evidence that the employee was doing it wrong—they did not completely understand the new concept. "Show me" can help to minimize or eliminate this problem.

Instead of asking the employee if they understand, you gently ask them to "show me" the new process in practice. Then, as their coach, you will get a much better understanding of their comprehension and mastery of the new process. Of course, your tone will make a big difference in how your coaching approach is received by the employee. Harshly demanding that the staff member show you what they are doing will imply that you don't trust them and that you might even think that they are incompetent—not exactly a helpful message in a student-coach relationship. But gently saying "why don't you show me what you've learned in practice so that I can see your learning progress," will usually be seen as fair and non-threatening.

A long time ago, during my work in the aerospace sector, a colleague leader and friend was telling me about how he learned the importance of "show me" first-hand. Every week, around the team huddle board, the team would meet and my colleague, as the supervisor, would go through the list of projects on the go and ask the team member who was the lead for each project if there were any concerns or challenges. If there were no challenges, the project had a green light indicator on the tracking board.

One particular project was being handled by a newer staff member who had very little project management experience. Every week, as this project was called out at the huddle board, the project lead called out "no issues," and the project kept its green light indicator to show that it was successfully tracking towards completion. Weeks before the customer's due date, my colleague also began to remind the project lead about the deadline when the status reports were being called out at the huddle meetings. Yet, each report was always the same, "no issues." That is, until right before the project was due.

At that last huddle meeting, the project lead suddenly announced that the project had significant challenges and that it wasn't even close to being complete to deliver to the customer. It would take weeks and additional help to solve the challenges. My colleague was obviously surprised, as was everyone else on the team. Why would this project lead not identify the issues with the project as soon as they arose, so that help could be redirected towards the project?

When my colleague and I dissected the situation together, we arrived at the conclusion that the project lead was new to project management and was still learning the approaches towards identifying project risks. The employee's inexperience likely, along with the fear of calling out one's problems in a group setting, contributed to the breakdown. But what was the solution then? To simply blame the employee? Well, the employee should obviously have handled the status reports differently. But to leave it at that would suggest that there was nothing that the leadership could have possibly done to prevent the situation. That was obviously the wrong answer.

Instead, we concluded that as leaders, and coaches, we have an obligation to do what is necessary to ensure that our employees truly are understanding new skills that they are learning, and then to provide additional coaching and support as required. My colleague and I realized that if the employee had been asked in a one-on-one setting to "show me" how the project is going, the problems would have been detected much earlier, and the situation could have been avoided. It was a learning experience for us both.

I, myself, have encountered this phenomenon a few times when serving as a project manager. A few times, when I've simply asked a team member how a certain deliverable was coming along, I've been told that everything was on schedule and going fine. But then, as we were trying to piece all of the deliverables together, I found that the team member wasn't even close to completing their piece of the project.

In one instance, I found that a key project deliverable, a significant technical design, wasn't even started—when I asked how it was going to get done, I was told that it would be finished on the plane on the flight to the installation site. Seeing as we had budgeted several weeks in the project schedule to develop the design, I didn't see how it was possible to complete it in a few hours.

I ended up flying to the installation site and developing the design myself over the course of a full week of long days—by sheer luck, this type of design development was something with which I had personal technical experience. I was disappointed in how the employee had been answering my questions about this work, but I realized that if I had simply asked "please *show* me how the design is coming along," all of this could have been avoided. Yes, the employee had dropped the ball with how they had represented the status of the deliverable to me. But I had failed in my responsibilities as the coach, and as a result, part of the problem was me.

As a senior leader, you need to apply the coaching principle of "show me" instead of "tell me," and you need to teach this principle to your leadership team to use when they coach their own teams. Make sure your leaders are careful with their tone when they start asking "show me," and you will find that the project and training surprises will quickly begin to diminish. When you do encounter a surprise where an employee wasn't doing something correctly for a significant length of time, check to see if the supervisor was following this principle in their coaching—it is very likely that you will be told sheepishly "Well, no, not in this case."

You've got to take the fear of blame off the table, and in order to do that, you have to take the need to blame the staff off the table. Then the staff start to believe that the leadership aren't looking to blame someone, then they will be more willing to open up about project or production problems.

In his book, Toyota Kata, Mike Rother describes the importance during coaching of the leader requesting that the student and leader go and see together the results of trying something new for the first time. In Rother's own words:[2]

> *"The words spoken most often at Toyota may well be, 'Show me.'"*

This part of the culture change for the leadership team might take some time to become routine as a part of the transformation to leaders as coaches instead of leaders as experts, but when it does, it will greatly help to properly shape the *Space for Change*.

# 46

---

*Change Principle #13: Use Visual Metrics Regularly to Teach and Reveal, Never to Assign Blame*

---

*"You can't manage what you don't measure."*

**Aphorism often attributed to Peter Drucker[1]**
*well-known management guru*

Part of the Lean methodology involves measurement. You don't even know where your process problems are if you aren't keeping score. If your organization hasn't been measuring things regularly before, this is definitely going to be a big shock to the system when you announce that the team is going to start posting metrics on the walls. We found that this was a huge part of the cultural shift in Manitoba Housing, and it was very challenging to get the people used to the idea. There was a lot of initial fear around the idea of performance metrics, and at times it seemed that I had to provide constant reassurance and reinforcement of our intentions to the staff, and to many of the leaders.

In the fall of 2015, our Lean consultant and our Lean practitioner worked with my branch leaders to develop two to four metrics each to post on the COO Scoreboard. Each branch leader would be responsible for publishing their metrics, either quarterly or monthly. In January of 2016, we went live with the first version of the scoreboard.

The Lean practitioner had a large whiteboard mounted right outside my office on a wall in the hallway on the way to the small kitchen. A few people suggested to us that putting it in such a high-traffic location was a mistake. We thought differently, as we knew we were trying to normalize a very difficult part of the culture change—therefore, placing the board in a high-traffic area was exactly what we wanted to do. The more that the employees were exposed to the board, the better. The Lean practitioner attached 8.5″ × 11″ clear vinyl pockets in a grid on the board, so that printed charts could easily be replaced when updated.

At first, we didn't have all of the metrics available because we were still setting up the data-gathering systems for some of them—in those cases, we put in the pockets placeholder announcement sheets. These were full-page signs stating (in a gigantic font) what metrics would go there in the future. In this way, we were committing ourselves to our staff about what we were going to measure right away, so that there was no hint of secrecy about what additional metrics might be in development.

In my experience, when you start this part of your transformational journey, you need to be prepared for some suspicion from staff, and also from some leaders. It is a normal part of the journey. Some leaders would be very concerned with what you do with the metrics data if things didn't go well in a month. As a result, you need to be tolerant and patient with these leaders. You will need to say over and over again: "These metrics are *not* for performance management of individuals. These are to identify areas where the teams need help, and I want to find out how to help those teams." At Manitoba Housing, I must have given a variation of this message well over twenty times in public forums over the year 2016, including HLT meetings and my senior leadership team meetings for operations.

You may even find that some leaders object to the concept of a "scorecard." This can be a fair concern, as the leaders may be worried that the scorecard is going to be used to facilitate a form of competition between teams. In Chapter 30 about Trust Principle #25: Eliminate competition in favour of teamwork, I talk about how it is so critical to stamp out all forms of implied or overt competition within the organizational culture. Therefore, you need to be very clear with your leadership team that metrics will never be used in this manner. At Manitoba Housing, I reinforced to my leaders many times that I would never pit one team against another. "But," I would say, "we don't know where we need to improve if we don't measure ourselves and keep track of how we are doing in the different parts of our business."

*When trying to understand metrics, we must always ask "why," never "who."*

I realized that my leaders would be carefully watching me, and I knew how I was going to behave when the data started coming in, and they would see that I had no ulterior objectives. With any group of leaders, you will find some who have had bad experiences in their work history with a previous supervisor who demonstrated a blame-and-punish approach to team performance challenges. For people with this kind of history, it can contribute to some concerns when you start using KPIs with your teams. I developed a favourite saying that seemed to really resonate with both staff and leadership: When trying to understand metrics, we must always ask "why," never "who."

When you get down to the root of the issue, the problem is not usually the people or the front-line leaders. The problem can, however, be you, as the senior leader, if you aren't prepared to be patient and help people through the culture change and the transition. At Manitoba Housing, the CEO and I had to be okay with providing constant reassurances, adapting our approach if needed, and listening to the leadership in order to hear and appreciate their concerns and fears. We had to recognize that changing a culture, especially in the public sector, is a marathon and not a sprint.

One of my favourite examples from Manitoba Housing of both the benefits and challenges of setting up metrics involves one of the teams that did not have any previous association with any type of scorecards or metrics. This team of dedicated staff were often working overtime to try to keep up with the demands of their program, but they were never quite able to catch up. One of the first metrics that the associated branch developed for the operations metrics board was a chart of the monthly average turnaround times for completing program applications. They recorded the date each application was received and when each application was completed, and calculated the turnaround time for each one as the difference in days between the two dates. They simply calculated the average of the turnaround times for the number of applications that were completed each month. The monthly metric was produced as a simple bar chart, where the height of each bar represented the average turn-time for that month.

This was a great practical first attempt at a metric for this team, and most importantly, what it measured was focused on what mattered to the client—how long they had to wait to get their application processed. The temptation for many teams new to performance measurement is to develop metrics that measure something that might be important internally, but is, in fact, irrelevant to the client or customer. Although internal metrics are appropriate in many instances, we should always be keeping the focus on the client when selecting our metrics.

This metric resulted from one of our earliest *kaizen* events, which involved developing some improvements to this program application processes. The *kaizen* was an excellent effort, with an enthusiastic team that was discovering that the senior leadership really was serious about listening to the input of the staff when making process improvements. They removed several administrative steps and greatly improved some of the forms that the clients were asked to fill out, consolidating and simplifying them to reduce the chances for errors requiring reprocessing. At the end of the *kaizen*, this team committed to tracking the application turnaround time on this posted metric, so that we could see how the process improved after the *kaizen* event.

For several months, the average process turnaround time gradually lowered month by month. Due to the fantastic nature of the *kaizen*, and the very promising results, this initiative was featured publicly and recognized in several write-ups about the Manitoba Housing operations excellence program.

And then, one month, the metric was absent from my board. I asked the branch leader where the chart was. The leader had to do some digging but was at first was baffled by various explanations as to why the metric wasn't ready by the regular due date. We then came to realize that the staff were worried because the process turnaround times had taken a turn for the worse that month. And then we discussed what was going on. This discussion was incredibly enlightening for me, and it served as one of my personal Lean management development milestones. It would seem that I was the problem.

Well, I knew that I wasn't really a problem, but the staff were not yet certain of that. As was completely normal in this type of transformational journey, the staff were afraid of what would happen when the leadership saw that the team performance went backwards after all of the improvements they had forecasted from the *kaizen* event that had received so much public praise. In other words, they didn't yet feel safe. So, the branch leader agreed to dig into the results from that month with our consultant and to focus on what we could do to help the team.

After a little research, they discovered that the number of applications received each month greatly varied, but yet the number of staff that the team had to support the program was fixed. In this one particular month, the number of applications had spiked by almost fifty percent, which led to a dramatic increase in the cycle time, as the staff struggled to handle all of the applications simultaneously.

Our Lean consultant, working with the team, made a simple addition to their bar chart, an overlaid red line graph to indicate the number of applications each month. This provided some extra context when reading the metric each month and provided an answer to the "WHY" when the reader would see a change. This was the first metric that we had that went through a revision, and it was an incredible coaching opportunity for me as the Lean champion.

The branch leader had learned something from using the metric that was previously not fully appreciated—the work volume varied greatly from month to month, and this can create turnaround time problems if the staffing complement was fixed. Now, the branch leader would be watching for surges in application volume and would be ready to temporarily re-deploy an additional resource from another area to support the team if required. Just by measuring something, we were able to help the team in a way that would not have been anticipated.

I had to close the loop from my end though. The reason that the staff were reluctant to hand over the chart in the first place was that they were somewhat afraid of what the senior leadership would do with the reversal of the positive performance trend. Since I was continuing to meet with staff on a regular basis, I took the opportunity to join in with the leader's monthly branch team meeting. In this meeting, the leader re-broadcasted the most recent HLT presentation, and then they had some discussion around topics relevant to the various branch teams. I had planned in advance with the leader a time in the meeting where she would ask me if I had anything to share with the staff.

When my time came, I first thanked the team for the hard work that they did, and I commended them on some of the branch initiatives that were discussed in the meeting already. Then, I asked if the staff had any questions for me. I told them, "You've got the COO hostage for a little while, ask me some questions!" A few brave people asked me a few questions, and I answered them the best that I could. When the questions slowed down, I segued to talking about the importance of metrics in our operations excellence culture. And then I tackled the elephant in the room, the program application turnaround time metric.

I mentioned how the metric this past month showed something unexpected. I could see the team members' eyes widen slightly with concern. But then I thanked them for honestly reporting the data when they must have been a little nervous wondering what I might think of the situation. I reminded them again that these metrics are never used for performance management of staff, but only as a means of trying to figure out how we can help teams.

I told the branch about what we had learned about the susceptibility of the metric to workload, and that we hadn't realized how that work volume could fluctuate so significantly. So now the leader would be on the lookout and would assist, if possible, with an additional resource to support a monthly surge in application volume. I told them that this wasn't a problem, but instead, it was a tremendous learning opportunity for all of us on how to make the process better. And if we hadn't been measuring the turnaround time in the first place, we would not have had these revelations. In a way, this was also an application of Trust Principle #13: Talk about problems openly, but focus on solutions (described in Chapter 18).

After the meeting, I asked the branch leader how it went. The leader reassured me that it was the right thing to do and that the timing was right. The story of the revision of this metric from Revision #1 to Revision #2 would show up in next month's HLT presentation, I decided then and there. The coaching moment for the staff was too good not to share with the broader population. And I did tell the story at that next HLT, and the leadership team seemed to appreciate the message about how the senior leadership positively handled what might look like "bad news" from one of the metrics.

But then something else happened with the program application turnaround time metric—it was modified again. Granted, this took a few months, but the evolution of this metric for me served as a microcosm of the ideal of Lean transformation for our organization. After a few months of following and more carefully managing the team using the Revision #2 cycle time metric, the branch leader became aware of something else. There were actually two very different types of work streams within the program application processing flow. There were new applications, from applicants who were not yet served by the program, and there were renewals from current applicants that wanted to renew their agreements and continue within the program.

The renewals were thought to be very simple to manage, and their turn-times were suspected to be quite short, compared to the new applications. In the case of new applications, they had to make sure that all of the necessary client information had been received and checked out, which took additional time compared to dealing with re-applications. When this became clear to the branch leader, and after working with our consultant and our Lean practitioner, the leader realized that in order to better manage the process, the metric had to be split in two. So, a couple of months later, the program metric consisted of two charts, one above the other on the same page. One was labelled "New Applications," and the other was labelled "renewals." This was the birth of Revision #3 of the metric.

Contrary to what was predicted, the new applications cycle time was doing pretty well, but the cycle time of the renewals work stream was struggling. So, after a couple months of learning by measuring, the branch leader concluded that an additional *kaizen* event was required, this time focusing specifically on the renewals process flow. This would be the first time at Manitoba Housing that a process would be reviewed more than once with a *kaizen* improvement event, and I loved it. This was true continuous improvement, as even very mature Lean management organizations never improve their processes only once, but rather, they continue to look for opportunities to improve them over and over again.

Every opportunity I had, I spoke to how impressed I was that the team and the leadership had learned so much about the program application process, and that these learning opportunities were sparked by the use of monthly metrics. Whether it was to our own staff, or to outside visitors who were now starting to ask more frequently to see our operations metric board, I gave a similar speech about this incredible story of organizational evolution.

In early 2017, the branch leader arranged for the second *kaizen* event to tackle the processing of renewals to the program. Since so many of the clients of this program were also clients of another program run out of a different government division, the branch leader made sure to get a manager from the other division to attend our *kaizen* event. This was a big milestone in itself, as it was the first time that Manitoba Housing reached outside its own staff for an "outsider" to join a *kaizen* event. We deliberately waited to do that until our own people were comfortable and trusting of the process, as we didn't want to confuse the environment with complicating factors too early. But at this point in our Lean journey, it was the right time. This *kaizen* event was to be facilitated by a staff *kaizen* facilitator from the branch itself and supported by the Lean practitioner.

I checked in with the *kaizen* group partway through the event, as I really wanted this one to be over-the-top successful. I would not be let down. The staff had done such a great job of mapping out the process, and the representative from the other division was really getting engaged with the *kaizen* process. This person came to our event with only minimal knowledge of what operations excellence was, and perhaps was initially a little skeptical, having had very little personal experience with continuous improvement. The conversion to enthusiasm apparently didn't take long.

The manager from the other division was one of the individuals that presented to me, the CEO, and the branch leader at the end of the *kaizen* event—and what a fantastic story they had to tell us. The manager proudly told us that it was clear that the program application process often got stalled when our staff was unable to quickly get the necessary information from the other program. To help solve the problem, this manager was going to arrange for our staff to get restricted access to the other program database—providing just the information necessary for our staff to be able to fill out the renewal applications, without bothering already busy program staff with trivial requests for basic information. This type of cross-divisional access to this database had previously never been allowed for any staff member at Manitoba Housing.

Because this team member had fully participated in the *kaizen* event, it was simple to quickly make a convincing case to their branch director to get approval for the system access. This branch director, who was also getting very involved with Lean in their own division, was thrilled with how excited the manager had become after participating in our *kaizen* event. At the end of the presentation, the manager gave a testimonial statement about now being a true believer in operations excellence and promised to spread the good word about continuous improvement back at their home branch.

The good news about what we were doing with our program was starting to spread beyond what we had initially envisioned. At the time, the idea of our staff obtaining restricted access to the other division's program database was considered mind-blowing within Manitoba Housing. For many years, our operations staff had tried to work across departmental or divisional boundaries to obtain basic information necessary for program applications or renewals with clients from the other program, with minimal success.

It wasn't for a lack of willingness on the part of the other program workers—this database contained information that would be considered highly confidential, so the program staff correctly protected the privacy of their clients. But in doing so, they unknowingly also made housing program access difficult for these same clients. It certainly wasn't intentional. And the challenges that our staff experienced in trying to get basic information about the other program's clients wasn't limited to the one housing program—it also regularly impacted hundreds of clients each month across Manitoba Housing operations. This lack of information access negatively impacted Manitoba Housing staff across the province, as well as the clients that we were trying to serve.

All it took was a single person from the other division participating in a Manitoba Housing *kaizen* event to take the personal responsibility to make a key change to fix the problem. Make no mistake; the manager was very careful to ensure that client privacy continued to be protected by ensuring that Manitoba Housing staff only had access to the minimal information that they needed for program applications or renewals. But that seemingly small effort made such a huge difference to our application cycle times, and as a result to the time that clients had to wait before hearing if their application was accepted or not. This meant better client service, and it also meant a better use of our staff time on more value-added activities. Our staff morale would go up as a result of participating in the elimination of some of the unnecessary steps of chasing down information.

The predicted results of the *kaizen* improvements were astounding. A ninety-three percent estimated reduction in renewal application approval time was forecast, as well as a reduction in staff time of fifty percent. This meant that the workload went from being impossible, even with significant overtime, to being just possible with the existing staff complement, if the new process was adopted. Of course, we all agreed to go with the recommendations of the *kaizen* team.

I couldn't wait to present about this *kaizen* event at the next HLT meeting. The leadership seemed quite impressed, especially with the access to the other program's database, as many of them had experience with struggling with that issue for many years. Immediately after this HLT presentation, I printed up the presentation material and took it to my regular meeting with our deputy minister. He had been encouraging his senior leadership team to see ourselves as one large department, and not a collection of independent silos, so I thought that this would be a good example of collaboration across divisions. He was impressed and asked if the *kaizen* team would mind giving the presentation again for him. I readily agreed, knowing that the team would not at all mind telling their story to an even more senior audience. The deputy minister loved the initiative and the partnership and collaboration that it represented, and he told the team as much. He also requested that the team develop an article for the deputy's weekly blog so that he could recognize this amazing cooperation of the staff, and yet another success of the Manitoba Housing operations excellence program. And to think that this all started simply by measuring something for the first time.

Once you get people to understand what Lean is, and to become familiar with the principles, then start with having your teams measure things about their work. Don't wait for perfection when trying to develop a metric—get started, and trust that by measuring something, almost certainly you will learn things about how that part of the business works. Learning by doing when developing metrics is absolutely okay.[1]

Be prepared to be patient with your staff as they become acclimatized to the idea of this new part of the organizational culture. An initial fear of process measurements is normal. Remember to ask "why," not "who."

The metrics are there to help everyone understand the business better and identify possible areas for improvement. Since we don't assign blame, which is completely unhelpful, there is no need to ask any type of "who" question when trying to understand a trend or change with a metric. "Why" questions are clearly directed at understanding the real problem. As we discussed earlier in Chapter 8, we follow Trust Principle #3: Believe that your people come to work every day wanting to do a good job.

> *Don't wait for perfection when trying to develop a metric—get started, and trust that by measuring something, almost certainly you will learn things about how that part of the business works.*

Do make sure that, whenever possible, your metrics are relevant to the interests of your client. In Chapter 23 on Change Principle #18: Set up a structure of aligned metrics to take you where you need to go, I will talk more about guidelines for what metrics to select for your organization and your teams.

Based on my experience in both private and public sectors, I offer a few cautions for when you begin the measurement stage of your organizational transformation. Be careful about your leaders or staff wanting to wait on posting metrics until an IT change is made. Although your people may not want to hear it, recording metrics manually, with Microsoft Excel, is always an option in situations where the staff are pushing for the convenience of a push-button report. Don't give in and let this crucial part of your Lean journey stall out before it begins.

Make sure that the leader who is responsible for the team performance is also accountable for the metric. Although the leader may delegate the data collection to an administrative or analyst team member, hold the leader accountable for truly understanding how the metric is calculated by making the leader explain the latest trends at monthly leadership meetings.

If a leader says that they don't understand how the analyst obtains the data in a metric for their area, then in a coaching session, ensure that the leader digs in properly to learn how the metric works. If as the senior leader you tolerate a lack of accountability by a leader to their own metric, then the leader will become disconnected from the metric, and the opportunities for improvements by learning by measuring will be lost. The culture that you are trying to build should have the leader being accountable for the metric and understanding what each trend means every month. As a result, they are always on the lookout for improvement opportunities.

# 47

## Change Principle #14: Embrace Huddle Board Meetings as a Part of the Culture Change

*"Don't blame your culture; use it purposefully. View it as an asset: a source of energy, pride, and motivation. Learn to work with it and within it."*

**Jon Katzenbach and Ashley Harshak**[1]
*leadership speakers and consultants*

Visual management systems are one of the hallmarks of Lean management. Simple, easy to understand, easy to read boards mounted up in a high-traffic and visible area, with critical information about a business area, are a part of the culture change. But the most important thing, I believe, is getting the staff and leaders used to meeting regularly around the board in their areas to discuss business.

Our approach at Manitoba Housing was to develop what we called "huddle boards." These were usually magnetic whiteboards that we would prominently post up on the office wall in different branches. On each board, the branch leader would post key branch metrics, and different schedules and items that they knew the staff for that branch would need to follow carefully to work together properly. At first, only the CEO and I had our own huddle boards around our offices.

On the CEO's board was the corporate business plan metrics, along with our internally-assessed scores of progress against each business initiative. The CEO also had a simple action list of hot items that the senior leaders were keeping track of each week, with a simple Red/Amber/Green traffic light assessment of each item, the owner, and an estimated completion date. The CEO would gather all of the senior leaders in the organization

224 • *Starting Lean from Scratch*

in his office first thing every Monday, and review the hot items list, as well as the corporate initiatives, as appropriate. After the CEO's fifteen-minute huddle board meeting, we would all head down one floor to my huddle board for the operations excellence huddle.

My own board was outside my office, in the hallway on the way to the small office kitchenette, so it had a lot of traffic going by it. It was a perfect location. My board had a set of my senior operations leaders' key performance indicators on it, and it also had a matrix of operations excellence actions that we were tracking each week. Similar to the CEO's hot items list, it had a Red/Amber/Green traffic light assessment, an owner, and a due date beside each item.

Eventually, after a few months, other Manitoba Housing leaders started setting up their own huddle boards in their own areas. I started having people want to show me their boards, to see what I thought. I praised each one that I saw. I wanted to provide as much positive reinforcement as I could for the leaders being willing to try out something so new.

*In the beginning, it's not so important what is on the huddle board, as long as the team regularly meets around it.*

In our HLT meetings, I would provide pictures of the boards, and recognize the business area for setting up the board and for being willing to start meeting around it. Supported with coaching advice from our Lean practitioner on how to set these boards up, the approach began to work. In our business, weekly huddle meetings seemed to be the right cadence, based on how rapidly things change, but in many industrial organizations, daily is a more appropriate cadence for the operations team.

Huddle boards began popping up organically around the organization. Out in various site offices across the province, leaders began setting up their own boards. In 2017, I started to make sure almost every one of my HLT presentations had a short feature on huddle boards and the culture change that we were trying to bring about within the organization. In the early stages of our journey, I would consistently say: "It's not so important what is on the huddle board, as long as the team regularly meets around it."

The board itself wasn't so much the culture change; it was the habit of the team meeting around the board on a regular basis to discuss what was moving and changing in their business. It was the act of innovating together as a team within a fifteen-to-twenty-minute weekly meeting to bring up repeating problems and have someone make a commitment to try out a solution and report back out how it went. It was the concept that the staff have great thoughts about how to make each branch better and more efficient, and that they just need to believe that the leaders are open to hearing about new ideas. It was the notion that the leadership would support experimentation on new ideas and be willing to try things out without expecting perfection the first time.

Once we had huddle boards appearing in various areas across the organization, we started providing some coaching, through questions, to each leader to try to help them learn from other types of boards across the organization. Some people started putting space on their boards where staff members could add items throughout the week that they wanted to be discussed at the next meeting.

Sometimes, the boards were actually located in a leader's office because the geometry of the office space in that area didn't allow for anything else that would support a meeting space. As a result, we might ask that leader if they thought that more ideas for the next meeting might come from the staff if the idea sheet was located on a bulletin board in the hallway instead of in their office.

Simple questions, like that one, were intended to get the leaders to think about how to get the most out of the intended collaborative engagement with the staff. We encouraged them to think about their own roles as the leader and how their authority might enhance or diminish innovation.

We suggested that huddle boards include graphics of the Deming cycle: Plan-Do-Check-Act, or the common updated version: Plan-Do-Study-Act. Getting people to come up with ideas, be willing to plan an experiment to see if it brings about an improvement, study the results, and then implement the change quickly into practice is a huge part of the culture change that the huddle board meetings can help to get going. But the design of the huddle board should evolve to one where it makes visible problems with how the business is operating, so that these problems can be tackled by the team. If problems are kept below the surface, they will remain there forever. This is the key idea of visual management, to bring problems out into the open for everyone to see.

When I visited the site offices, one of the most rewarding things for me as the Lean champion was to watch huddle board meetings in progress, knowing that one year earlier, nothing like that would ever have happened. To be able to be a part of the live-action evolution of the organizational culture, from a top-down, hierarchical, siloed organization to one where leadership and staff met weekly to discuss issues, and toss around ideas to try out, was absolutely fantastic. This was a part of the true tipping point when I knew that the Lean management approach was taking hold.

Make sure that whatever approach you use involves everyone on each team, so that there is no exclusion. Make sure each team board is in a visible, open, and accessible location. Try to make each one look as neat as possible and maintain them properly. A sloppy-looking huddle board implies that the organization doesn't take this part of the culture seriously. Involve your teams in creating their own huddle boards, guided by some experienced Lean practitioners—you can make a team-building activity out of designing a huddle board.

Don't be too quick to let the technical people convince you that you don't need a huddle board, that a TV monitor connected to a computer will suffice. The simpler, the better. It might be manual, but the simple magnetic whiteboard will work without requiring someone to edit and update a rotating slideshow of some sort. As a part of my "Lean Blackbelt" training, I had the opportunity to tour several facilities in Japan in 2017, including Nissan and Toyota, and both of these organizations were using whiteboards for manual huddle boards on the factory floor.

Remember that visual metrics are important. As discussed earlier, the development of the *Space of Trust* requires transparency between the leadership and the staff, so whatever metrics you are using should be posted up on your walls for all to see. If you have a computer system for scorecard reporting, that's fine, but print up the key metrics, post them on your huddle boards, and discuss them together in huddle board meetings.

# 48

---

## Change Principle #15: Realize That in an Office, 5S Doesn't Just Mean Cleaning off Your Desk

*"Let there be a place for everything, and everything in its place."*

**Benjamin Franklin[1]**
*American inventor, civic activist, politician, and diplomat*

One of the foundational elements of Lean management is the concept of 5S. It really is considered a fundamental part of Lean management, so it shouldn't be overlooked when you are considering your own Lean transformation. The origins of 5S are five Japanese words, but there are English equivalents:

1. Sort (*Seiri*)
2. Set in Order (*Seiton*)
3. Shine (*Seiso*)
4. Standardize (*Seiketsu*)
5. Sustain (*Shitsuke*)

The concept of 5S was originally developed for industrial factory settings to optimize a production workspace to support the efficient flow of work. This approach has more recently been applied to other sectors, including government. In the public sector, instead of physical products, it is often information that moves through the workspace. However, in an office environment, the benefits of 5S are not as readily apparent as they are in the factory environments from which Lean management originates.

*227*

I completely understand—in an office environment, it looks at first like simply cleaning off a desk. First impressions can be hard to shake. Of course, once someone goes through a properly-facilitated 5S redesign of their workspace, they end up thinking critically about how they manage and organize their work. At that point, the individual usually ends up changing their mind about their original preconceptions regarding 5S.

To maximize workflow in an office environment, a 5S optimization of the workspace can be tremendously helpful. The Set in Order step of 5S is the critical one, where you would figure out why that pile of paper forms every week on the desk and change the process to do things a better way to prevent the pile from forming the way that it does. Of course, this might require the workplace owner to form new habits.

*In an office, the 5S approach is intended to not just clean the pile of paper off a desk, but to address the process problems that cause the pile to form in the first place.*

I was, and rightly so I think, concerned that early in our Lean journey at Manitoba Housing, many of the staff who were just becoming aware of what Lean means, would view the concept of 5S in an office space as some kind of misplaced industrial witchcraft that didn't translate from the private sector to the public sector. It might appear to many of the staff that we were trying to bizarrely claim that, by cleaning their desks, they would magically become more efficient.

So instead, what we did was let the staff get some familiarity with operations excellence from the *kaizen* events, where they could see and participate in the engagement side of Lean. We worked this way for a whole year before we unleashed the 5S approach on our staff. I would recommend this sequencing for any group in the public sector that is at the very beginning of their Lean journey, especially when the Lean terminology and toolkit will be completely foreign to the vast majority of the staff.

We were careful to point out that in an office, the 5S approach is intended to not just clean the pile of paper off a desk, but to address the process problems that cause the pile to form in the first place. I also believe that the more skepticism there is around a part of the toolkit, the more the senior leadership needs to first model the way themselves, before asking the staff to participate.

As I mentioned in Chapter 31, Trust Principle #26: Be congruent, The CEO and I elected to "model the way," and to be the first people in the organization to take our offices through the 5S transformation process. My own office 5S event took place on December 21, 2015, and although I was the Lean champion for the organization, I still remember it as an eye-opening experience. I was challenged to think about how I handled this pile of work or that one, and to change my strategy for how I organized everything.

At the end of the transformation, which took about half a day, we took a photograph of my office. Everything was polished up, and my desk had a rectangular pin-striped space outlined for my daily folder of work. Any other folders I needed would be moved to the in-bin behind my desk and get moved to the out-bin when done. Other than my one large daily folder (with files for every meeting of the day), my computer, my phone, and my family photos, my desk was clear and clean.

The unexpected, but beneficial, side effect was that I quickly found that my stress level went down, and noticeably so. Previously, every morning I would show up to a desk with various piles of work on it and see it as a testament to my failure to get things done the day before. The very sight of the piles often evoked a disappointing and depressing start to each day. But now, I had a system and a process for sustaining the new workspace configuration.

Coupled with my new-found approaches for time management (CI Principle #2: Study and adopt methods of time management, described in Chapter 61), I was able to arrive at work every day to a clean desk, and quickly get to work in a much more efficient and effective manner. No more searching through a pile for the correct files. To borrow the old phrase often referenced in Lean management, there was a place for everything, and everything was kept in its place. The CEO's experience with his 5S transformation was much the same as mine, as was his personal reflection on his stress level after the event.

Remember, you are trying to get your staff to approach their work with a whole new mindset. You want them to view everything they do as a process, because processes can be improved. And viewing your own workspace and your own personal work processes as worthy of optimizing through Lean, is one way to imprint this mindset in a continuously visible way throughout the organization. It shows commitment to the cause. Just remember that once you commit, you can't give up on it, or you will lose credibility with the staff.

# 49

## Change Principle #16: Be Ruthless When Setting Strategic Priorities

*"The essence of strategy is choosing what not to do."*

**Professor Michael Porter**[1]
*author, speaker, economist, and professor at Harvard Business School*

One thing that I think many organizations struggle with is strategic focus. There are so many things that the leaders want to accomplish, that it is hard to say "no" to some things so that you can focus on the others. But focus is absolutely critical to getting things done effectively. In short, you can't be all things to all people or stakeholders.

Some of the more well-known approaches to strategic planning all strongly emphasize the criticality of strategic focus. In his book *How to Run a Government So that Citizens Benefit and Taxpayers Don't Go Crazy*, Michael Barber outlines a methodology for achieving strategic goals within government, sometimes known as Delivery or Deliverology.[2] Throughout the book, Barber outlines the rules of the methodology. The first two rules speak to the importance of focus: "Rule 1. Have an Agenda," and "Rule 2. Decide on Your Priorities (really decide)."

David Kaplan and Robert Norton in 1992 published a paper in the *Harvard Business Review* entitled "The Balanced Scorecard— Measures That Drive Performance."[3] The paper was incredibly popular, and it was followed by another paper in 1993, and in 1996 by a book, *The Balanced Scorecard*.[4] After the year 2000, Paul R. Niven authored a series of books intended to help organizations better understand and implement the balanced scorecard methodology.[5] The approach consists of first developing a series of strategic priorities, and then a graphical map of strategic objectives balanced among four perspectives (most commonly:

Customer, Internal Processes, Employee Learning and Growth, and Financial). Measures and targets are then developed to follow the progress of the organization towards achieving these strategic objectives.

The development of the strategy map will make the senior leaders of an organization painfully aware when they lack strategic focus, simply because the strategy map will clearly look like a jumbled and complicated mess. Having a simple and easily-understood strategy map shows that an organization is committed to focusing its limited resources and energy on its true priorities.

The Lean management toolkit also includes an approach for strategic planning, or as it is known in Japanese, *hoshin kanri*. This methodology calls for setting strategic priorities or goals, and then strategic objectives, followed by selecting the necessary initiatives to achieve the objectives. Measures and targets are also selected to be aligned with the objectives, and sometimes the strategic planning is mapped out using a tool called the X-matrix, or X-chart, although it is not used by Toyota. However, Toyota does follow the approach of *hoshin kanri* for its strategic planning and has instead produced graphical strategy maps. This approach also requires a clarity of focus by the organization, if it is going to be successful in achieving its strategy.

At Manitoba Housing, we were about to begin incorporating X-matrices into our corporate strategic planning process towards the end of 2017, and we had done quite a bit of development work in this regard already. When the Manitoba Government indicated that they were going to adopt the Balanced Scorecard methodology, Manitoba Housing was able to quickly shift gears and to begin using this approach instead. We had been following a structured approach to strategic planning for about five years already, but we were missing a few things.

Our strategic planning approach after five years lacked focus and consisted of a very large number of strategic objectives, and a much larger number of corporate initiatives, on the go at any given time. Our lack of focus was evident in our corporate reporting, where we regularly had several corporate initiatives showing little or no progress since the last report. We knew what the problems were with our strategic planning process, and we wanted to fix them with a different approach. But we also understood that corporate strategic focus would be absolutely crucial to success in achieving a strategy.

Strategic focus means saying "no" or "not right now" to ideas that might sound really good. And that is very hard for organizations and leaders to do. But if you can't say "no" to things when developing your strategic plan, then all you will do is disappoint your stakeholders, and frustrate and disengage your staff. Instead, choose a thoughtful strategy, and be ruthless in setting your strategic priorities.

Don't set the bar too low to guarantee success, because you will miss the chance to galvanize and motivate your organization towards an exciting, visionary future state. But setting the bar too high will demotivate your team and reduce the credibility of your leadership team with the staff. Choose wisely and strike the right balance.

# 50

## Change Principle #17: Value How an Objective Is Achieved as Much as the Achievement Itself

*"Sometimes it is better to lose and do the right thing than to win and do the wrong thing."*

**Tony Blair[1]**
*former Prime Minister of the United Kingdom*

There are many risks to simply setting strategic objectives, measures, and targets, and asking your staff and leaders to drive towards them. Such an approach would be analogous to the somewhat discredited methodology of management by objectives, or MBO. This methodology was first described by Peter Drucker in his 1954 book, *The Practice of Management*.[2] The idea of MBO was to empower people, limit micromanagement, and encourage accountability by clearly articulating goals and objectives across the organization, and allowing people to figure out how to best achieve them.

However, the approach has drawbacks. As Jeffrey Liker and Gary Convis suggest in *The Toyota Way to Lean Leadership*:[3]

> *"By essentially ignoring the ways in which managers and workers achieve the objectives that are laid out, MBO creates ample space for unintended consequences. There are many cases in which MBO leads to people cutting corners to meet their targets."*

As Liker and Convis explain, a new trend then developed to counteract the problems caused by MBO, called MBM, or Management by Means. This approach assumes that if managers pursue their jobs in the right way, positive outcomes will follow. But without targets to follow, how can anyone in an organization possibly know where they are going?

In my experience, in order for an organization to be successful, it is important to have a unified strategic plan, and objectives clearly understood across all departments and teams. Objectives and targets set at the corporate, branch, and team levels should all be aligned with the corporate strategy.

But be warned that when you define objectives and set up measures to track progress towards them, you will get what you measure, whether you want it or not. What I mean is that the staff in any organization often will take seriously what is measured and tracked by management. As a result, this will often lead people to take extreme measures to achieve the targets that the organization appears to desire. A common phrase is: "What gets measured gets done," but perhaps the more accurate saying should be: "What management pays attention to gets done."

In a way, this can be the workplace demonstration of the truth behind the observer effect, also known as the Hawthorne Effect, a term coined in 1958 by Henry A. Landsberger.[4] The concept is a natural reaction in which individuals change their behaviour in response to the awareness of being observed or measured. In other words, workers behave differently when they know that aspects of their work are being measured.

*But be warned that when you define objectives, and set up measures to track progress towards them, you will get what you measure, whether you want it or not.*

The challenge, therefore, is to minimize the risk of unintended consequences or perverse behaviours resulting from implementing measurements into your organizational culture. Unfortunately, it sometimes takes experience to understand how to do this properly. You need to ensure that your staff comprehend the intent behind each measure, and that the organization establishes the measures to allow each team to learn about its business and then to facilitate process improvements. You don't want your staff stomping over each other, and leaving a trail of human wreckage, as they frantically drive towards achieving your measurement objectives.

As is often the case, balance is essential. I believe that, while the organizational culture should support everyone working to achieve their objectives and targets, a constraint is required. This constraint, I suggest, is a comprehensive set of principles to guide the organizational behaviour while everyone is driving to achieve the objectives. The leadership principles contained within this book, divided up into the Three Spaces of *Trust, Change,* and *Continuous Improvement,* serve this purpose.

Ensure that these principles are made a part of your leadership culture *and* follow every one of them. They must be communicated to everyone, well understood by all leaders, and enforced vigilantly at all levels of the organization. If you do this, you will have a proper constraint built in against the risks of management by objectives.

# 51

## Change Principle #18: Set up a Structure of Aligned Metrics to Take You Where You Need to Go

*"If you don't like change, you're going to like irrelevance even less."*

**General Eric Shinseki[1]**
*U.S. Army*

Setting up alignment among the metrics in an organization is something that will become an obvious necessity after you start "measuring stuff," and you will need to make that alignment a part of your culture. It's one thing to start measuring things that operationally seem to make sense as business metrics to get your people used to this new part of the culture. It's another thing to get the entire organization to the state where each part of the business knows that they are "measuring the right stuff." It's even better if they can point to an overarching strategy with which each of their metrics is aligned.

The Lean management methodology of *hoshin kanri* provides an approach to aligning your business measurement system with your strategy. Often, you hear *hoshin kanri* associated with tools such as the X-matrix. What an X-matrix does is allow you to put on the same page your long-range goals, shorter-range objectives, immediate initiatives, your associated measures and targets, and finally the organizational resources that would be associated with each objective and initiative. The downside is that this tool *looks* frighteningly complicated for the uninitiated when they see it for the first time.

When the first impression that someone has of your strategic plan produces a visceral reaction of fear, it's not a good thing. And you often find that people need training to understand how to read and X-matrix, so that doesn't help very much with using it as a method for publicly communicating your corporate strategy across the organization. If you want alignment of all your team members with your strategy, your strategy needs to be something that can easily be communicated.

At Manitoba Housing, in 2017, we were going down the path of transitioning our strategic planning methodology to adopt the use of X-matrices. Although there were some downsides to the tool, it would help align our measurements with our strategic plan, and we were sorely missing that in our organization. I had myself invested countless hours during that year in developing sample corporate X-matrices and attempting to cascade the X-matrices to the next management level, the branch level.

It turned out to be incredibly fortunate that the Manitoba Government indicated in late 2017 that it was going to adopt the use of the balanced scorecard as a strategic planning and business metrics methodology system across the entire civil service. At first, we were a little disappointed because it seemed as though we would have to reverse course. We were concerned that we would have lost forward progress in our journey. I obtained the book *Balanced Scorecard, Step-by-Step for Governments and Non-Profits*, by Paul R. Niven.[2] I read it over Christmas and discovered more similarities than differences in the methodology. And I found that this methodology addressed some of the shortcomings of the X-matrix approach. *The Balanced Scorecard* approach called for the development of a graphical strategy map, which was much easier for the average person to understand when passing by and seeing it posted on a wall, with virtually no training required.

*The Balanced Scorecard* methodology basically frames strategic planning around four key "perspectives": Customer, Internal Processes, Employee Learning and Growth, and Financial. Giving equal emphasis to each of the four perspectives in strategic planning, as well as in the scorecard measurement system, is what provides the "balance" to the system. The four perspectives seemed to me to very closely align with our developing culture. I loved that this approach called for the development of employee-based metrics as a part of the corporate strategy, as this closely matched up with our existing corporate values—in fact, one of our organizational values was called "Learning and Growth." And recognizing internal processes as a perspective for strategy development fit well with our continuous improvement operations excellence program, as our program was designed to help improve internal processes.

I'd highly recommend that you consider learning more about *The Balanced Scorecard* methodology for strategic planning and business measurement. The concept is quite simple to understand. The structured approach can take you from the very initial development of a mission and vision statement, if you don't already have one, to the development of strategic priorities. From there, you develop a map of strategic objectives across each of the four perspectives. You next select performance measures and associated performance targets—these last two items form the basis of the actual corporate metrics scorecard. The final stage in this development is the identification and prioritization of corporate initiatives to help you achieve your objectives.

The evolutionary step for Manitoba Housing in going down this path was moving away from focusing on our corporate initiatives in our scorecard reporting, to instead focusing on measures designed to assess the progress towards achieving our strategic objectives. Tracking the initiatives was, in retrospect, micromanagement of our senior leaders who should be left accountable for the objectives and any associated initiatives that are required to achieve the objectives. If the performance measures indicate that progress has stalled towards an objective, then it should be within the job of the senior leader accountable for that measure to call for additional resources, or to adjust the initiatives designed to move the organization forward in the right way.

But the best part was that we had a very clear and structured approach to cascade the strategy maps and scorecards down to lower levels in the organization. In this way, every branch and team in the organization would have their own strategy map of objectives, performance measures, and targets, that would be in complete alignment with the corporate strategic plan and scorecard. When a team looked at a particular metric each month, they would know why they were tracking that measurement, and they would know how it fit into the corporate strategy. We would move from "measuring stuff" to "measuring the right stuff."

Earlier, I used the phrase: "What management pays attention to gets done." The system of aligned metrics that you need to build will provide the structure for management to regularly pay attention to things that are relevant, and therefore, should drive organization activity in relevant directions.

While there are different methodologies that you can use in your organization, I think you need to assess a method of ensuring alignment between your corporate strategy, and the business measurements and targets towards which you want each branch and team to drive. Without this, the staff struggle to understand how they fit into the "big picture" of the organization, and you can get teams moving in different directions. The alignment serves as a force multiplier for your teams, and as an engagement tool in its own right. When everyone understands the "true north" of the organization and believes that they are all moving in that direction, it is a really strong motivator.

# 52

## Change Principle #19: Drive Towards Thoughtfully Selected Targets on Your Metrics

*"You have to set goals that are almost out of reach. If you set a goal that is attainable without much work or thought, you are stuck with something below your true talent and potential."*

**Attributed to Steve Garvey**
*former Major League Baseball player*

In the previous chapter, Change Principle #18: Set up a structure of aligned metrics to take you where you need to go, I reviewed the importance of setting up a system of metrics across your organization that align with your strategic plan and priorities. Setting the targets is where you really begin to drive performance within your organization. But you need to be cautious of driving unintended consequences in the organizational behaviour. As discussed in Chapter 50, Change Principle #17: Value how an objective is achieved as much as the achievement itself, establishing a comprehensive set of leadership principles and enforcing and modelling them across the organizational management team is the recommended approach to minimizing the risks of unintended consequences from measurements.

You will need to set targets towards which you want your team to drive. This can be a more difficult task than it sounds if you are having teams are very new to measuring things in their business. For instance, the first time you start to measure something, such as a process completion time, you may not know right away what a "good" completion time should be. Sometimes it takes a little while to work with the measure before you begin setting a target.

Although others may have different opinions, I am of the mind that part of the transformation involves leading people through the change. I think that the first part of the change is just getting people used to measuring business performance in the first place and talking about areas for improvement. Once people begin to trust that these measurements are not punitive in nature, they will be open to really looking at the intended purpose, which is demonstrating trends, helping to identify areas for improvement, and measuring progress towards targets. Because the first step is to engender trust, I don't mind too much if people hold off initially on setting targets while people become acclimatized to the use of the metrics.

Having said that, you do need to get there, and the sooner, the better. You need to be able to establish a target that will be beyond what the team can deliver today, and they need to understand that they have to drive improvements towards achieving the targeted level of performance.

The concept of striking a balance will be necessary when setting the targets. If you are too aggressive in setting your targets, you will quickly appear to your staff to be overzealous and simply unrealistic. Your team will quickly disengage from attempting to achieve what they believe to be impossible. However, if you compensate too much in the other direction and set easily achievable goals, you will miss a valuable chance to galvanize and engage your workforce towards something great.

In his literature on *The Balanced Scorecard* methodology, Paul R. Niven suggests selecting a major long-term ambition for the next ten to thirty years.[1] Paul invokes the terminology of James Collins and Jerry I. Porras from their book *Built to Last: Successful Habits of Visionary Companies* when he suggests that organizations should set for themselves a BHAG or big hairy audacious goal.[2] The most frequently quoted example of a BHAG that worked to inspire and motivate an entire country was the pronouncement of U.S. President John F. Kennedy on May 25, 1961, when he announced: "I believe that this nation should commit itself to achieving the goal, before this decade is out, of landing a man on the moon and returning him safely to the Earth."[3] Although he was assassinated years before the success of

> "Standards should not be forced down from above but rather set by the production workers themselves."
> **Attributed to Taiichi Ohno**
> *Industrial engineer, and founder of the Toyota Production System.*

the Apollo moon-landing program, the BHAG of President Kennedy was achieved on July 20, 1969, before the decade was out.

If you set up a major long-term goal for your organization, you will need to consider setting up mid-range and short-range incremental targets to break down your BHAG into manageable pieces. Your team will need to see success periodically, and celebrate it, in order to maintain their perseverance towards the long-term goal, as we will see in Chapter 54, Change Principle #21: Celebrate team accomplishments, large and small. So, help them out, and map out the long road ahead into shorter pieces so that everyone can prove to themselves that they are making progress. But each target should be a stretch target of some type.

When looking to set your targets, Paul Niven suggests a few helpful sources of information, including your past data baselines and trends, industry or sector averages, customer/client and stakeholder feedback, other companies or agencies, best-in-class benchmarking investigations, and most importantly, employees.[4]

I believe that employees should be consulted partway through the research process after you start to learn what might be possible from looking outside your organization. This information can be shared with the employees to show them what other organizations can do, and then put the challenge to them to help you set the mid-term and short-term goals to achieve the long-range vision that you desire. And, the employees can be a useful double-check for you on the realism for the targets that you hope to set. But don't let yourself be too quickly talked out of a challenging goal in order to keep things easy.

It certainly will be much easier to motivate and engage the staff if they participate in the development of the targets for the organizational measures. Participation will lead to ownership by the people. Ownership leads to engagement. And engagement is what you are trying to achieve with this cultural transformation.

# 53

---

## Change Principle #20: Say "Yes" More Often Than "No" at First, Then Be Selective

---

*"Leadership is the capacity to translate vision into reality."*

**Warren Bennis**[1]
*former president of the University of Cincinnati*

I often have had people ask me what approach I recommend for prioritizing improvement projects. I'm a little embarrassed to admit that Manitoba Housing didn't really have much of a structured prioritization system at first when we started our Lean journey. But I've realized that this was okay, that it was a useful part of building the *Space for Change*. Getting people used to the organization viewing their work as processes, was part of the cultural evolution, and so was getting the organization comfortable with the idea that the leadership trusted the staff to fix process problems. So, in that regard, in the beginning, it really didn't matter what improvement projects we selected, as long as they addressed some pain points that the staff were feeling, and that they provided some clearly demonstrable improvement in business performance.

However, once you move past this initial stage, you need to start thinking about how to focus your process improvement efforts on the right things. In Chapter 51, Change Principle #18: Set up a structure of aligned metrics to take you where you need to go, I talk about matching your metrics with your corporate strategy in a cascading structure from the top of the organization to the bottom. This structure can also help you to prioritize the improvement projects. When you develop a map of your corporate strategy, this can provide the guidance for which internal process problems deserve attention from your organization's limited resources. And your structure of aligned metrics will already be set up to track the improvement in performance on the scorecard.

In the very early stages of an organization's business evolution, you will likely find several situations where you don't even have a defined process or standard for some work. In the earliest days of our Lean journey at Manitoba Housing, we called some continuous improvement events *kaizens*, even though they were actually simple process-mapping events. We realized in these situations that the biggest problem was the total lack of a defined process. Most of the effort went towards creating a standard where none had previously existed. That's okay, because, as the saying goes, "Without standardization, there can be no *kaizen*." Defining the process is an investment for future continuous improvement opportunities. It is likely that each time the team will find some waste in the process that can be eliminated, and that success can be celebrated. Don't overlook the benefit of simply creating standardized processes from chaos.

Early on in your journey, don't worry too much about what improvement projects you take on, as long you can point to some benefit. Once you get people comfortable with the *kaizen* approach and toolkit, and able to trust the leadership, then begin the shift to being more selective with your improvement projects. You do want to get the organization to the state where it uses its limited resources carefully, instead of on "random acts of improvement." When you can see that people are trusting the culture change and the leadership sincerity around Lean, start to align your improvement initiatives to your corporate strategy and your metrics.

# 54

## Change Principle #21: Celebrate Team Accomplishments, Large and Small

*"Remember to celebrate milestones as you prepare for the road ahead."*

**Attributed to Nelson Mandela**
*former president of South Africa*

In order for the initial step towards Lean management to really resonate with the staff, you need to be prepared, as the senior leader, to create a pattern of constant positive reinforcement. The leadership need to show the staff, with their presence, that they are backing the Lean activities. The Lean champion, as well as the senior leader for the affected area, should be present at every *kaizen* event kickoff, as well as the final presentation at the end of the event.

There are only two things that a senior leader should say to staff after listening to the presentation on the results of a *kaizen*: "Well done and thank you." The project team has just worked for two, three, or more days straight to redesign a business process that may have been broken for years, to try to improve efficiency. Likely, some of them are nervous about presenting for an executive as well. As the senior leader, you have an obligation to the employees to associate positive recognition with their efforts that are supporting the program. When the team members go back to their regular jobs, they will have upbeat feedback to give their colleagues when asked: "So, what did the big boss think of your solution?"

Conversely, think about what message it would send to the staff if, after three days of hard work trying to fix a business process at your behest, you walked into the team's final presentation and said: "Not bad, but you missed the boat on a few things. We can't do it the way you are recommending, but nice try anyways." How would you feel if you were on that *kaizen* team? You'd likely be pretty upset, and angry that the big boss never bothered to tell the team in advance if he or she had expected the team to make the final answer look a certain way. You would be frustrated that the boss expected the team members to be able to read his or her mind. Think about, in this scenario, which message would be relayed back to the colleagues of the *kaizen* team members when they returned back to their regular duties. They would tell everyone what a waste of time it was, and that the boss over-ruled the team at the last minute.

This is *not* the reinforcement you want associated with Lean. In fact, if you are the Lean champion, you need to work to avoid any negative associations with the Lean program. The concept of carefully planning your Lean events well in advance to ensure that the final results are always accepted by senior leadership is described more fully in Chapter 67, CI Principle #8: Scope your projects with care. If you consistently handle your Lean events the correct way, the staff will appreciate the senior leadership for showing gratitude for their efforts to improve the processes. Then, when you call on them to tackle a bigger challenge, they will be more willing to do it, knowing that you recognize their efforts.

> *Don't just thank people for the major successes—thank them for the small ones too.*

In Chapter 20, Trust Principle #15: Thank your staff personally when they do something great, I give an example of a short employee survey that we took of the Manitoba Housing staff in January of 2016: eighty-five percent of the people said that it was important to them to feel that their work was valued and appreciated. I strongly believe that this is a universal trait among people in the workplace.

Although you don't want to inadvertently foster competition in the process, you need to get into the habit of providing constant positive reinforcement and recognition for your teams. Show your gratitude for the hard work the teams are doing, and make sure the other leaders in the organization are doing the same.

Don't just thank people for the major successes—thank them for the small ones too. Don't make them wait to celebrate a milestone, even if it's a small milestone. On every team in your organization, the people are doing great things every week. Grab each opportunity and let the staff feel great about their accomplishments, and make sure each leader in the organization is doing the same with their teams. It will help to make the next milestone seem closer than it did before.

# 55

## Change Principle #22: Recognize the Power and Primacy of Intrinsic Motivation

*"Our prevailing system of management has destroyed our people. People are born with intrinsic motivation, self-respect, dignity, curiosity to learn, joy in learning. The forces of destruction begin with toddlers – a prize for the best Halloween costume, grades in school, gold stars – and on up through the university. On the job people, teams, and divisions are ranked, reward for the top, punishment for the bottom. Management by Objectives, quotas, incentive pay, business plans, put together separately, division by division, cause further loss, unknown and unknowable."*

**W. Edwards Deming**[1]
*author*

It seems to be a "management best practice" to provide tangible rewards for certain workplace behaviours or accomplishments. If someone achieves a target, they should be rewarded with a bonus. It can often be hard to dispute the notion that people will work hard to reach a target if they know that there is a financial target attached to it. But over my career, I've evolved significantly in my thinking about this type of compensation system within an organization.

I've come to believe that the most powerful type of motivation is intrinsic motivation, which is defined as the desire to do an activity for the inherent satisfaction rather than for some consequence or reward. Remember, you are trying to move your organization along a path of culture change to foster innovation and creativity, and much of this can only be supported with the intrinsic motivation that is already residing within your staff.

Extrinsic, or tangible, rewards will only get in the way and will serve to confuse your teams.

Dan Pink, author of the book *"Drive: The Surprising Truth About What Motivates Us,"* in a July 2009 TedGlobal talk entitled "The Puzzle of Motivation,"[2] outlines his belief, supported by extensive references, that traditional, extrinsic motivation systems in the workplace only are effective for maximizing productivity with repetitive and mechanical tasks. He outlines several examples of studies which conclude that, for any tasks that require innovation or creativity, extrinsic motivation actually reduces performance.

In an often-referenced 1962 publication in the *Journal of Experimental Psychology*, Princeton researcher Sam Glucksberg explains his experimental use of "The Candle Problem" to test motivational theories on performance.[3] The Candle Problem was developed by Karl Duncker and first published in 1945, as a cognitive performance test to measure the influence of functional-fixedness on an individual's problem-solving capabilities.[4] The Candle Problem involves giving an individual a task: how to fix a candle to a cork-board wall, and light it, in such a manner that the candle wax will not drip onto the table below. The individual is presented with a candle, a book of paper matches, and a box of thumbtacks.

Most of the solutions that creative individuals imagine when presented with the problem will not work. The answer is to use the empty thumbtack box as a platform to support the candle above the table and to use the thumbtacks to attach the box to the wall. The challenge comes when people have trouble seeing the thumbtack box as something beyond its original intended purpose as a container for the thumbtacks—this is what is meant by functional-fixedness. It is a self-imposed limitation on how things are perceived.

A second variation of The Candle Problem involves providing the same supplies to the test subject, but the difference is that the thumbtacks are outside of the box. Usually, in this variation of the problem, the test subjects are much more easily able to arrive at the problem solution because the problem of functional-fixedness is alleviated by the method of presentation of the supplies.

In his experiment, Sam Glucksberg offered one group of test subjects varying levels of financial incentives, depending on how fast they took to solve the problem. The second group of test subjects were not offered financial incentives. The study found that the group of test subjects offered financial incentives had poorer performance in solving the first variation of The Candle Problem, which requires cognitive skills.

However, further testing with a group of subjects who were provided financial incentives demonstrated better performance at solving the second variation of The Candle Problem, which requires less creative thinking. The basic conclusion that resulted from this experiment was that extrinsic rewards systems do not improve performance in situations where innovation is required, and can actually make things worse, but that they are effective in improving performance in other types of work. In his book *Drive*, Dan pink suggests that extrinsic motivation systems are only effective in algorithmic problems, where there is a set path to follow. Heuristic problems, on the other hand, require a break from the path to discover a novel solution, and extrinsic motivators can actually hinder performance with these problems.[5]

In 2009, an article published in *The Review of Economics* outlined the results of several experiments conducted at MIT, the University of Chicago, and in rural India.[6] In these experiments, they gave test subjects different tasks to complete, and offered different performance-contingent payments, from large to small. The test in rural India was conducted to see if the standard of living or culture played a significant factor in the results. The conclusions from the researchers stated that: "With some important exceptions, we observed that high reward levels can have detrimental effects on performance."

In June 2009, the London School of Economics hosted a workshop, entitled "When Performance-Related Pay Backfires," to unveil over fifty studies of financial incentives in employment relations. Dr. Bernd Irlenbusch, from the London School of Economics Department of Management, stated: "We find that financial incentives may indeed reduce intrinsic motivation and diminish ethical or other reasons for complying with workplace social norms such as fairness. As a consequence, the provision of incentives can result in a negative impact on overall performance."[7]

Dan Pink makes his own case about the negative aspects of extrinsic rewards systems when trying to foster innovation in the workplace, and he suggests that these traditional tools of management are effective at fostering compliance but fail to engage creativity among workers. Pink states that "For too long, there's been a mismatch between what science knows and what business does."[8] He suggests that extrinsic rewards tend to narrow one's focus and concentrate the mind. This is fine for repetitive or mechanical work, but it is completely unhelpful for work requiring innovation.

I think that when you are trying to get the people of an organization to develop a culture of innovation, to being willing to look at their business processes differently than they had in the past, you need to ensure that your incentive systems do not work against what you are trying to accomplish. I believe that extrinsic rewards systems are not congruent with your destination of teamwork and innovation, and therefore, should either be a minimal part of your organizational culture, or even better, absent entirely.

In Chapter 9, Trust Principle #4: Understand that people become a product of their environment, I outline my perspective that humans are highly attuned to their respective environments, and that their environments can change their behaviour quite drastically. I suggest that a working environment where management reinforces with a compensation system that the organization feels the needs to pay for great performance tells the staff that the employer believes that the people will not be intrinsically motivated to perform superbly with their base salaries (assuming they are fair to begin with).

As a result, the organization trains the staff only to engage and innovate when they can see the prize that is being offered. I don't think that this is in keeping with the culture that you should be trying to foster in a continuous improvement journey. I think that you want staff to be truly engaged, and to be intrinsically motivated to offer improvement ideas all the time, and not just in a manner that fits into a rewards system.

Ask yourself if your current incentive system will truly take you where you are hoping to go with your goal of organizational evolutions towards a continuous improvement or Lean management culture. Does your current system require the regular, systematic ranking of your staff against each other in order to assign bonuses or other financial compensation? If so, you need to consider that you are violating Trust Principle #25: Eliminate competition in favour of teamwork (described in Chapter 30). If you want teamwork to thrive, you need to stamp out anything that implies that you support competition.

I realize that this principle will put me at odds with many people in the business world, and I can appreciate their beliefs and perspectives. However, as I suggest in Chapter 31, Trust Principle #26: Be congruent, I maintain that if you are trying to change a culture, you need to remove everything from the leadership behaviours that deviates from the model of the culture you are targeting. Remember that for where you are trying to go, the latent and inherent intrinsic motivation of your staff should always have primacy over other types of motivation.

This is not to say that bonuses or incentive programs should be completely eliminated, or that they have no place in any organization. I do think that they would have the best chance of success in producing the intended results when they are rewarding behaviour at the level of large teams, or divisions, or even across the whole organization. If you want teamwork, then ensure that everything you put in place as a management system is consistent with rewarding and celebrating teamwork.

If you create an incentive program that works at the individual level, you are supporting an environment where your people will think of themselves as individuals before they think of themselves as part of the team. This may lead to forms of competition between individuals as they strive to maximize their own compensation, and potentially at the expense of behaviours that best support the team goals.

Your people want to be free to innovate where possible, to support your organization's mission. They want to be a part of something bigger than themselves, to believe that what they do really matters in the big picture. In many ways, all you have to do is create the structure and system to let them do this, and to remove the impediments and barriers.

# 56

## Change Principle #23: Teach Your Leaders to Operate in the Gray

*"Life isn't black and white. It's a million gray areas, don't you find?"*

**Ridley Scott**[1]
*film director and producer*

I think that one of the hardest things for new leaders to figure out is how to "operate in the gray space." What I mean by this, is how to interpret the best steps to take when the known rule book does not clearly apply to the situation at hand. I don't think that there is an easy way to describe in writing how a new leader should navigate this gray space. But I do think that senior leaders have an obligation to coach and teach their leadership team members approaches to use when they each encounter their own gray situations.

Perhaps the struggle for new leaders comes from learning to operate without direction, when, for so many years, they have had a supervisor tell them what to do next. When they begin to advance to higher-level positions in the organizational structure, the direction they are provided from their superior becomes less tactical and more strategic and broader. Eventually, they are given general objectives to accomplish, and the "how" is left to the leader to determine. Without a rule book, some leaders will struggle. And if there is a rule book but the situation places them in between two different situations, each with different recommended solutions, the leader can be paralyzed into indecision and inaction.

A paradox, sometimes referred to as Buridan's donkey, named after the 14th-century French Philosopher Jean Buridan, imagines a situation where a donkey that is equally hungry and thirsty is placed exactly midway between a stack of hay and a bucket of water. Unable to choose which option is better, the donkey dies of both hunger and thirst. Although it is completely unfair to compare a person to a donkey, I think that we have all at some point in our careers encountered a leader that seemed just as paralyzed by indecision as the donkey in this paradox. In my experience, the likelihood is small that two different options are exactly equal as possible courses of action. To break the tie, gather more information quickly. Talk to the people involved daily in that situation to learn more about it. A true perfect tie in the real world is very rare.

In the public sector, I have seen people get stuck on how to proceed with the interpretation of policy for a special situation. Usually, I have found it helpful to refer to the policy rationale statement, which explains the intent and purpose behind the policy. This, I believe, can help a leader make a correct interpretation in a situation which the policy-makers could never have possibly envisioned when the document was crafted. In other words, seek out the WHY behind the rules.

Understanding and placing primacy on the idea of "intent" of the rules or policy is a useful approach to navigating the gray space as a leader. There will always be situations that come up that land you in between two or three established rules and directions. Sometimes the best course of action will be a unique direction that follows the intent of the policy but is specific to the special circumstances of the day.

Some leaders try to avoid these situations by documenting every possible situation that they can think of that might confuse their staff. But no matter how diligent you are, you will never be able to craft a manual of "if this then do that" statements that can cover every possible circumstance. It's a fool's errand, I think, to attempt to obviate decision-making for staff and leaders, and it is extremely dangerous. In an innovative organizational culture, you need your team members to be able to make think and decisions on their own.

Some leaders go down this path because they have seen some of their staff make poor decisions in the past that had resulted in negative outcomes. But the answer isn't to remove decision-making from the hands of workers; it's to train people on how to make better decisions.

You need to accept that you cannot encode a solution to every possible problem in advance. Therefore, you need to be prepared to select a course of action in a new situation. You need to teach your people how to do this, too. The more people that appreciate and understand the decision-making process, the better. The culture change through which you are leading the organization needs many people who can solve unique problems, not just a few.

# 57

## Change Principle #24: Protect the Culture Change

*"So goes the leader, so goes the culture."*

**Simon Sinek**[1]
*leadership author*

As a senior leader, you will often face challenges, sometimes framed as feedback or suggestions, to the culture change that you are trying to facilitate. The difficulty, I think, is identifying when to bend and compromise, and when to hold fast. We've all seen leaders who hold fast on issues where it seems to make no sense. These leaders can be seen as amusing and misguided, or, in another light, arrogant and stubborn. So how do you know which path to take?

As an executive, I have struggled with this choice myself and I have come to realize that, as a leader of a culture change based on continuous improvement, a culture where people are celebrated when they challenge the status quo, you only hold fast on items that would stall or hurt the culture change itself. Ask yourself, will making the suggested change impair the positive culture journey on which the organization is travelling? If the answer is "yes," then you should reject the change.

At Manitoba Housing, we expected the leaders in the organization to re-broadcast the monthly housing leadership team presentation to their staff within two weeks of the HLT meeting. If we were to receive a suggestion from some leaders that we could reduce the meeting frequency to quarterly, we would reject that change because it would imply that we don't believe in regular communication with our staff—it would send the message that the inconvenience to the leadership was making us question our commitment to transparency and communication.

If we were to be asked if we could stop presenting the financial information periodically at these HLT meetings, because people were too busy to prepare the relevant reports, we would say "no," because that financial information was a part of the message of trust that we had for our staff. We were showing them information that wasn't typically shown to staff in the public sector, and they knew it and appreciated seeing the financial situation of the corporation. Cutting out this type of information would send a terrible message that we had changed our minds about the level of trust that we had with our staff.

If we were to be challenged that we don't need to bother with preparing metrics for our scorecards each month, because people need to get "the real work done," we would say "no," because we are now an organization with a measuring culture. We measure things in our business because it teaches us things about our business that we didn't know before, and because it helps us to improve our business.

Now, if someone points out that they are spending lots of time preparing data for a metric that no one ever looks at or uses, then that is a concern worth considering. Apply a method of root-cause analysis, such as the simple 5-Why approach, to understand the true problem. Why isn't that metric used? If the metric doesn't help us to truly understand that part of our business, then change it to something that provides more relevant information.

If, however, the metric is appropriate, but isn't used because the leader simply doesn't want to be bothered, then that is a problem with willingness, and that problem with that leader needs to be addressed right away, as described in Chapter 21, Trust Principle #16: Discipline only the unwilling, but know that they are few. The leaders all will need to become supportive of the measurement part of the changing culture of the organization.

This book contains the leadership principles that, I believe, embody the essence of the culture change that people want for their organizations *Do not handle this in a group setting and ask your leadership team to vote on it, or you will quickly lose control and compromise the culture change you are trying to facilitate.*

when they attempt to bring in a Lean or continuous improvement program. As a result, you need to look at what elements are key to the culture change and resist suggestions that would compromise the culture journey. At the same time, you must be willing to change other elements that aren't critical to the culture.

It won't be easy, and you will encounter situations where you aren't sure what to do. That's okay, and that's normal. Talk to some of your most trusted senior leaders one-on-one to give them your thoughts and get their input. But keep the final decision for yourself to make. Do not handle this in a group setting and ask your leadership team to vote on it, or you will quickly lose control and compromise the culture change you are trying to facilitate.

Remember, culture change is very hard and uncomfortable. Even within your trusted leadership team, there will be those who would prefer that things stay the way they are right now or go back to the way they were. They may not admit it outright, but if you give them a glimmer of hope that you are prepared to compromise, they may move more aggressively to make you reverse course.

I think it is best to be completely transparent about why you might say "no" to a particular suggestion that someone might have. Tell them your rationale about how it would compromise the culture change, and that this is the reason why you need to hold fast on that issue. Remember, you are promoting a shift to a continuous improvement culture, and if you say "no" to every suggestion about change within that shift, then you will start to appear hypocritical.

This will compromise your integrity and weaken the trust that you have been working so hard to build and to maintain. But if you share your thought process and your rationale, you can differentiate this situation from a case of simple stubbornness. In fact, you may distinguish it as an example of thoughtful leadership.

# 58

## The Space for Change—Concluding Thoughts

*"Everything changes and nothing stands still."*

**Heraclitus[1]**
*ancient Greek Philosopher*

When the Space for Change is developing, you will know it—in fact, you will feel it. You will see it in the faces of your people, and in the energy levels that the staff and the leadership bring to work every day. The positivity that you sense in different offices becomes palpable and noticeable.

Manitoba Housing, between 2014 and 2018, had several major strategic initiatives ongoing simultaneously. A new IT system was being developed for the operations staff, and the entire social housing policy and procedure set was updated and being rolled out across the organization. And while all this was going on, we were adopting Lean management practices as well. To support these changes, we invested in consulting services for organizational change management.

The consultants recommended that we develop an OCM framework, like an organizational chart, to support change management across the corporation. At the top of the framework were the change sponsors, typically the executives and executive directors. At the next level were the change champions, usually leaders such as directors or managers. At the third level were the change agents, the people who supported change at the front-line level. These were identified and selected individuals in each branch who were trained to be able to answer questions from staff and colleagues, and to provide feedback and concerns up through the levels of the OCM framework, so that we could respond before the concerns caused problems.

One of the most visual examples for the CEO and myself that caused us to realize that we had reached a milestone in the development of the *Space for Change* was a photograph that was sent to me by the executive director of a branch. This photograph was of three leaders who were proudly sporting brightly coloured T-shirts that they had made for themselves with the words "change champion" emblazoned across the front.

These leaders probably regretted posing for that picture because I insisted on including it in many presentations later on when speaking about the importance of developing the *Space for Change*. But it was a great visual statement of how change can be not only a positive thing but how it can actually be embraced and supported, instead of reviled, by people within the organization.

Work carefully to build and shape the *Space for Change*, and to sustain it. You're going to be needing it for a long time to come.

# Part IV

# Understanding the Space for Continuous Improvement

# 59

## The Space for Continuous Improvement Explained

*"Continuous improvement is better than delayed perfection."*

**Attributed to Mark Twain**
*American author, humourist, entrepreneur*

This space is the third and final space described by the Three Spaces model. The *Space for Continuous Improvement*, or the *Space for CI*, refers to each individual event on your Lean journey. It could be a *kaizen* event, it could be a regularly-scheduled facilitators meeting for sharing best practices, or it could be a Lean *hoshin kanri* or balanced scorecard strategic planning event with the senior leaders. The point of this space in the model is the recognition that each individual CI event needs to be carefully shaped in advance by the Lean champion and the Lean practitioner, especially in the early days of the organizational transformation.

After about one year of great progress in our operations excellence program at Manitoba Housing, our Lean practitioner asked me if we would still need a Lean champion to drive forward the concepts, or if we could just at that point delegate it to the various senior leaders. I thought about that idea for some time before answering. I replied that we were not nearly at the point yet where we could consider Lean as an integral part of the organizational culture, where it would seamlessly continue without the constant nudging and course corrections of the Lean champion.

At the four-year point in the Manitoba Housing program, I believe that this diagnosis was and remains accurate. Even after over four years, I believe that the operations excellence program still needs the guiding hand of an operationally-minded Lean champion to adapt the next set of tools from the Lean toolkit for incorporation into the corporate culture.

268 • *Starting Lean from Scratch*

But the goal of having all senior leaders delegated to champion Lean in their own areas is exactly the target towards which every organization must drive.

In the early days of your Lean program, the Lean practitioner will be most heavily involved in shaping these events, by carefully planning each event in advance. At the beginning of your journey, you are still trying to build trust and confidence in your people, with something that is strange and foreign to them. As a result, you want to get as many staff involved with successful and positive events as possible. I believe that success in these events breeds comfort and confidence with the staff.

The more staff that have rewarding and productive experiences in *kaizen* events the better, as these staff all go back to their home positions after the event and will likely provide good feedback to their colleagues when asked: "What was it like?" If a *kaizen* event has eight staff members attending it who all share positive experiences with five people each, that means forty people receive a positive endorsement of the program. Do that a few times in a row, and you are rapidly building an encouraging vibe with the staff. Even the naysayers, who are likely sitting on the sidelines just waiting for the program to fail and disappoint people, will struggle to complain after a while.

I need to point out that this book is heavily based on developing an event-based Lean culture within an organization. This, I believe, is a necessary evolutionary step for organizations just beginning their cultural journey, because events can be shaped and planned for success—and you want the teams to have success so they will begin to believe in the culture change. However, I strongly believe that the long-range destination of a cultural journey needs to be a continuous system, such as that described by Mike Rother in his book *Toyota Kata: Managing People for Improvement, Adaptiveness, and Superior Results.*[1]

In this desired state, your supervisors are all acting as coaches for the people on their teams, and they are behaving in line with Lean culture all the time. The teams are identifying problems and using experimentation and structured problem solving themselves every day to constantly make improvements to processes. The need for Lean facilitators drops substantially, as *kaizens* become much more infrequent, as they are used only for larger problems. As the teams begin to embody the two *katas* (or patterns), the improvement *kata* and the coaching *kata* into how they operate, the organization transitions towards a truly continuous improvement culture. However, at the very beginning, I do not believe that many managers are ready for this type of approach, and the trust of the staff is still building. I remain firm in my belief that there is tremendous cultural learning and transformation that takes place as you develop an event-based Lean system as the first part of your Lean journey. Just be aware that true continuous improvement will require your organization to evolve beyond the event-based system to a proper continuous system—otherwise, your people will forever see Lean as something that is "done by others."

To properly adjust your organizational culture to take full advantage of *kaizen* events, you will need to build and shape and maintain the *Space for CI*. The focus and energy required in this space are quite substantial for the Lean practitioner, and occasionally for the Lean champion. But the investment of time and effort will definitely be worth it in the medium and long run, as it will serve to strengthen the organization's trust in Lean in general.

# 60

---

## CI Principle #1: Defend Continuous Improvement as an Investment, Not a Cost

---

*"If you always do what you always did, you always get what you've always gotten."*

**Jessie Potter (but often attributed to Henry Ford)**[1]

*educator*

Sometimes, senior leaders who don't understand the Lean management approach say that their teams are "too busy to improve." They believe that they are serving as the champion of the front-line people, protecting them from this foolish waste of time. From their perspective, all that the Lean training and Lean events do is consume valuable work time. Their people are so stressed, they say, and they have been asked to do "more with less" for so long that they are exhausted. So, please, no more "initiatives." The people have had enough, and they have no more bandwidth to handle any additional effort. They are just getting by, and they are hanging from a thread.

Let's carry this thought process through to its logical conclusion. Do we think that it is good leadership to tell the organization and its people that the situation is so dire, that, as the senior leaders, the only thing that we believe we have left in our toolkit is to bemoan the hopelessness of it all? That our solution is to continue with the status quo, all the while complaining about it, without even attempting

> *"A leader takes people where they want to go. A great leader takes people where they don't necessarily want to go, but ought to be."*
>
> **Attributed to Rosalynn Carter**
> *former First Lady of the United States.*

to take the team down a path that is, by its very nature, intended to help bring about efficiency improvements so that the team can do more with less? Do we think that, by choosing to do nothing differently, things will change?

Is this what our people deserve from us as leaders? I believe that our people deserve better. I think that it is important to remember that, as leaders, we need to be prepared to persevere through tough challenges if we are going to take our team to a place that is better in the end.

One story that I have found helpful in explaining the need to take on an improvement challenge, even though you don't think you have the time today, is from *The Seven Habits of Highly Effective People*, by Stephen R. Covey.[2] The last Habit, "Sharpen the Saw," speaks to the need for an individual to continue to study and learn, to be taking the steps needed to perpetually improve as a person. I think that the story of the saw also pertains to taking on process improvement initiatives at work when everyone thinks they have no time. The story goes like this:

> *"Suppose you were to come upon someone in the woods working feverishly to cut down a tree.*
>
> *'What are you doing?' you ask.*
>
> *'Can't you see?' comes the impatient reply. 'I'm sawing down this tree.'*
>
> *'You look exhausted!' you exclaim. 'How long have you been at it?'*
>
> *'Over five hours,' he returns. 'and I'm beat! This is hard work.'*
>
> *'Well, why don't you take a break for a few minutes and sharpen that saw?' you inquire. 'I'm sure it would go a lot faster.'*
>
> *'I don't have time to sharpen the saw,' the man says emphatically. 'I'm too busy sawing!'"*

When I have explained it this way, I have seen many leaders have an "aha!" moment. The toughest people to convince may not be those leaders that report to you, but your peers. Either they have their own "aha!" moment, or they must be told to get on board by their boss. There is always the possibility that, after your team starts to show the efficiency improvements and the benefits of Lean management the staff in the adjacent branch or division will be asking their leader "why can't we give that approach a try?" This results in peer pressure from the bottom up, which can also be effective at reducing the leader's resistance.

I think the new way of the world is to learn how to do more with less, and that is what Lean can help your team do. I don't think anyone really believes that governments or private sector businesses are going to start blindly injecting more resources into organizations to help fuel inefficient processes. The answer, of course, is to make those processes more efficient so that your teams can actually manage them effectively. That's why Lean management is so important in today's constrictive business environment.

The phrase "do more with less" has become quite clichéd, but a very realistic alternate scenario, I find, is to be asked to do "the same with less." With this reality facing nearly every organization today, we need to have the foresight to view improvement efforts as investments in a more efficient future.

# 61

## CI Principle #2: Study and Adopt Methods of Time Management

*"The key is not to prioritize what's on your schedule, but to schedule your priorities."*

**Stephen Covey**[1]
*leadership author*

You need to be able to strategically plan to complete some initiatives, while still getting the day-to-day business done. This is harder than most people think, and it is a large part of why leaders might say that "We have no time to improve." So how can you ensure that you are able to insert new objectives into your calendar, and make sure that they get done, when you already feel that you are busy enough?

In my own case, the time-management lessons I adopted seemed to help. I learned from the fundamental principles identified in Stephen Covey's *Seven Habits*, Habit 3: "Make First Things First."[2] Although he identifies a complete document template that he recommends for use in time management, I found that I could achieve what I wanted simply by regularly updating an electronic list of my long- and medium-range priorities.

I would then put placeholders in my calendar between two and four weeks out from the current date where I could either focus myself on creating a deliverable for an initiative or it would be a milestone meeting to keep a priority initiative moving along. I called this my "planning horizon," and it was very different from the one to two-day-ahead planning horizon with which I used to work. The most critical thing to remember is that you need to protect those placeholders diligently. It seems to me that this problem is very common with leaders—so many of us keep such a shortened focal-length view of planning our work, that the day-to-day busy-work takes over and we never feel like we accomplish anything. This is Parkinson's Law taking over.

Cyril Northcote Parkinson published an essay in 1955 in which his original conclusion was that bureaucracies expand at a nearly predictable rate over time.[3] He provided data from the British Civil Service to back up his claim—in particular, he noted that the British Colonial Office had its highest number of employees while Great Britain's foreign overseas empire was in decline. The bureaucracy had continued to increase its ranks even though there were fewer and fewer colonies to administer. Parkinson theorized that the predicted increase of five to seven percent of employees per year, was "irrespective of any variation in the amount of work (if any) to be done." He rationalized that this increase was due to two motive causes, or factors:

1. "An official wants to multiply subordinates, not rivals, and
2. Officials make work for each other."

As someone who moved from the private sector into the public sector, and who also believes strongly in Lean principles, I cringe at the idea of these assumptions being applied to my organization. However, the version of Parkinson's Law that is quoted in practice today comes from the first sentence of the 1955 essay, and I am convinced that it holds true for time management. Parkinson's Law states that

*"Work expands to fill the time available for its completion."*

I find that the busy-work and the day-to-day reactionary fire-fighting issues of high urgency, but low strategic value, absolutely follow Parkinson's Law. However, I have found that if I put my priorities in my calendar weeks in advance and let Parkinson's Law fill the time *around* these priorities without displacing them, then I was able to keep the priority work progressing in a way that I never could before. But you must be steadfast about protecting those priority time blocks from the so-called "urgent" needs of the day. I believe that the answer is not to tightly plan every day in ten-minute increments, as that leads to frustration and despair when urgent issues show up at the last minute, which they will. Rather, the secret is to ensure that your calendar allows time for the urgent issues to fill in at the last minute. You need to give your calendar a degree of freedom for urgent issues so that you have space for them to go without immediately feeling that you have to displace your priorities.

If you embrace this type of approach, you should find that it will go a long way to reducing your stress level at work. Your feeling of effectiveness as a leader should increase as you will see yourself actually getting important things done. It may feel to you as though the workplace, which previously was a swirling vortex of actions and reactions, has slowed down and that you are now in the calm eye of the storm, able to get things done when you used to feel tossed about, helpless, and ineffective.

You may need to coach your team with this concept as well. In Chapter 60, CI Principle #1: Defend continuous improvement as an investment, not a cost, I discussed situations in which leaders push back against transformational initiatives, stating that they and their teams are "too busy to improve." Time management solutions to prioritize extra projects, despite a busy schedule, will be a necessity if you want to get your team used to these Lean concepts.

Learning a time-management philosophy that allows you to keep a longer-range planning horizon is absolutely critical for anyone that is going to be leading an organizational transformation. You need to be looking beyond the horizon to keep planning the next steps—if things work well, the organization will achieve the first few targets that you set, and you will need to have the next targets figured out.

# 62

## CI Principle #3: Let Those Who Do the Job Develop the Improvements

*"If you want a successful business, your people must feel that you are working for them—not that they are working for you."*

**Sam Walton**[1]
*founder of Walmart*

One of the traditional management clichés that you will need to break as a part of the culture transformation is the idea that management is responsible for all improvements. In a way, this is an extension of the different role of the leader that was discussed in Chapter 27, Trust Principle #22: Understand the true source of your value as a leader. Your value as a leader comes not from your subject-matter expertise; rather, it comes from how you can coach the people on your team to become better at their jobs and work better together as a team.

Therefore, the job as a leader changes from the traditional paradigm of the "answer-provider" to that of coach. And a coach is not there to give out the answers, but rather, to teach the people how to answer their own questions, as outlined in Chapter 29, Trust Principle #24: Coach with questions, not answers. So, since we believe that the staff are important, and that they have valuable input into how to improve the business processes, then we need to structure all continuous improvement events to reinforce that message.

*Remember, the staff won't want their own ideas to fail.*

This means that the senior leadership, and the other levels of leadership, need to believe and state that the people working with the processes every day are the best ones to identify improvements to those processes. This will

---

become a principle that you must use when identifying and selecting the right people for a continuous improvement event.

As described in Chapter 29, Trust Principle #24: Coach with questions, not answers, Toyota uses the Shu-Ha-Ri model of coaching and mentorship for its people. In this model, it is at the *Ri* (meaning the Freedom to Create) stage of development, that an employee is in the best position to be able to innovate with a process in their area of expertise. These *Ri*-type experts, are the ones for whom you should be searching when you are trying to select a team for a continuous improvement event.

If your staff develop the improvements, then they will be motivated to make them work in practice. Allowing your staff to obtain the benefit of travelling the journey of discovery will dramatically help with the change management during the implementation stage. Remember, the staff won't want their own ideas to fail.

In Chapter 65, CI Principle #6: Choose the right people for an event, I review the importance of adding a few other types of team members to the mix, in order to create some diversity. But the basic principle that you need to remember is that the experts that are doing the job every day are crucial to improving how that work gets done. And that means that the leader of those experts has a role to play that goes beyond developing the improvements for the team.

# 63

---

## CI Principle #4: Plan for Success Every Time

---

*"Failing to plan is planning to fail."*

Reverend H. K. Williams[1]

---

### GET SOME EASY WINS GOING

To get some momentum in your Lean transformation, you need to get some wins under your belt. They need to be ones that the team can see for themselves, and the more staff that see the wins, the better off you are. The best idea is to search for several small, easily attainable wins to build the team's confidence in the Lean toolkit, and in the Lean approach itself. When you implement what the team comes up with, this will also help to further develop and strengthen the *Space of Trust*. You absolutely must avoid the temptation to target a big win right away, to tackle that huge broken process that everyone knows is out there—that's a huge risk that you should not take on too early. Fail at that one at the outset, and you will lose momentum in what you are trying to do, which is to advance the organizational culture. In the beginning, you want to get your people to *believe*.

It might seem disingenuous to deliberately select small initiatives that you know will be successful, but you need success as a part of the change management approach to get your people on board with the methodology. Your staff Lean facilitators will be new to the approach, and you might be new as well. Your consultant and your Lean practitioners should have some more experience, but other than that, you will initially be very thin on actual successes.

When trying to figure out where to start with your first *kaizen* events, look for these key attributes:

1. The branch leader owning the process in question appears enthusiastic and supportive of the new Lean management approach, and is willing to be an "early adopter";
2. The results of the complete *kaizen* will be very visible to outside branches, making this a "demonstrator" event that buys you additional positive advertising power with staff beyond the affected branch;
3. The affected process crosses relatively few boundaries, and all the impacted leaders are also very supportive; and
4. The *kaizen* is simple enough that you think it should be able to be completed in one day. And then schedule it for two days.

Once you get a few of these wins racked up, word will start to spread through the staff. Remember that every successful event has eight or so *kaizen* participants each of whom go back to their regular jobs when it is over, to be grilled by colleagues who will ask them "So? How was it?" You want those answers to be positive every time.

Conversely, imagine that due to poor planning, the staff hear bad reviews of the *kaizen*, and right at the time when you are trying to build the organizational confidence and trust in Lean. Trust me; it's worth the effort to select carefully for your first few events.

Get several successful events going in a row, and now you have multiple groups of people hearing positive things about the program. This is the type of foundation you need to have to be able to start to tackle the more challenging issues, gradually building in complexity, of course.

## LATER ON...

I've said several times to people who were asking us how we made our Manitoba Housing operations excellence program work so successfully: "If you think that a *kaizen* event involves just picking eight random staff, throwing them in a room for a couple days and hoping for the best, you are crazy." While our events might look like they only had a nominal amount of structure to them, in fact, they were extensively planned for several weeks in advance.

First, the Lean champion definitely has a large role to play early on in the journey in selecting what *kaizen* events to do, and when to do them. I found that the best *kaizen* event options started to become obvious to me after I began spending time out visiting staff in their office areas across the province. When you talk to your people and ask them what their challenges are, eventually you will hear some common themes.

Contained within those themes, are likely absolute gems of ideas for *kaizen* events in which the staff can participate. If you select the events this way, the staff will usually not question the topic of the *kaizen* because you can easily say that the process was selected based on challenges that the staff told you about during your visits.

But you will need to define the *kaizen* project scope very carefully. I think that many organizations getting started down the path of a Lean journey want to see big successes quickly. As a result, a common mistake is that they select improperly large *kaizen* events at the beginning of the journey to show the value. This error will lead to disappointment and quickly-fading enthusiasm for the program. Remember, you want successes, regardless of the size, so start small and collect those guaranteed wins right away.

Early on, it's more important to build the trust with the staff than it is to impress outsiders. Be very careful not to choose *kaizen* project scopes so large that it is unlikely that the team can finish the event in the two or three days you have reserved for the event. You're trying to have the staff improve a process; you're not trying to have the staff solve the problem of world hunger in three days.

Even if you have a proper "size" of *kaizen* event selected, you will need to work deliberately with your Lean practitioner to define what parts of the process will be considered "in scope" for the project, and what parts will be "out-of-scope." In other words, it may be in the best interest of the team to deliberately ignore some pieces of the process, if the odds are that those pieces will just drag the team down a

*You're trying to have the staff improve a process; you're not trying to have the staff solve the problem of world hunger in three days.*

rabbit-hole of confusion, with little hope of solving those issues within the allowed time frame. These pieces may, at the time of the project, be truly dependent on processes completely outside of the control of the team, or perhaps on some decision that has not yet been made. Rather than setting up the team to be frustrated with their lack of control in these areas, define the project scope so that it only includes the elements of the process about which they can make decisions.

In previous chapters, I spoke about the importance of authority, the leadership chain of command, and proper delegation. I think that the most important realization that I had during the development of the operations excellence program was that a *kaizen* event is actually an exercise in the delegation of authority by the senior leadership.

If the operations executive can be assumed to own all of the key business processes and procedures, then that person also owns all of the authority to make changes to those processes. A *kaizen* event involves deliberately taking that authority from the executive and giving it to the group of staff for the duration of the event. In order for this delegation of authority to be effective, a few things need to be set up properly beforehand.

First, the operations senior leader needs to be front and centre during the delegation exercise. If some functional leader is there instead of the operations leader, it will be obvious to the team members attending the *kaizen* event that this person has no authority to delegate to the team. In the case of Manitoba Housing, I, as the operations executive was made the Lean champion, and this seemed to work very well for us. Since I had control over the vast majority of the operations processes, and a large fraction of the organization's staff, this helped to bring authority where it was required for our operations excellence program.

Second, as the Lean champion, you need to make sure that all of the leaders understand that once the *kaizen* event kicks off, the leadership have committed to delegating their authority to the staff to change the process. In order to get the employee-engagement benefits from the Lean event, that delegation needs to happen, and it needs to be completely sincere.

If the senior leader walks into the *kaizen* closeout presentation and over-turns the staff's ideas, then they will see right away that the leadership wasn't honest about wanting the staff to solve the problems, that they weren't sincere in saying that the staff had the answers. That is why it is absolutely critical that the Lean champion and the Lean practitioner work with the branch leadership in advance of the *kaizen* event to correctly define the project scope.

The scope of the *kaizen* project needs to be carefully and thoughtfully defined such that the senior leadership can confidently say, before the *kaizen* even occurs, that they are prepared to accept whatever comes out of the event. Sometimes, that takes more thought and preparation than you might think. You may find that you need to tighten up the scope and pull some elements out of the consideration of the *kaizen* event to be examined another time. If there are a few "must-haves" or "don't-touch areas" in the project scope, then you need to be completely up-front with the *kaizen* team before they start and put those items on the table as soon as possible.

The team members need to know early on what freedoms they have, and within what constraints they must work. Just be careful that you aren't so constrictive on the project scope that the team has no room to manoeuvre at all because that will cause them frustration as well.

Believe me, defining the scope more clearly at the beginning of the process will save a huge headache later on when you are trying to dig yourself out of a hole caused by poor planning and scoping on your part. Remember, once you start down the *kaizen* path, you have committed something to the staff, and you break that commitment at the risk of endangering the *Space of Trust*.

# 64

## CI Principle #5: Look for the Barriers in Advance, and Remove Them

*"The leader is the servant who removes obstacles that prevent people from doing their jobs."*

**Max De Pree**[1]
*businessman and leadership author*

One key piece of preparation before the *kaizen* event takes place is the search for, and removal of, barriers to success. As the project charter starts to take shape, the Lean practitioner should be walking around talking to key leaders and some subject-matter experts well before the *kaizen* to get input on issues that might come up during the event. When barriers are identified, they need to be reviewed with leaders right away to see if they can be quickly removed. When that isn't possible, they need to be escalated immediately to the Lean champion for resolution.

Sometimes, the answer to barriers is to tighten up the project scope to remove the problematic part of the process where changes are not yet possible. This, of course, assumes that the remaining project scope still allows the team the ability to succeed in moving the needle on the process efficiency. In other cases, direct action either by leaders or the Lean champion is required. In one particular case, we at Manitoba Housing had an excellent *kaizen* lined up in one of the cities outside of Winnipeg. It was unique for us at the time, as it involved the use of the 5S toolkit on a filing system.

In Manitoba Housing, as in many parts of government, there was a heavy reliance on paper filing systems at the time. In one branch, the files for a particular program were large, cumbersome, and they contained a tremendous amount of material of questionable value. When you would look at a file, it was clear that there were no decisions being made about what needed to be filed or not filed—every transaction record was filed, without question. This made the files simply scrapbooks of memories of our engagement with the clients. Some of our clients would be very long-term clients, participating in the program for many years—the result could be files that were well over four inches thick.

Many files tended to retain every notice that had been sent to clients. Our computer system could reprint any notices if we ever needed them, but our staff believed that they needed to file the paper copies because, on rare occasions, they used them for dispute resolution. However, the world had long since evolved, and electronic records had become accepted and commonplace.

The Lean practitioner and I were very excited about this *kaizen*, as we were forecasting the opportunity for tremendous reductions in tenant filing, along with the associated time savings for the staff involved. This event had a lot of potential to be a huge win for the staff, and for operations excellence to really demonstrate the value of continuous improvement. And the best part was that this *kaizen* had been suggested by staff in the regional office, instead of me. It had come from the front-line staff, so I really wanted this one to succeed.

But then, two days before the *kaizen* was to take place, the Lean practitioner came into my office and told me that there was a huge problem on the horizon. He had been told by some subject-matter experts that the paper copies of the notices could never be eliminated from the files, and that paper was essential to the dispute resolution process, so the risk was too high to consider not filing these items.

Yes, our database could reprint the notice document, but it would put the current date on the reprint, instead of the actual date that the notice was issued—this would be a problem if it couldn't be validated when the notice was issued. The problem was that allowing the staff to remove the notices from the files was expected to result in over half of the waste reduction opportunities of this event. If this was made a constraint, there wasn't going to be much left for the *kaizen* team to recommend. The event might fizzle out after a day. This had quickly become my problem to solve.

I walked over to our legal advisor's office and asked for an opinion on the matter. I explained what the upcoming *kaizen* event was about and relayed the concern that the notices needed to be in paper form for the dispute resolution process. I suggested that electronic records were a part of everyday government life now, and that they must be admissible in judicial situations. He agreed with me.

I then asked the crucial question: What would need to be essential about the electronic records in order for them to work for our purposes to support dispute resolution? The answer was actually quite simple. Our database system could work if the staff included a short text string in the notes field beside the notice about what the notice was for and the date on which it was delivered. With those simple additions, it was felt that we could let the notices be removed from the paper files, and that the staff would be able to have everything that they needed in the event that they had to defend a disputed case.

The *kaizen* went ahead two days later, and it was the resounding success for which we had hoped. A staff member from the corporate legal support group was part of the team, along with staff from a variety of roles. The savings were tremendous—about 500 clerical staff hours per year were saved. This was the time that we could reinvest back into the value-added duties of serving the client, instead of wasting that time filing papers that no one needed. Cleaning up the files also meant that other operations staff had an easier time reviewing files. Every time they pulled a file, it would take less time to find what they needed and get back to the important work. Every new file that was started by this office followed the new filing protocol the defined was to be included in the file, and what didn't need to be filed. But the legacy files still followed the old, cumbersome filing method.

The office staff then elected to tackle these files themselves to bring them up to the new standards. This was beyond the scope of the *kaizen* because we only committed to developing the new Standard Operating Procedure that would apply to newly-created files. But they were excited to make it happen. They invited a few other people from different areas over to the office to help them out. This had the added benefit of spreading the good word to different offices about the new streamlined way of filing that a group of front-line staff had developed. They were quite impressed that the COO had immediately endorsed a procedure at the final presentation that front-line staff had created.

The best part was that the savings didn't end there. Our new IT system was in development at that time, and the system was being designed to make almost all files to be electronic, without any need for paper files. All files would be scanned into the new system that would be rolled out in a couple years. Any savings in paper files today would reduce, by potentially hundreds of thousands, the number of records that would need to be scanned into the new IT system in the future.

The story was so good that we even made a video about it. A few months after this *kaizen*, the Manitoba Government was hosting a Lean conference, and there was a call for short videos telling a story about a Lean success from different departments. We decided that we would submit a video about this *kaizen* event. The Lean practitioner ran with this and was able to get some professional videographer support to produce a very high-quality short video that covered the entire *kaizen* story-arc in just a few minutes, including the problem, the 5S process used, the end solution and the benefits realized. This video was unveiled at the conference in October of that year and was widely regarded as a fantastic story. In fact, the video was posted on YouTube and ended up being used by several departments across the province as mandatory material for their Lean training for government staff. The message really resonated with people, as every department had a paper filing system that was inefficient and messy.

And to think that the *kaizen* would have been a flop if I hadn't fulfilled my duty as Lean champion to remove that obstacle before the *kaizen* started. None of the team members ever knew about what I had done, and they didn't need to know. All they knew was that they solved a huge problem, and that management supported their ideas and their efforts.

# 65

---

## CI Principle #6: Choose the Right People for an Event

---

*"Problems can become opportunities when the right people come together."*

**Attributed to Robert Redford**
*actor, director, producer, environmentalist, philanthropist,*
*founder of the Sundance Film Festival*

---

### HOW IMPORTANT IS TEAM DIVERSITY?

In Chapter 62, CI Principle #3: Let those who do the job develop the improvements, I discuss the importance of using the expertise of those deeply experienced with the business processes when trying to improve those processes. While it will likely be easy to identify several subject-matter experts, you will have to narrow your options and make choices when you are trying to build a small team for a continuous improvement event.

It's quite obvious that the people who are selected people for a *kaizen* team can greatly influence the outcome and the chance of success of the event. You might be tempted to think that this should lead you to carefully select only those who are of the "right mindset" for the *kaizen* events, so that everything will go as planned. Unfortunately, striving for complete homogeneity in the selection of the *kaizen* team members will actually cause you other problems, such as groupthink.

Groupthink was widely researched by Irving Janis, a psychologist from Yale University—it is a group behaviour phenomenon where the desire for unity or conformity within the group leads to senseless or poor decision-making results.[1] Groupthink has been often associated historically with such events as the U.S. failure to anticipate the Japanese invasion of Pearl Harbour in 1941, the Bay of Pigs invasion fiasco in 1961, and even the ill-fated decision by NASA to launch the Space Shuttle Challenger on January 28, 1986, despite the cold temperatures that were known to negatively affect O-ring seals on the rockets.

A diversity of viewpoints is more likely to lead to innovation and out-of-the-box thinking. Challenging the status quo is what is really going to improve the process, and that takes different viewpoints. Having said that, in any large organization, there are always a few people that speak or act in a manner that make others wince and wish they were somewhere else. While there are some extreme cases when these aren't the people that you would want to be a part of a *kaizen* event, you shouldn't shy away from selecting people who might be outspoken. You might want to select "easy" groups at first to build some early momentum in your Lean program, but then you need to accept the fact that to really prove the process works, you need to involve some dissenting views. And, quite honestly, dissenting views will lead to better improvement results anyway.

When you are at this stage, it simply needs to be part of the advance planning and preparation. When you involve that outspoken individual on the team, talk to that person's supervisor in advance to find out how he or she responds in group settings, and to different situations. Find out from that person's leader how to calm them down in challenging situations. Have the Lean practitioner work with the Lean facilitators to get a contingency plan in place in case a situation in the *kaizen* event starts to escalate.

Maybe it involves setting a time limit for part of the debate to ensure that the team reaches a key milestone by the required time. Maybe it involves setting up the "parking lot" for items that require further discussion, but clearly aren't going to get solved in time for the completion of the *kaizen*. The important thing is to get that individual contributing to the event and to the team and making sure that all voices and ideas are heard and considered.

Make sure that the Lean practitioner is at the back of the room in the *kaizen* event, ready to step in and help out the facilitator, in case things get out of hand. Having that more experienced person in the room as a backup support will feel reassuring to the facilitator.

Although deep experience with the processes in question is absolutely critical for a continuous improvement event team, I have also found value to including the "outside set of eyes." This should be someone who is involved with the processes but perhaps is newer to their job. There are two key benefits to including such an individual:

1. The individual will benefit from the training opportunity of deeply dissecting a key business process, and from the exercise of identifying waste in that process alongside experts in the field; and
2. The team will benefit from the new person seeing things for the first time that the more experienced people may miss because of familiarity.

Once when I was working in the aerospace sector, I was assigned to a four-month business redesign project within one cell of a business unit on the factory floor. A business redesign, sometimes referred to in Lean terminology as *kaikaku* (meaning large change), is much larger in scope than a typical *kaizen*. As described previously, a *kaizen* is typically a 2–5-day event intended to remove waste to improve a process that otherwise could be effective. A business redesign, however, is a large project, typically lasting several months, where the value stream is so fundamentally ineffective that it needs to be broken up completely, and put back together in a new form to serve the current needs of the business.

At any rate, on this redesign project, I was assigned as a facilities engineering support to the team, but I enjoyed equal footing with the rest of the production staff on the team when we would conduct a process-mapping exercise. I had very little knowledge at first about how the product moved through that particular cell. As a result, the production staff would sometimes roll their eyes when they had to explain something to me during a workshop.

But during our first process-mapping exercise, my outside set of eyes was helpful. When looking at the current-state map for the process flow of a particular part through the cell, I asked why that part went back to the grinding station three separate times, instead of just once. Everyone in the group looked over at the senior technician who quickly answered that they had always sent the part to the grinding station three times. From the team's introduction to redesign training, everyone knew that you had to be prepared to challenge the status quo and not simply accept an answer of "because that's the way we've always done it." So, I asked the senior technician, "Why is it that we can't change the process to just send the parts to the grinding station just once?"

The technician furrowed his eyebrows, thought about it, started to give an answer, and then interrupted himself, and blurted out, "Hey, yeah, why do we send that part to grinding three times?" After further investigation, we found that we couldn't trim the process down to only one stop at the grinding station, but we did eliminate one of the three grinding steps. Even though I was an "outsider," I felt that I had contributed to the project by forcing the team members to challenge the status quo.

The lesson that I learned that day, many years ago, remained with me well into my change of career into public service. I see an outside set of eyes on a *kaizen* or redesign project team as a useful check against the confirmation bias towards the status quo. Ensure that you staff your continuous improvement teams with those who know the process, as they are likely the ones to have the best answers on how to improve things. But always be on the lookout for the benefit that an outside person can bring to the team. They will tend to challenge the experts to look again at the value of the steps in the process that most people take for granted as necessary, and that is a good thing.

I think everyone, at some point, has seen an instance where someone completely unfamiliar with a situation has walked in and pointed out a problem that the experts have all missed. We chalk that up to being "too close to the problem." In psychology, the concept of someone who is foreign to an area of subject-matter knowledge is sometimes referred to as having significant "knowledge distance."

In my experience, the outsider can be very good at asking "why?" when they are confronted with a process that is new to them. Given that asking "why" to get to the root cause of a problem is also one of our leadership principles (CI Principle #12: Solve the right problem, as described in Chapter 71), this is quite desirable to the culture we are trying to foster. A person with knowledge distance

*Therefore, I find that adding one or two less-experienced staff to a team of subject-matter experts can balance the confirmation bias with the questioning that naturally comes from knowledge distance.*

is going to be seeing everything about the process for the first time, and they are more likely to question the rationale behind the steps and the sequencing of tasks in the process. The more experienced people, while incredibly knowledgeable, bring with themselves the inherent handicap of confirmation bias, which is the tendency to search for, or interpret, information in a way that confirms one's preconceptions.

Therefore, I find that adding one or two less-experienced staff to a team of subject-matter experts can balance the confirmation bias with the questioning that naturally comes from knowledge distance. A variation of this approach is to deliberately cross-pollinate the team with one or two people from another division, branch, or team. This can sometimes provide the dual benefit of the outside set of eyes to the team, and the benefit of positive Lean exposure to the individual from a part of the business that maybe hasn't yet started working with Lean—that person may be an ambassador in their home business area for the continuous improvement culture after participating in a successful event.

In addition, since every process should be customer-focused or client-focused, it can be hugely beneficial to bring onto the team a customer or client representative. However, if your team is very new to the culture change, you might want to let your staff start to get some familiarity and associations with the Lean concepts before you bring people from outside your organization into the mix. But the sooner you can, the better, because seeing waste in a process identified by your clients or customers is an insight that many staff don't often get.

## SELECTING THE LEAN FACILITATOR

Selecting the right staff member as the *kaizen* can be important too. Don't worry too much about subject-matter expertise—in fact, I have found that you can have fantastic *kaizen* events when the facilitator was "cross-pollinated" from a different branch or division. I think that the role of the facilitator needs to be respected as the person whose job it is to help lead the team to their own answers, and to be knowledgeable about the *kaizen* process and the Lean toolkit. The team is supposed to provide the subject-matter expertise, and if the *kaizen* facilitator is the expert, then the team will quickly start to feel irrelevant, and that they are not being engaged to solve their own problems.

For this reason, we often took facilitators from a different area than the one in which the process resided. Now, the facilitator has some homework to do in the weeks leading up to the *kaizen* event, working with the Lean practitioner to get familiar with the process and the terminology involved—however, the goal of this homework is simply for the facilitator to become *conversant* in the process, not an expert. Having the facilitator become conversant in the current process respects Trust Principle #19: Go and see to truly understand (described in Chapter 24). I am not suggesting that the facilitator can't be an expert in the process; the question is, can the facilitator set their expertise aside and take on the role of being the coach of the team to help them find the answers? When I trained a class of 18 new facilitators from across the Department of Families in the fall of 2018, I repeated over and over to them that their job is to help the *kaizen* team be successful—to get them a "win."

It's a good idea to rotate through your team of facilitators so that they all get some experience. With your first few *kaizen* events, with the spotlight of suspicion shining on the operations excellence program, you will want to choose your facilitators carefully so that the events have the best chance of success. We would usually choose the team first, and then select the best facilitator for that group, and the type of process being reviewed. But you have to respect that all of your facilitators need a chance to perform in a *kaizen*. Once you successfully get past your first half-dozen *kaizen* events, the trust starts to build in the workforce, and you don't have to be as selective with the facilitator choices.

# 66

## CI Principle #7: Get the Leadership out of the Room

*"A great asset for a leader to have is to know when to get out of people's way."*

**Mark Wager**[1]
*leadership consultant*

One of the most challenging aspects of adopting a continuous improvement culture is for the leaders to accept that they might need to leave the room for a *kaizen* team to be able to succeed. Part of this challenge for leaders, I think, stems from an inherent misunderstanding of the role of a leader.

As we discussed in Chapter 27, Trust Principle #22: Understand the true source of your value as a leader, the role of the leaders in your organization needs to shift from that of "answer-providers" to that of a coach of a team. This can be very hard for some leaders, even frightening. Asking a leader who is known as the foremost expert in their field to let the staff innovate on a process that the leader may have developed themselves can make that leader cringe. But if you want to build trust between the leadership and the staff, sometimes, this is what you have to do.

In Chapter 62, CI Principle #3: Let those who do the job develop the improvements, I identified the importance of those who do the work every day being allowed to identify the best improvements to their work processes. But in Chapter 13, Trust Principle #8: Remember that authority matters, I highlighted how important it is to remember that the corporate hierarchy impacts many situations for the leadership team.

Here is a great example of a situation in which a leader's authority will hinder what you are trying to achieve. If you are trying to set up a *kaizen* event with a team of front-line staff and you are trying to encourage them to improve a business process, you need to consider the possibility that the presence of the senior leader for that business area in the room will negatively impact the ability of the team to innovate. In many cases, it is very reasonable to expect that the presence of the senior leader will result in the staff simply looking to the executive to dictate the final answer to the team. Sometimes, the staff may not be very comfortable or familiar with the executive and will simply stop collaborating and openly sharing out of fear of embarrassment.

At any rate, I've found that the easiest thing to do is to get the leadership out of the room. It can be a show of trust in the staff when you explain why you are doing it. Tell them that you trust them to have better answers than yourself as a leader on how to fix the process, and that you look forward to seeing what they come up with at the end of the event. Tell them that you understand that they will feel more comfortable innovating without the senior leadership in the room, and then excuse yourself. In most cases, you will really earn respect from the team for doing so.

A few times in my career, I've seen managers who are in the room during a *kaizen* event cause more harm than good. Usually, the common thread between these cases is that the managers believed that their role was to be the prime subject-matter expert among the members of their team. They usually did not yet see themselves as coaches for their people. They believed, at that time, that their job was to make all decisions for their team, to answer every technical question, and to come up with the best processes for the team. Why? Because they were the experts, that's why.

Once, I heard about a *kaizen* where the manager was in the room and was talking over the staff who were trying to offer up suggestions for improvements to the process under review. Finally, at a break, the facilitator politely, but firmly, suggested that the manager should leave the room to allow the staff some freedom and space to be creative. Reluctantly, the manager agreed. However, soon after, the staff started passing their phones around, shaking their heads, and groaning. The manager had taken to sending text messages to the staff members, demanding to know what was going on in the *kaizen*. Clearly, the team felt, the manager wanted to be in control at all times and was not comfortable giving the team any authority. But this had the unfortunate

*Tell them that you understand that they will feel more comfortable innovating without the senior leadership in the room, and then excuse yourself. In most cases, you will really earn respect from the team for doing so.*

effect of pouring cold water on the ability of the team to develop something exciting. And it was completely incongruent with the organizational message of trust between the leadership and the staff.

This isn't to say that you can never have any manager or director in the room during a continuous improvement event. But I do suggest that you need to carefully ask yourself if the manager's presence will help or hinder what you are trying to accomplish with the event. It's completely understandable that many leaders will question this concept, and that they would be concerned about the staff possibly taking the process in an improper direction. But the answer isn't to micro-manage the *kaizen*; instead, the answer is to define the boundaries for change to the process up-front to the staff. This is discussed in more depth in Chapter 67, CI Principle #8: Scope your projects with care.

If you are serious about having your continuous improvement events produce truly innovative results, you likely should consider getting the leadership out of the room. It may be the only way the team will be able to really develop something out-of-the-box. But I guarantee you this: if you do get the leadership out of the room and do it properly, it will definitely help boost the trust relationship between the leadership and the staff.

# 67

## CI Principle #8: Scope Your Projects with Care

*"How to manage a project: Limit it in scope. Make it simple. Get success. Then iterate."*

**Attributed to Auren Hoffman**
*CEO of SafeGraph*

One of the worst things that can happen during the early days of a Lean journey is for a senior leader in the organization to reject the solutions provided by a continuous improvement team. Some leaders, I know, would object to my statement, and they would say that they simply cannot give a blank cheque to staff to redesign their policies or procedures. I agree that you don't want to give a blank cheque to your staff in that regard. But, that's not what I am advocating either. I think that when this type of rejection happens, it is due to the lack of planning and foresight by the senior leader during the project scoping stage.

Remember what you are trying to accomplish: culture change. You are trying to transform the environment of the organization to one where the people all believe that the organization values them and their talents and efforts. You are trying to transform the environment to one where the people believe that they can challenge the status quo, and that the leadership will support them in helping to make the working processes better. You are trying to transform the environment to one where the leadership recognize the value of the experience from the staff doing the work every day. You are trying to transform the environment to one where the leadership recognize their roles in the organization as coaches, not as answer-providers. And coaches work to set the stage so that the people can successfully learn by doing.

A senior leader who is going to arrange for a continuous improvement project in his or her area has responsibilities to help properly shape that continuous improvement space. That senior leader cannot delegate these responsibilities completely to a more junior person, although a junior person can support you in your duties. Properly scoping each project well in advance of starting is a key responsibility that you can share with a Lean Practitioner and your Lean Facilitator, and that can be supported by the Lean Champion, in the weeks leading up to the event.

You need to work with your support resources to ensure that each project is scoped properly so that each project has the best possible chance for success from the team's perspective. Because for each project that is successful, you have a set of team members that each goes back to their regular day jobs as energetic ambassadors of the cultural transformation. Each project that is unsuccessful means that a team of people will each go back to their home roles with negative messaging about the transformation. So, you need to deliberately and carefully work to scope each project so that it can be a win for the team and for the organization.

There are a couple factors to consider:

1. Ensuring that the boundaries of the project are properly chosen to guarantee a success; and
2. Ensuring that the mandatory conditions of the solution are clearly identified by the senior leadership in advance.

The first factor means that you need to carefully identify what is to be included in the process assessment by the project team, and what is to be excluded from the project. Sometimes you need to zero in on a piece of the process, instead of trying to tackle the entire process. Look at the time duration that you are prepared to allot to the project time and be realistic about whether or not the breadth of the project scope is too wide to be completed. Although you may wish that the team could address all of the key problem areas with the process under review, you may have to get choosey about it. Remember, you want a success at the end of the Lean event.

*You cannot expect a team to be capable of reading your mind.*

The second factor means that you need to identify what aspects of a final solution would be considered essential by the senior leadership, and these aspects need to be communicated clearly, and understood by the team, before they start. If there are a few key things that you or the other leaders would consider must-haves for the project solution, then these should be stated to the team in advance. Don't worry that they will be upset that you are dictating part of the solution to them. They will be okay with it, as long as they still have some freedom to manoeuvre and to innovate. They will be upset, however, if you don't tell them about mandatory conditions, and then you reject their solution after the event is complete. You cannot expect a team to be capable of reading your mind.

When I train leaders within the Department of Families on the topic of leadership principles to support innovation, I tell them that if they cannot accept the recommended changes from a *kaizen* team that is almost always evidence of a failure of the leadership to scope the project properly. This is rarely the fault of the *kaizen* team.

Scoping the project in advance is a joint responsibility for the Lean champion, the Lean practitioner, and the leaders that owns the affected process—but the final accountability for properly defining the scope of each CI event rests with the senior leadership. Think carefully during the planning, and work to set up each project for success and celebration.

# 68

## CI Principle #9: Take Each Project over the Finish Line

*"Perseverance is not a long race; it is many short races one after another."*

**Reverend Walter Elliot[1]**
*religious author*

Most people incorrectly think that when the *kaizen* event is over, the work is over. In fact, this is when a lot of the real work begins. In many cases, you will find that some of the actions that need to occur to improve the process cannot actually take place in the *kaizen* timeframe itself. This is a key judgement call on the part of the Lean facilitator, deciding what the team can actually do in the event, and what needs to be assigned as a follow-up action after the *kaizen* is completed.

For instance, the team may decide that a new checklist will help the staff to better understand what the steps are in the process—developing that checklist might be a reasonable action to handle during the *kaizen* event. But developing multiple complex spreadsheets, one for each type of workflow, might not be reasonable in the timeframe of the *kaizen*. In this case, the Lean facilitator might assign that action to a *kaizen* team member to complete by an agreed-upon due date a few weeks after the *kaizen* event, so that the process improvements can occur. This was not uncommon in the Manitoba Housing operations excellence program. However, we found that the Lean practitioner was kept very busy following up with team members about the tasks they promised to complete after the *kaizen* events.

We found that there was a period of goodwill after a *kaizen* when people fondly remembered the positive experience of the project and their willing commitment to complete their actions. Typically, this timeframe ranged from about two to six weeks maximum. If an action item wasn't completed within this timeframe, it was likely going to be a big challenge to get it finished.

I think that our Lean practitioners felt like, at varying times, cheerleaders, nagging spouses, auditors, school principals, or people calling from a collection agency, depending on the project. It seemed as though once the *kaizen* team members went back to their home positions, they sometimes got swallowed up by the typical busy-work of the day-to-day grind, and they felt it difficult to set aside time to fulfill their action item commitments. But in most cases, I don't believe that this was due to a lack of willingness on the part of the employee.

So, who owns the leftover action items? Don't for a minute think about having your centralized team (the practitioners or the champion) take responsibility for them. That absolves the *kaizen* team of their duties—the *kaizen* ideas should come from the staff and be implemented by the staff. While it might be acceptable for a short time for the Lean practitioner to work with the Lean facilitator to chase down the incomplete actions, you need to be prepared to quickly place the accountability where it belongs.

As soon as possible, the ownership should be handed to the senior leader in the area (who should have been on board at the beginning as a supporter of the *kaizen*), and that leader should become responsible to run down the final items to completion. At Manitoba Housing, we kept a tracking table on the huddle board outside my office, with a list of the open action items, the owners, and the due dates for all to see. I would periodically check with the senior leader owners to make sure that they got their action items finished.

After all, in order to have the staff continue to trust in the operations excellence program, they need to believe that things about the business will actually look different after the *kaizen* event, and that the program doesn't just involve a lot of talk but no action. You want a list of 100% complete *kaizen* events, not a list of 95% complete *kaizen* events, if you want your staff to believe that the organization really is committed to Lean.

# 69

## CI Principle #10: Receive with Gratitude and Implement the Efforts of Your People

*"Leaders who don't listen will eventually be surrounded by people who have nothing to say."*

**Attributed to Andy Stanley**
*author and pastor*

In Chapter 63, CI Principle #4: Plan for success every time, I discuss the concept that a continuous improvement event, such as a *kaizen* should really be viewed as an exercise in delegation of authority. In order to delegate without negative consequences, you need to set the parameters of that delegation in advance. In other words, you need to clearly define what is in scope and what is out-of-scope for the team to change. If the process change must have a certain characteristic in order to be acceptable, you need to identify that up-front before the team starts. They will be okay with that. I call this "defining the working space" for the team, and this is closely related to CI Principle #8: Scope your projects with care (described in Chapter 67). This principle really requires that the senior leader decides in advance what types of solutions would be acceptable and what would not be acceptable, and then use those rules to define the working space for the team well before the continuous improvement event takes place.

Typically, this definition exercise is performed in conjunction with your Lean practitioner and the selected Lean facilitator. The Lean facilitator needs to know what the solution boundaries are, so that he or she can properly navigate the team within that space. This way, when the team hands back to you the finished product at the end of the event, you can accept it without concern.

But your job as the senior leader is not to warily accept a solution from a team—rather, your job is to accept the team's solution with gratitude and then implement it. In Chapter 63, CI Principle #4: Plan for success every time, I talked about how important it is to ensure that your continuous improvement teams are set up to be successful with whatever projects they take on. This takes planning, of course, but the attitude of the senior leader also plays a huge role.

Once, I witnessed a *kaizen* event report out to the senior leadership of the organization. The *kaizen* team was absolutely bursting with pride with what they had developed—and it truly was impressive! They had every right to be proud. But immediately after they finished their presentation, the manager for the area (who had been asked to stay out of the *kaizen* room, so the team could operate freely) piped up and thanked the team for coming up with most of the ideas that he had already developed himself.

Ouch. I was immediately alarmed as I saw the team begin to deflate before my eyes. What a backhanded acknowledgement to a hard-working group of individuals. I don't think that the manager really intended to come across as he had. In fact, I think he was probably feeling threatened because he wasn't a part of the *kaizen* over the previous few days. He wanted to re-affirm his subject-matter expertise value to the executive. But this wasn't the culture that we were wanting to reinforce. Fortunately, the executive in the room quickly jumped in and began to lavishly praise the team for their efforts and thank them for their innovative ideas. The executive closed off the discussion with a promise to implement the team's set of solutions, and the team was thrilled.

The team wants to see that the senior leadership is grateful for their efforts. The team wants to feel that their contributions matter, the that their ideas will make a difference to the success of the organization. The team wants to see that the leadership values their improvement ideas so much that they will adopt them into the current business practices. And it is up to you, as the senior leader, to tell them these things.

# 70

## CI Principle #11: Teach Them about the Types of Wastes

*"The most dangerous kind of waste is the waste we do not recognize."*

**Attributed to Shigeo Shingo**
*industrial engineer and expert on the Toyota Production System*

In order to start your people down the path of continuous improvement innovation, they need to know what to look for. In many organizations, one of the first things you can start to teach your employees at the beginning of a Lean journey is the different types of wastes. It is these wastes that you will want *kaizen* teams to eliminate. But before they can eliminate waste, they first must need to know how to identify it.

I found that many of the wastes that were visible to me, as an outsider coming into Manitoba Housing, were at first almost invisible to many of the staff. It seemed to me that many of the employees and leaders had become so accustomed to the processes that they were mandated to use, that the fire-fighting, the duplication, the unnecessary approvals, the large portion of non-value-added steps, had faded from the foreground of everyone's sight to the background. Much like the familiar art on the walls of one's home, most people eventually stopped noticing it. And when you don't notice it, you can't question it. And when you don't question it, it won't change.

To be fair, the legacy culture also was based on a "compliance management" mentality. When this is a foundational principle of leadership, it tends to strongly discourage people from challenging the status quo, and from asking if there is a better way. You are rewarded for following the rule book (despite how ineffective it might be) and you are spoken to if you don't follow the rules. This cultural history was probably the more compelling reason as to why people hadn't been pointing out the waste in their work when I joined the organization.

I love the visual language from the title of the classic Lean guide book *Learning to See*, by Mike Rother and John Shook.[1] In my view, the title of this book explains so well what you need to teach people to do at the very beginning of a Lean journey if the organization is truly starting the journey from scratch. If they are going about their business every day and they don't see the waste all around them in their processes, then you need to help them to "learn to see" their work differently than they have been. First, people need to learn to see their work as part of a process, and a larger value stream. Then, they need to learn to see the waste, the overburden of certain resources, and the unevenness of the process flow. Only when this happens can you have the staff engage in continuous improvement initiatives.

Taiichi Ohno, the father of the Toyota Production System, developed categorizations of waste, or *muda*, in Japanese, known as The Seven Wastes.[2] Later, an eighth waste, that of underutilization of employee talents, was added by the Lean community to the original list of seven. The eight wastes are sometimes represented in English by the acronym DOWNTIME:

1. Defects
2. Overproduction
3. Waiting
4. Non-utilization of talent
5. Transportation
6. Inventory excess
7. Motion
8. Excess processing

Whether you are in an office environment, or a manufacturing setting, these different types of wastes can be found in just about every process in use. Since these waste categorizations were first originated in Toyota in the manufacturing sector, it is usually quite easy for factory workers to see the relevance of these types of waste to their day-to-day production work.

But sometimes in office environments, you need to provide some relevant examples to make it real to the staff. Remember, many office staff will be initially skeptical that something from the manufacturing world could possibly be relevant to their jobs, so you need to think about your workplace and train the staff with relevant examples of wastes that they will likely encounter on a regular basis. Don't make them stretch their imaginations to understand the application of Lean to their work. Make it easy for them.

Defects might look like client applications or other forms filled out improperly, or missing information, that requires calling the applicant back to fix the problems. Poorly designed forms with unclear instructions, or the lack of an accompanying checklist or guide document are common causes of this type of waste.

Overproduction is a little harder to identify in office work. In the manufacturing sector, it often involves producing in advance of the customer demand for the product. However, in much of government work involving programs that provide benefits to clients, a government worker can't provide a service to clients that haven't yet shown up to apply for the benefit. But it is possible, and common, to find situations where government workers are collecting unnecessary information from clients that isn't actually necessary for the program operation.

The waste of waiting, in an office environment, commonly results from a worker batch-processing similar types of work. The thought process by the worker usually is that it is more efficient to enter a bunch of the same types of forms all at once—they feel that this way, they can get a "rhythm" going. The only problem is that entering the one type of form once a week adds a one-week delay on the overall process for an action that might take thirty seconds.

Non-utilization of talent looks similar in both manufacturing and office environments. Usually, the culture in the organization has not yet evolved to the point where creativity and innovation is widely celebrated and supported. As a result, people who have capabilities well above their current job are pushed to "keep your head down and your tail up" and just focus on doing the job the way you were taught. When the culture of an organization begins to transform to that of a continuous improvement culture, you begin to see additional talents in the staff that were previously hidden from view.

Transportation in an office environment is becoming less common as a waste, as electronic documentation becomes more and more common. However, in some government environments, you still find a legacy of paper-based systems. The problem with this is that multiple approvals (a different waste in itself) can require that a document actually be physically transported around for each signature before the process can move forward.

Inventory excess looks somewhat different than it might in the manufacturing environment. It is usually defined as a supply in excess of true customer demand, which masks the proper flow of production. In many cases, in an office environment, this can look like unnecessary document or record storage, of information that is never used. In my opinion, you should also look for the unnecessary buffers of time that people put in place for information flow. These time buffers are the excess inventory, as they are often put in place to compensate for other problems, such as an unreliable supplier to the next step in the process, or poor tracking systems for the process. The answer, of course, is to solve the problems of the unreliable supplier, or the poor tracking system, as opposed to putting in time buffers.

Motion in an office environment can include the obvious carry-over wastes from manufacturing, such as poorly laid out office workstations that require unnecessary motion by the worker. But they can also include motion wastes such as double-handling of work packages by the same person or sending something back to the same person multiple times in the process flow.

Excess processing often shows up in government environments as unnecessary approval steps in a process. It can also manifest as excessive reporting requirements or re-entering the same data multiple times.

All of these wastes increase costs, the time it takes to complete processes, and they take your people away from working to serve the client or customer, the work that actually adds value. There is a simple approach that the manufacturing sector sometimes uses to challenge whether or not a step in the production process is waste: They ask themselves for each step if that step is something that the customer would pay for. If not, they try to find a way to eliminate that step.

Sometimes, in government work, people try to escape the discussion about waste by saying that "we have clients, not customers." But you can still apply this thought process to office environments and government work. Ask yourself if the majority of citizens would consider each step of the process to be adding value, and if they would consider it a good use of taxpayer money. If you find yourself struggling, that step is likely a form of one of the eight wastes, and you should look at removing it from the process.

When I was teaching a *kaizen* facilitation training class in the Department of Families, I had the privilege of watching a class full of employees all have their "aha!" moments together as we talked about the wastes, overburden, and unevenness, and then we shared examples often found in our different offices. We talked about the inherent inefficiency of batch-processing compared to single-piece flow, and the problems caused by pushing work downstream instead of allowing the downstream process to pull work from the upstream station. I said to the students, this waste, this ineffectiveness, has been going on around you for years, invisible to almost everyone—I want you to learn to see it, so that you can challenge it for elimination. When we did our *hansei*, our reflection, at the end of that day, several of the students pointed out how they had their eyes opened to their own work, and that they already could see so many opportunities for improvement in how workflows in their offices. It was like watching people look around and see the world in clear focus for the first time. They had truly "learned to see."

# 71

## CI Principle #12: Solve the Right Problem

*"A problem thoroughly understood is always fairly simple."*

**Charles Kettering[1]**
*American inventor, engineer, former head of*
*research at General Motors (1920–1947)*

One of the hardest things for people to learn when leading their organization down the journey to adopting a continuous improvement culture is proper problem-solving. And it may be hard for you as well. It is possible that the previous culture of your organization was that the leadership solved whatever problems that were presented by the staff. If this was the case, then any problem-solving skills that the staff did have may have atrophied, or they may never have developed the skills in the first place. Problems may have been seen as something to dump on the manager's desk to them to solve. But this is not where you are going with your cultural transformation. Where you are going, everyone needs to understand basic structured approaches to problem-solving. And the job of the leadership will be, in many cases, to help coach their staff to solve their own problems, instead of being the answer-provider.

The first concept that needs to be well understood is the principle of *genchi genbutsu*, or as I call it, Trust Principle #19: Go and see to truly understand (described in Chapter 24). You simply cannot coach people to solve problems from your office. You need to get out to where the problem is in order to truly understand the problem. If you do not understand this first crucial step, it is very likely that you will solve the wrong problem.

What I mean by this is that you will misunderstand the true nature of the problem due to your shallow understanding of it, and as a result, your solution will not properly address the root cause of the problem. It will only address the symptoms of the problem.

In an article written by Thomas Wedell-Wedellsborg entitled "Are You Solving the Right Problems?"[2] he suggests that the biggest challenge that most people face in problem-solving is the improper framing of the problem statement. Thomas gives the example of what he calls "The Slow Elevator Problem" in this article to support his point.

The Slow Elevator Problem goes like this: the owner of an office building finds that they are getting a lot of complaints about the elevator being very old and slow. The building tenants are getting frustrated with having to wait for the elevator, and some are considering breaking their leases if something isn't done to fix the problem. When your average person is asked for solutions to the problem of the elevator being too slow, they often will consider mechanical solutions to the speed of the elevator, such as an upgraded elevator control system, a new motor, or replacing the elevator cab itself. From my own experience in property management, I know that very few upgrades to elevators are ever inexpensive.

But the author of the article suggests that building managers may take a different approach to the problem—they would redefine the problem from being stated as "the elevator is too slow" to being stated as "the wait for the elevator is annoying." This definition of the problem statement leads the building managers to consider very different, and novel, solutions to the problem, such as putting up mirrors on the walls next to the elevator. The mirrors serve the purpose of reducing the annoyance element of waiting by distracting the building tenants—they now get to look at themselves (which is much more interesting) instead of counting the seconds until the elevator arrives. The complaints are drastically reduced for a fraction of the cost.

I think that this story is a great example of how deeply we need to dig into problems before we can confidently state that we are about to attempt to solve the right problem. How many times have you heard someone insist that a technology solution is the only way to address a challenge? That the only way to fix an issue is for everyone to get a new computer program at great expense, or that everyone needs to get new iPads or the latest smartphone?

I can admit that I have stumbled myself in my career when trying to apply this principle correctly. I believe that many times, we jump quickly to the first solution that is presented to us if it comes from an extremely credible and expert source. But if that person is not highly skilled in structured problem-solving methodologies, they could be making the same rush-to-judgement about solutions as most people tend to do with the elevator problem.

In many cases, I believe that the primary flaw in our problem-solving approaches is to prescribe a solution in our definition of the problem. Once, when I was providing Lean support across the Department of Families (under which Manitoba Housing reported), I was asked to lead a problem-solving exercise with a group of program staff across the rural and northern areas. They travelled so much from client to client that they often found that they didn't have the ability to keep up with their work.

In some cases, they reported that they would commute one hour to a meeting in one town, and then commute another hour back to the office just to send an email or make some case notes into the system, and then commute another hour back to where they were for a second meeting. Since most of the program staff had limited access to technology, such as smartphones, cellular data connectivity, etc., I initially saw an early version of the problem statement along the lines of "the program staff need to replace their current phones with smartphones."

While I realized that there was certainly going to be a technology requirement of some form in the solution we would eventually propose, I insisted that the problem statement be taken up a level to instead state: "The program staff lose effective working time due to extensive travel for work." This type of problem definition would keep us grounded in ensuring that we look at the problem of the amount of travel and how the work was being done, instead of jumping to buying everyone iPhones. This led us to consider root causes and solution options, such as:

- Lack of planning protocols to support travelling staff to minimize ineffective work time;
  - What about giving staff more autonomy to set their own schedules and coordinate meetings to minimize downtime?
- Lack of access to other office locations for different government departments around the province to allow staff to use access the government network in locations not served with an office by the home department;
  - What about management paving the way to ensure that staff are welcome to enter any government office in the province to use an available network connection to work?

- What about giving staff VPN (virtual private network) login access to enable them to securely connect to the government network wherever there is a wireless network available?
- Lack of consideration around flexible starting locations for the workday
  - What about developing a policy to allow workers to, with approval, start certain workdays from home instead of the office, in order to minimize travel to particular locations?

Taking the problem statement up a level, until a solution was not prescribed within it, was crucial to allowing a better problem-solving exercise.

Sometimes you will find people with a solution that is in need of a problem. In other words, they want to try a new approach, but it is clear that they haven't clearly identified in their own mind what the problem is that they are trying to solve with the new approach. Often, this situation arises when an exciting new technology application becomes available. People can sometimes want to adopt the new technology, without stopping to think if the technology will actually address a challenge that the business is facing. Sometimes, you need to slow people down by simply getting them to answer: "What is the problem you are trying to solve?"

Early on in this book, in Chapter 6, Trust Principle #1: Know that culture change is the goal, not the implementation of Lean tools, I encourage you not to focus on tools, but rather to focus on the mindset of your team. I think that this lesson is analogous to what is necessary to understand in the principle of this chapter. This is where the leaders need to truly act as coaches to encourage their workers to first look at changing how the work is done, instead of prematurely focusing on replacing the tools of work.

*"By repeating why five times, the nature of the problem as well as its solution becomes clear."*

**Taiichi Ohno**[3]
*founder of the Toyota Production System.*

Teach your people the structured problem-solving approach and keep the approach simple. The easiest and most common approach for people new to Lean is the 5-Why method. Credit for developing this methodology is widely given to Taiichi Ohno, the founder of the Toyota Production System. The approach is based on the statistical likelihood that, by repetitively interrogating and iterating upon each answer by asking "why?" five times, the problem solver should arrive at the true root cause of the problem, and at the best idea of the solution.

The key is that the problem solver needs to avoid logic-traps and common assumptions that would steer the problem-solving ship off course. The problem solver needs to keep the train of thought based on processes as the likely source of the problem, and not the people. As I said in Chapter 46, Change Principle #13: Use visual metrics regularly to teach and reveal, never to assign blame: always ask "why," never "who."

Fishbone, or Ishikawa, diagrams can be useful tools to support a 5-Why analysis of a problem. But sometimes, you need a more rigorous approach. Although the Toyota Production System, the predecessor to Lean, uses the Toyota 8-Step Method to problem-solving, an underpinning of Toyota problem-solving is the Deming cycle, known as PDCA, or Plan-Do-Check-Act.

In his book, *Toyota Kata: Managing People for Improvement, Adaptiveness, and Superior Results*, Mike Rother references the PDCA cycle as the approach to guide scientific thinking and experimenting to solve problems.[4] However, Rother interestingly highlights the fact that Toyota modified the PDCA cycle by adding the words "Go and See" to the centre of the typical cycle diagram. I agree that this addition is tremendously powerful.

Another common approach is the DMAIC methodology, usually associated with Lean Six-Sigma. This acronym stands for the five steps that one should follow for the problem-solving approach: Define; Measure; Analyze; Improve; and Control.[5]

Since I am more focused in this book on outlining the leadership principles necessary for a continuous improvement culture change, I leave it to you to study these, or other problem-solving methodologies separately, and to practice them enough yourself so that you can teach others.

You may find it hard to follow the discipline of the methodology that you choose. You will need to fight the urge to take shortcuts, or to jump to a solution far too early, just so that you can move onto something else that is more urgent (though, sadly, often not more important). Don't give in to the temptation to bypass the structured path that can take you to the correct answer to the right problem, and instead choose a fast answer to the wrong problem.

As a senior leader, you need to be cautious about being overly-specific to your team members when giving direction. I've caught myself many times being too prescriptive of the solution that I envision for a problem. Instead,

I had to back up and simply quantify the properties of the outcome that was desired and let the team or the staff member solve the problem of defining the "how."

Lean problem-solving is commonly used in association with something that is often called the A3 report. This is a one-page reporting structure named for the A3 metric size of paper used in Europe and Japan, which is closely equivalent to the 11″ × 17″ size paper in North America. The purpose of this type of report is to serve as a guide to walk the supervisor and their employee through the problem-solving approach. It is sometimes also used as a standardized method of communication to share best practices across teams and across organizations.

In *The Toyota Kata Practice Guide*, Mike Rother suggests another approach called a "learner's storyboard" to guide the student and the coach through the steps of experimentation and problem-solving.[6] Rother suggests bringing a whiteboard into the workspace with spaces dividing up the board to identify the Process in question, the Challenge you are trying to achieve with the process, the next Target Condition for the process, the Current Condition, and then spaces for the Experimenting Record and the Obstacles Parking Lot. The whiteboard is filled or updated by the student before each coaching session with the latest information that they have available about the process under examination. This method would replace the need for an A3 report and ensures that the problem-solving approach remains collaborative between the student and the coach. I love the idea behind the storyboard, and I believe that many staff would find this approach easier to use than the typical A3 reports.

Many people, myself included, have at times forgotten why Toyota invented the A3 report and simply felt that they had to copy the use of this template because that is what you need to do as a part of your Lean journey. But this A3 template is what Toyota found worked for its iterative coaching model. I've seen organizations that use the A3 report as a final summary of an improvement event. I don't think that this is the purpose of an A3—it's meant to be a tool to support coaching between a leader and a worker. If the A3 doesn't work, then consider something else, like the storyboard approach.

There is no right or wrong template to use for an A3 report, and many examples can be found online to serve as starting points for your organization. I do recommend that you tailor your template to follow the problem-solving methodology that you adopt, such as the Improvement Kata, PDCA or DMAIC. But above all, remember the purpose of the

A3—to structure the path through the problem-solving approach. If your A3 tool doesn't do this, reconsider why you are using it.

You absolutely need to consistently follow a structured approach to problem-solving, and there are several approaches available for you and your team to study and practice. But before you jump in and start using one of these methods, make sure you are certain that you and your team are going to solve the right problem.

# 72

## CI Principle #13: Run an Experiment to Improve Something

*"The most exciting phrase to hear in science, the one that heralds new discoveries, is not 'Eureka' but 'That's funny…'"*

**Attributed to Isaac Asimov**
*science fiction author*

One thing that senior leaders need to get used to when fostering a culture of innovation is the concept of experimentation. Unfortunately, in many organizations, it seems that the leadership expects that anything new that is attempted should work perfectly the first time—if not, blame and shame are assigned to the implementers for their failure. This cannot be the approach that you take in your organization.

You are trying to support and spur innovation, and innovation means trying things that have never been tried before. It means experimentation. Experimentation, in the context of Lean, is like exploration, as you are going to places to where you have never been before. You want your people to try out new ways of doing things, using a structured approach of course, to improve your business processes and create efficiency and better customer or client service.

But there is a side effect to experimentation—failure. Sometimes an idea will sound good on paper but will not work out well in practice. That is perfectly normal, and you will need to get used to failures during experimentation. You can't condemn people when they follow your direction, which is to innovate, and then try a new way of doing something, only to find out that the idea didn't work out as intended. You need to be supportive of mistakes made in good faith and remember that this is all a part of experimentation. Remember what was discussed in Chapter 49, Trust Principle #16: Discipline only the unwilling, but know that they are few.

Ask yourself, "What are the risks of failure if this idea doesn't work?" In many cases, the risks are quite minimal, and easily localized to one part of the business. There may be other checks and balances in place that would serve as secondary containment systems to capture problems. But, in other situations, the risks might be quite high, such as poor-quality product escaping to the customer, or client service standards being inappropriately compromised. In these situations, you should consider inserting counter-measures into the experiment to minimize the risks of failure.

There are things that can be done to minimize the collateral damage that might result from innovation failures. Limit the scale of failure by running a pilot project in a small area before rolling out the new idea across the whole organization. Conduct a lessons-learned evaluation after the pilot, identify further improvements, and then decide if you are ready to roll out the idea across the other business areas.

> *"Similarly, doing small-scale experiments helps you ensure that unexpected results don't cause harm; they limit the blast radius, so to speak."*
>
> **Mike Rother[1]**
>
> *The Toyota Kata Practice Guide.*

You can also attempt to limit the scope of failure. Try implementing only a limited number of improvement ideas at one time, so that you can carefully identify what contributes positively or negatively to the process. Too much change all at once can make it difficult to identify the causes of failures, and quite frankly, further complicate the change management support needed for the staff to ensure a successful implementation. In fact, Toyota teaches its people to test a single improvement at a time to ensure that the cause-and-effect relationship on the process is very clearly understood.

Experiments don't have to involve big process changes. Sometimes, they can be very small simple things, such as a shop-floor employee wanting to try out a new kind of tray for sorting consumable materials. The risks from this type of experiment could very likely be very low, and so this might be something that a front-line manager tells the staff member to "just-do-it." Have the employee try it out for a week or two, keep some records of how it works out, such as time-trial records, so that the efficiency improvements of the new tray can be compared with the previous baseline time-trials. The manager should encourage the staff member to return back to the rest of the team with the results of the experiment at a huddle meeting, with a short update report.

Never make the experimentation reporting requirements so rigid or onerous that it becomes a barrier to the staff to innovate. Make sure that the reporting requirements are appropriately scaled to match the complexity of the problem. In Chapter 76, CI Principle #17: Drive towards effective daily *kaizen*, I refer to a hierarchy of problems, based on size and complexity, starting with the "just-do-it" problems.

Some people tend to struggle with describing a problem concisely. These are the people who will complain to you that your project charter template or your A3 report template should allow multiple pages. Strangely, they always seem to believe that the template is the problem, not how they are writing. I do think that it is a poor sport that blames his or her equipment. Being able to properly define concisely a problem, the root cause, the solutions, and the results, will take practice for everyone. You will need to get your leaders comfortable with how to coach this type of reporting for their leaders and the staff.

The book *Toyota Kata*, along with the associated *Practice Guide*, by Mike Rother, are both excellent reading to describe an approach to helping organizations develop a culture of experimentation to foster continuous improvement. I highly encourage you to study the Kata methodology and consider its adaptation into your own Lean journey.[2,3]

Regardless of the experimental methodology you adopt in your organization, it is going to be crucial that your leadership recognizes that trying something new will often result in challenges. Most times we try something for the first time, it won't work as expected. These challenges are what teach us new things, and they are not reasons to be critical of our people. Embrace this understanding, and watch your organization grow in its Lean journey.

# 73

## CI Principle #14: Share Widely Best Practices

*"Men and women range themselves into three classes or orders of intelligence; you can tell the lowest class by their habit of always talking about persons; the next by the fact that their habit is always to converse about things; the highest by their preference for the discussion of ideas."*

**Henry Thomas Buckle[1]**
*history scholar*

The Lean principle of sharing best practices is often known by the Japanese term *yokoten*. The term in Japanese is usually understood from its origins in Toyota to involve horizontal deployment. The term "horizontal" is important to remember because ideally, there should be no top-down force driving the deployment. It should be peer-to-peer.

But that part of the culture transformation takes time and encouragement. If your people aren't sharing best practices naturally among their peers right now, they won't automatically start doing it themselves to support your desired culture change. You will have to drive and encourage this behaviour with your leadership until it becomes a pattern of behaviour that forms habits.

It may not be easy at first. I've seen many leaders who become very comfortable with their own methods of how things are done, and they sometimes take a very dim view of ideas that were "not invented here." You will need to be on the lookout for this type of leadership behaviour and address it very quickly. Any leader on your team that refuses out of hand to consider improvements to the business processes of their area is sending the wrong message to their staff about the cultural transformation. The leader needs to be quickly reminded of Change Principle #7: Challenge the status quo continuously (described in Chapter 40), and that person needs to be reminded that as a leader, he or she plays a key role in modelling the desired culture in front of their staff.

The benefits from *yotoken* happen when it occurs between teams of front-line staff. But the sharing needs to take place beyond silos, beyond branches. In many cases, lessons learned in one area can be applicable in a completely different part of the organization. You will need to set up opportunities for when best practices sharing can occur. Typically, monthly team or branch staff meetings can include opportunities for people to share exciting best practices from which others can learn. Higher-level leadership meetings can also be opportunities for sharing ideas across branch or divisional lines, in order to ensure that good ideas don't stay trapped in one segment of the organization.

It really helps to develop a standardized reporting template, and the simpler the better, at first. At Manitoba Housing, we developed a very simple *kaizen* reporting template that we called a 4-up report. This was a single page PowerPoint document, with lines dividing the page equally into four quadrants. The title of the *kaizen* project was across the top of the page, and the top two quadrants contained a description of the purpose of the project and a photograph of the project team. The bottom two quadrants contained the observations found by the team about the problem, and the improvements developed by the team. The text was kept simple, so that the font size would be large and easy to read.

This reporting template allowed best practices from *kaizen* events to be shared in leadership presentations with virtually no reformatting required, since PowerPoint presentations were often in use at team meetings anyway. The team photograph was always a huge hit. The pictures would always show an enthusiastic and smiling group of team members, capturing the positive energy that the team felt during the continuous improvement event. This provided excellent positive reinforcement to staff to see their colleagues being celebrated as teams that helped to solve problems and making the business processes more efficient.

The only downside to this reporting format was that it didn't allow the sharing of the thought process for more complex problems. But, in the very early stages of an organization's Lean journey, that's okay. Simpler will definitely be better at first. When you start moving into structured problem-solving, you may feel the need to develop a different type of report to share more details about the best practices. In Chapter 71, CI Principle #12: Solve the right problem, I refer to the use of the A3 report template that follows the PDCA or DMAIC problem-solving methodology. This type of report can serve the dual purpose of supporting a leader to coach the staff through the problem-solving approach, as well as providing a vehicle for *yokoten* with others in the organization. The only downside to the A3 report is that, due to its size, it requires summarization and reformatting to include it in a standard PowerPoint presentation.

A key element of proper best practices sharing is that, in order to be executed correctly, it requires the application of Trust Principle #19: Go and see to truly understand (described in Chapter 24). Those that are hoping to adopt the best practice themselves must go to the real place where the practice was developed in order to properly understand it. Only then, can they begin to imagine the proper adaptation of the idea into their part of the business. The A3 report, or the 4-up presentation slide, are merely methods to alert a leader or staff member to something that is worthy of further investigation.

But best practices cannot be rigidly imposed across the organization; rather, the ability to adapt during adoption of best practices is critical.

# 74

## CI Principle #15: Adapt and Innovate When You Adopt Best Practices

*"Intelligence is the ability to adapt to change."*

**Thomas W. Faranda[1]**
*business author*

One of the most interesting revelations for me in my Lean studies was the realization that the leaders of Toyota, the origin of Lean thinking, never advocated the "copying" of best practices everywhere. They rarely mandated practices of "how" to perform certain processes. Of course, Toyota would establish corporate quality standards for their products, which they would never compromise. But the manufacturing processes used to achieve the quality standards for the products were always up for innovation.[1]

In *The Toyota Way to Lean Leadership*, Liker and Convis recount a story about how a team from Toyota Motor Manufacturing Kentucky (TMMK) visited a subsidiary in Japan called Central Motors.[2] Central Motors had developed an innovative way to convey parts around without containers, called *minomi*. The TMMK team at first attempted to outright copy the method of *minomi* back at their home facility, only to learn that their own parts and processes didn't work well with the tooling setup used by Central Motors. So, the TMMK team adapted the approach to suit their situation and innovated on the tooling required to support the concept. The new system worked very well. So well, in fact, that a team from Central Motors visited TMMK to view the innovative adaptation of their own approach. The Central Motors team took the knowledge back home to Japan, and applied the new tooling design to their facility, but with the addition of robot automation to further streamline the process.

The TMMK team soon afterwards adopted the Central Motors automation idea and added further automation innovations of their own. This type of iterative innovation of best practices just isn't possible if best practices are pushed down from the top of the organization with the direction that "everyone must now do things this way."

It can be very tempting for leaders of very large organizations, especially in government, to take the mandating approach to implementing best practices. But this approach will have the contradictory effect of stifling creativity and innovation. You just cannot blindly dictate a best practice for everyone to follow and expect that innovation will continue around it. Therefore, you need to encourage, and allow for, the adaptation of the ideas when they are adopted by different parts of your organization. This concept is crucial for your senior leadership follow in order to stay congruent with your messages about the value of continuous improvement. You can't roll out a best practice as an improvement and then forbid further improvements to it.

Furthermore, sometimes a best practice from one area just will not work in another area without some modifications. It's even possible that forcing the implementation of a practice from one area into another could make the second area less efficient if the approach just isn't a good fit. But these modifications to the best practice provide additional learning to the organization, and they can also result in fantastic additional innovations.

The challenge of course is understanding when to force standardization, and when to allow for freedom of movement. This challenge is discussed further in Chapter 75, CI Principle #16: Strike the balance between innovation and standardization.

# 75

## CI Principle #16: Strike the Balance between Innovation and Standardization

*"Almost all innovations are actually improvements."*

**John Shook[1]**
*lean author, speaker, and senior advisor within*
*the Lean Enterprise Institute*

The previous two chapters provided a mandate to share best practices (yokoten), and a degree of freedom in how a new idea is implemented in a different location. But there is an important constraint to the concept of *yokoten* that leaders new to the Lean way of thinking may find difficult to understand. That constraint is the necessary balance between innovation and standardization.

As discussed in Chapter 74, CI Principle #15: Adapt and innovate when you adopt best practices, you cannot mandate that every branch or team in your organization copy a best practice without allowing for the adaptation of that approach. There are two reasons for this:

1. The approach may not actually work well when copied into a new location, and may essentially make the business process less efficient than it was before; and
2. Refusing to allow adaptation during adoption is incongruent with your desire for innovation across the organization.

The challenge, though, is that you don't want chaos across your organization with everyone doing their own thing and with no standardization at all. This is where understanding the balance is critical.

I have found that it is helpful to think about the controls that you are going to put in place to allow for innovation in different aspects of your business. Think about what level of leadership approval you would want before you would allow changes to different things.

You usually do want standardization of the big things, such as the product, deliverable, benefit, or service provided to your client or customer, and the quality standards governing your product, deliverable, benefit, or service. You might be open to changing these things (hopefully to the benefit of the customer or client), but you likely would want the formal approval of a senior executive in your organization before doing so. In government, this could also involve consideration of changes to program policy.

However, you may be willing to allow lower-level leadership in the organization to approve changes to the methods or processes used by your staff to create or provide the product, deliverable, benefit, or service— assuming, of course, that controls and testing ensure that the quality or the output itself is not compromised during the innovation.

Smaller process changes might be approved by front-line managers, while more complex changes might require the approval of the branch director, or executive director, or vice-president. The important thing to remember is that you need to develop change-control guidelines or policy for your organization, that describes which approvals are required for different types of changes.

In the social-service sector of government work where I was working, the simplest and broadest way to describe guidelines around when to seek higher approval was as follows:

1. Would the change impact the client's eligibility for a program?
2. Would the change impact the quantity of the client's benefits with a program?
3. Would the change negatively impact the quality of a client's benefit or engagement within a program?
4. Would the change serve to increase the costs of the program?
5. Would the change serve to significantly increase the work of another branch, department, or service provider?

If the answer was "yes" to any of these questions, then the idea should be escalated up to the appropriate senior leader to assess before any innovation is attempted with actual clients, as a program policy impact assessment would likely be needed before the idea is considered further. Appropriate guidelines for your own organization will obviously look a little different.

In the process of developing such change-control guidelines, remember that your focus should not be on preventing innovation, but rather clearly identifying for the staff and the different levels of organizational leadership the freedom that they do have to innovate. Make it the purpose of your policy to describe the freedom to change, instead of to describe what people are not allowed to do. It will sound very different when it is written. Be clear and define the working space that you are giving your leaders and teams to innovate, and then let them surprise you with the results.

# 76

## CI Principle #17: Drive towards Effective Daily Kaizen

*"The key to the Toyota Way and what makes Toyota stand out is not any of the individual elements – but what is important is having all the elements together as a system. It must be practiced every day in a very consistent manner, not in spurts."*

**Fujio Cho**
*former Chairman of the Toyota Motor Corporation*[1]

It became clear to me at Manitoba Housing, after a couple years, that our operations excellence program, despite its many successes, was not sustainable in its current form. Its activities were too closely dependent on the involvement of our Lean practitioners and me. The unfortunate side effect of this dependence was that the staff were being trained to think that Lean was something that "those people" did. I realized that this would not truly change the culture in the organization.

A continuous improvement culture change truly happens when front-line team managers can handle structured problem-solving on their own without calling for help. It happens when a team huddle meeting outside of the headquarters building initiates a *kaizen* event and the team handles it using the methodology on their own. It happens when all staff realize that they have the power and the leadership support to improve how business is done in the organization, with minimal bureaucracy to hold them back. A true culture change in an organization really happens when the staff recognize continuous improvement as something that can take place every day, instead of being the exclusive domain of corporately-scheduled *kaizen* events.

I struggled with how to handle this problem, as at that time we had not yet provided much hands-on training in structured problem-solving to our front-line managers. We had given some presentations about it, but that wasn't enough to really change the culture, as we find in Chapter 44, Change Principle #11: Understand that a presentation does not equal training. The practical challenges of how to provide over-the-shoulder coaching to a large number of front-line managers made the problem seem overwhelming.

My answer came in a Lean conference in Toronto when a presenter from a large health authority talked about a very similar challenge that he had faced with his organization.[2] He had tried, with his small Lean support team, to spread training across a huge number of teams and managers, and quickly found that they were accomplishing very little, like too little butter spread over too much toast. So he changed his approach. He started providing deep and focused coaching and mentorship with his support team to only a few teams at a time. When, after a few months of coaching, a team and the leader had achieved the level of training and comfort with the methodologies that they required to be self-sustaining, the Lean support team moved on to an adjacent team and repeated the process. The results were markedly different, and the teams on the "waiting list" tended to be clamouring for their turn to receive the coaching support. I think that, as with strategic planning, focus is critical in providing coaching support.

This is the approach that we have begun to adopt within the Department of Families, and it is the approach that I would recommend to most organizations. Developing that structured approach to problem-solving is crucial, as discussed in Chapter 71, CI Principle #12: Solve the right problem. But it is very important to remember that your goal should be that front-line managers develop a Lean-thinking mindset where they can solve problems with their teams on their own, every day if necessary. That is the culture change towards which you are driving. Again, I would highly encourage you to consider the Kata methodology (described by Mike Rother) to develop a true culture of daily *kaizen* within your organization.[3]

Another key aspect of how daily *kaizen* can really work in an organization is the concept of a Lean problem escalation system. In some organizations, they define different classes of problems, with very basic descriptions of problem size, risk, and complexity.

A possible hierarchy of Lean problems, from simplest to most complex, might look like this:

1. The "quick hit" problems;
2. The team-level problems;
3. The branch problems; and
4. The divisional or corporate problems.

The "quick hit" problems are the simplest problems, and often the proposed solutions can be quickly implemented by just one or two people. To keep the continuous improvement momentum going, you don't want to impose a lot of unnecessary bureaucracy to hold back the person with the idea. The best way to address these situations is to let the person with the idea run with trying out their proposed solution and then report the results back to the group in a subsequent huddle meeting a week or two later. If the experiment was successful, the group can consider adopting the solution into their practices.

I've seen some organizations that work to minimize the bureaucracy around reporting for simple fixes by having a set of pre-printed "quick hit" idea tickets at the huddle board. These basically just have the user fill out the problem, the solution idea, who is going to own the trial of the idea, and the check-back date. These tickets, once filled out, are magnet-posted to the huddle board in the "quick hit" area. This keeps some accountability on the person to complete their experiment and report back to the group. It also allows the team to keep track of how many ideas they have on the go at once.

More complex problems can use the next level of problem reporting, like the A3 report, or the Kata learner's storyboard.[4] You may also need to train people on how much detail they need to add to an A3 or a storyboard, based on the complexity of the problem. Keep it to the minimum needed to solve the problem. I find that some people sometimes have a problem with leaving blank space in a template, as though they think that they will be criticized for not filling in every square millimetre of white space—they just need to understand that brevity can be okay if they clearly get their point across.

The team-level problems are more complex than simple just-do-it problems. These are the problems that a group from the team can run through your problem-solving methodology, either under the guidance of the team manager, or someone else experienced in facilitating a such an exercise. These problems may or may not require a *kaizen* or similar Lean event to resolve. But the key point is that this type of problem can be solved independently within the team without the need for external expert support, especially if the team has a trained *kaizen* facilitator in the ranks. The team should summarize their findings on the appropriate report for best practices sharing with other teams or across the organization.

The branch problems are larger in scope and typically require escalation to at least the branch leader for support in engaging people in the other teams of the branch. The key characteristic is the recognition by the team that they cannot solve the problem alone in their team, and that they need to cross boundaries to develop a solution. These problems may require a *kaizen*, or a major business process redesign to resolve. Since the problems are larger in scope, the more experienced corporate Lean practitioners may need to support the efforts. There needs to be a system understood by the team leaders on how to escalate these problems to their branch leader and to the corporate Lean support team.

The divisional or corporate problems are quite large in scope, complexity, or risk. These problems are recognized by the necessity to cross many organizational-chart boundaries in order to develop a solution. As with branch problems, these ones may require a *kaizen*, or a major business process redesign to resolve. These problems will definitely require the support of the more experienced Lean practitioner support team. Note that this doesn't mean that front-line staff Lean Facilitators can't support the events, but the Lean practitioner should at least be providing a supporting coaching role, given the complexity of the problem. Again, there needs to be a system understood by the team leaders on how to escalate these problems to senior management, and to the corporate Lean support team.

In trying to develop a problem classification and escalation system at Manitoba Housing, I struggled greatly. Eventually, I realized that by over-thinking the classification system, I was taking the accountability away from the managers. This would also hinder the culture change that I was trying to facilitate, by keeping the managers from feeling that they had a responsibility to lead problem-solving with their teams.

*Don't design your system around the limitations of today, or you will reinforce those limitations.*

The solution was to decide on a very important assumption: *that front-line managers are responsible for enabling problem-solving in their teams and to escalate the problem for assistance only when they have exhausted all options available to them.* The temptation, when you are setting up a system for the first time, is to develop a command-and-control system, where the escalation and classification criteria are overly defined. This greatly complicates the system, and it adds incongruent bureaucracy into a program that is supposed to reduce bureaucracy in the first place.

The initial inexperience of the management team early in a Lean journey can also drive a Lean champion to attempt to be overly-prescriptive in developing a system like this. The answer, I believe, is to design the system for the future state, and then to look for skill gaps and simply use those gaps to identify where training and coaching is required. Don't design your system around the limitations of today, or you will reinforce those limitations.

We landed on a much simpler system than I had thought we would. Given that everyone could intuitively recognize a "quick hit" (sometimes also called a "just do it") problem as something that offered a modest value gain, but required very little effort to implement, we kept that as the first level of the hierarchy. The term "quick hit" was also identical to a label from our 2×2 matrix value-effort graph that we often used in *kaizens* to prioritize solution options after problem solving. That matrix usually looked like this (Figure 76.1):

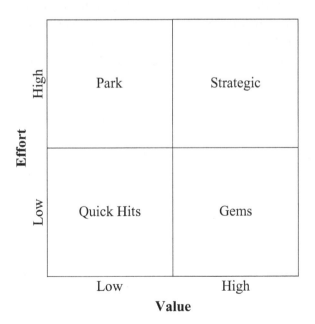

**FIGURE 76.1**  Value-effort matrix.

We simply decided that if a problem wasn't a quick hit, it was a more complex problem. Managers would have to be trained in how to support that problem-solving methodology with their staff, and in the continuous improvement leadership culture that was necessary to foster innovation in the workplace. The expectation placed on each manager was that they would be responsible for gathering any resources that they needed to solve that problem, including obtaining a Lean facilitator, or any other resources to which they had access. We would trust that the managers would know when they needed to escalate something to the leadership above them in order to get additional support to solve a larger or more complex problem.

One important point that also needs to be understood for success in an escalation system like this is capacity management. It is common that some organizations impose constraints on how many of each class of problem each team is allowed to have active at any given time. I've seen examples where teams only allow three to five "quick hit" problems at once, and only two or three branch problems on the go at any given time. The actual numbers for your team will vary depending on your team size and maturity level, of course.

But establishing some kind of capacity constraint will be appreciated by your team as a formal recognition of the necessity to balance the need to change with the need to get the day-to-day work done. Once the organization is more mature, I think that the leadership on each team will be able to select for themselves how many problems they can have active at a time, as problem size and complexity can greatly vary. However, I still think that early on in your Lean journey, embedding capacity constraints into your system will show your team that you recognize that there are limitations to what everyone can do in a workday.

The sooner you start to set up the infrastructure and system in your organization to support daily *kaizen*, the sooner you will be able to begin to truly embed the culture change into your people and your leadership.

# 77

## CI Principle #18: Plan for Your Obsolescence

*"One of the things we often miss in succession planning is that it should be gradual and thoughtful, with lots of sharing of information and knowledge and perspective, so that it's a non-event when it happens."*

**Attributed to Anne Mulcahy**
*former CEO and Chairperson of Xerox Corporation*

In Chapter 27, Trust Principle #22: Understand the true source of your value as a leader, I cover the concept that, in order to be successful in your transformation of the culture in your organization, you will need to accept the concept that a leader is more valuable as a coach than as a subject-matter expert. That doesn't mean that you don't *want* subject-matter expertise in your leaders—far from it. But you want your knowledgeable leaders to remember that their true value lies in coaching their people to improve in each of their roles.

The ultimate form of this mindset is for the leader to strive for the goal of their own obsolescence. In other words, you need to plan and design your coaching model for your team with the goal of getting them to the stage of not needing you anymore. This, obviously, can be extremely frightening to many leaders. But what appears to be a selfless and altruistic goal is also a means of changing how you behave as a leader to become more effective.

When you are concerned with trying to protect your current job as a leader, it affects your actions. You tend to centralize decision-making to yourself. You don't share your thought processes with your people. You hoard information. You isolate yourself. You don't make decisions in the best interest of efficiency, or the client or customer, or the organization— you may steer reorganizations towards increasing your span of control.

But this is all wrong. Instead, you need to demonstrate the opposite of each one of these behaviours. Therefore, I believe that you need to adopt, in your own mind at least, the principle that you are trying to coach your people to the point where they can operate effectively without your presence.

This type of leadership principle will take a tremendous amount of courage and self-confidence. You will, in many cases, feel like you are on the trapeze without a safety net underneath you. It also will depend a great deal on the leadership style of those above you. If the board, executive, or deputy minister is of a different mindset from the principles in this book, then this will be a difficult, or even risky, approach for you to embrace.

I truly believe that if you commit yourself fully to this leadership principle, then in most cases, your leadership value will become apparent to everyone around you. Your team will appreciate everything that you are doing, and the performance of your team will speak for your leadership more than you could possibly advocate for yourself.

Adopt this principle and remember it always when you are coaching your leaders. Watch how it forces you to think differently about the learning opportunities that you give your people, and the information that you share with them. When you are planning for any of them to succeed you someday, it really makes you think differently about how you should behave as their leader-coach.

Envision in your mind the day when you are no longer around, and keep asking yourself, "what do I have to do to prepare my team to be ready for that day?" Then do it. Plan for your own obsolescence and watch your value and worth as a leader skyrocket, alongside the performance of your team.

# 78

## CI Principle #19: Reflect and Improve

*"Self-reflection is the school of wisdom."*

**Baltasar Gracián y Morales**
*17th Century Spanish Jesuit, writer, and philosopher*[1]

One of the final principles that I myself only began to understand recently is the one known in Lean circles by its Japanese term, *hansei*, which means "reflection" or "introspection." I once heard the term *hansei* described by the assembly of the Japanese symbols for the word *han*, to "look back," and the word *sei*, which is an overlay of the character for "eyes" and the character for "small or narrow." In other words, *hansei* means to look back upon recent events with one's eyes narrowed in thoughtful contemplation. I think that mastering this concept by those brought up in Western cultures can be one of the most difficult things to accomplish because it requires the student to forget much of what they have previously known.

However, when you study the application of the concept in Japanese organizations, in some cases, you come across an association with shame for one's mistakes. While I would never suggest that people should be comically proud of their errors, I believe that teaching an association of *hansei* with shame to Western people will result in an aversion to the concept.

When I talked about the concept of *hansei* at Manitoba Housing with some of my senior leaders, some pointed out to me that many people already suffer psychologically with being overly self-critical, and therefore these people would struggle with the concept of adding *hansei* as a standardized management practice. It was then that I concluded that, in Western cultures, the proper application of *hansei* must involve the concept of balance, in order to accomplish that which is desired—improvement. This balance I can only describe as the idea of being "productively self-critical." While I recognize that these words aren't normally associated together, it is the only way that I can properly describe what is required with this leadership principle. If you focus simply on the need to avoid mistakes, you will focus on admonishing yourself for each error in the drive towards perfection. However, as perfection is only an ideal state, and an impossibility for humans to achieve, this will result in a pattern of unproductive self-criticism, where failures are highlighted repeatedly until one's self-esteem is left in tatters. Improvement, not depression, is the goal of *hansei*. Growth, not self-loathing, is desired.

For many people, I see them avoiding true *hansei*, because they are afraid of the negative feelings of confronting their own mistakes, and the internal humiliation to which they subject themselves. But this is a missed opportunity for these people to grow and to learn. Unfortunately, this principle is not one that people can easily learn by reading. They must also follow Change Principle #10: Remember that we learn by doing (described in Chapter 43). Only *practicing* this principle of reflection over and over, with the focus on being productively self-critical, can allow someone to learn how the principle should truly work.

> *Only practicing this principle of reflection, with the focus on being productively self-critical, can allow someone to learn how the principle should truly work.*

You must let go of your fear of what others will think of you if you admit that you made a mistake. This requires remembering Trust Principle #6: Free yourself from the need for external validation (described in Chapter 11). You must be prepared to confront your own needs for recognition from others, and ask yourself if, in this instance, that is holding you back from being willing to admit an error. You cannot improve until you admit that an improvement is required in the first place.

If you can place yourself in a position of not being threatened by the admission of mistakes, but rather seeing them as areas for improvement, you will be much better positioned to be able to properly apply this principle in practice with yourself. If you cannot apply this principle for yourself, there is no way that you can ever model the way and teach this principle to your leadership team and your staff. You need to be able to ask yourself as the senior leader, "is it possible that I might be somehow contributing to the problem?" Challenge your natural confirmation bias

*You need to take blame off the table for errors made in good faith by your people.*

that will cause you to look for information that supports your desired view of the world, and to ignore information contrary to your preconceived views. Fight your tendency to believe that it's your people who are the problem—in almost all cases, that's not true. In many cases, we as senior leaders inadvertently behave in certain ways that either cause, or exasperate, our challenges that arise during a continuous improvement journey. Have the courage to look first at yourself.

I think that, as leaders, so many of us are afraid to admit mistakes, because we are so concerned about what others think about us. We value the esteem of our superiors, our peers, and our subordinates so much, and we foolishly worry that this esteem is completely dependent on the perception by others of how flawlessly we can conduct our business each and every day. We worry that a single mistake will detract from how others will perceive us, and as such, we can be loath to admit errors, even when our mistakes are as blindingly obvious as a sunrise.

Although there are executives out there that will punish their subordinates for each and every error they make, you will need to be different. You will need to be prepared to admit your own mistakes freely, without self-destructive paralysis, and be productive about looking for improvements. Take joy from the freedom of no longer feeling compelled to hide your failures from others and embrace the knowledge that you are going to be better at the end of the day than you were when you woke up. Those around you will likely admire your strength and courage.

It is only when you can begin to properly apply the principle of "reflect and improve" privately with yourself, that you can begin to use this principle with your teams. When you can begin to teach this principle to your leadership team, it can then be applied at the team level, when problems arise. Remove the aspect of shame and blame when looking at problems. Remember Trust Principle #13: Talk about problems openly, but focus on solutions (described in Chapter 18). As I said in Chapter 46, Change Principle #13: Use visual metrics regularly to teach and reveal, never to assign blame, when assessing problems, always ask "why," never "who."

Your staff likely have been trained over the years by the old culture to hide problems to avoid blame and punishment by superiors. You need to take blame off the table for errors made in good faith by your people. Each error is an opportunity for reflection by your team, and you would be foolish to let those opportunities go by without seizing them. But be very careful about how you proceed—in many cases, it will be obvious to the staff if an individual was responsible for a mistake, and you need to make it clear in your actions that you are not trying to subtly humiliate anyone.

When you begin to understand how to *hansei* in a way that is productive and not destructive, you may feel as though the fast-paced world around you has begun to slow down to a more manageable pace. When you stop viewing mistakes as things to be hidden at all costs, and you begin to view them as learning points on your journey of improvement, you will feel more in control of yourself and your self-image than you ever imagined. Understand how to reflect and improve, and how to be productively self-critical yourself, and then teach your leadership team. Model the way and embed this crucial principle in your organizational culture until it happens everywhere.

# 79

## The Space for Continuous Improvement— Concluding Thoughts

*"Improvement usually means doing something that we have never done before."*

**Shigeo Shingo[1]**
*industrial engineer, and expert on the Toyota Production System*

The *Space for Continuous Improvement* is the third and final space in the Three Spaces model. This is where you adopt the mindset that every continuous improvement event needs thoughtful planning to ensure that it will be successful.

A successful event means a group of staff people who can be supportive ambassadors of the culture change that you are trying to foster. Every positive Lean event means that several people can talk about the success to their colleagues—that's a lot of people per event that can hear a positive message about the program if you work to make each one a success.

Remember the concept from the Three Spaces model that each space needs to be *shaped*. I find that when you consciously think of *shaping* each continuous improvement event for success, it tends to help remind you of what you need to do. What you want is a win for each team that is associated with continuous improvement, because you are trying to get your people to believe in the new way, and the new culture. This is what reinforces the *Space of Trust* and the *Space for Change* in the minds of the staff.[2]

Each of the CI Principles in this part outline things that I have learned through experience over many years, both in the private sector and in the public sector. I believe that my experience with Manitoba Housing, leading a continuous improvement culture change from scratch, was the most beneficial for me in learning what was important as a Lean Champion. You cannot pick and choose which of these principles you will apply. You must apply them all, as in many cases, one principle will act as a constraint for another.

Many of these CI Principles are quite intuitive, once you see the headings. The final three principles, I believe are among the most challenging to understand. But they are also tremendously important to the success of your culture change.

Driving towards *daily kaizen* is absolutely important if you want the culture change of Lean to really stick with your people. You need to get teams doing this on their own, without thinking that they need to call you for permission, or to get you to assign a Lean Practitioner for support for a simple 5S event. You won't be even close to *daily kaizen* at the very beginning of your journey, and that's okay. Many organizations will likely be on their journey for longer than a decade. But always remember that you are driving towards the goal of effective *daily kaizen*—begin with the end in mind, as Steven Covey would say.[2]

Planning for your own obsolescence is a hard concept for people because it's scary. It might feel like you are giving your employer permission to fire you for doing a good job. That's not what is meant by this concept. It means you adopt the mindset that you need to coach your leaders about *everything* that they need to know so that you can move on effectively to your next leadership challenge without leaving behind people that are dependent on you. If you commit yourself fully to the idea, adopting this ultimately selfless mindset as a leader will change everything that you do and say as a leader. Do this well, and you will be truly in demand as a treasure of your organizational leadership.

The concept of *hansei*, I think, is one of the hardest to appreciate. I know that, for myself, I will be a student learning to master this principle for many years to come. I believe that mastering this principle of self-reflection, to use the Star Wars terminology, separates the Lean Padawan Learners from the wiser Lean Jedi Knights. Accept that you make mistakes and admit it in front of your team. Welcome improvements to your ideas by considering and incorporating the ideas of others. Modelling the way of *hansei*, in this manner, will make you stronger as a leader, not weaker, in the eyes of your people. Lower your defenses and gain strength from doing so.

Adopt these CI Principles and watch your success rate of continuous improvement events climb significantly. And when each Lean event is successful, your culture change can really take root as your people will begin to believe that this can work. You will begin to change the culture, as your people start to recognize that their workplace is changing for the better. It will become a workplace at which they want to work.

Watch as you start to learn more about your people and the different skills about which you never before knew. Watch as your staff begin to "switch on" their true engagement, bringing with it increased productivity and efficiency and improved client or customer service.

# Part V

# Understanding the New Way

# 80

## Putting the Spaces Together

*"Lean is a way of thinking, not a list of things to do."*

**Attributed to Shigeo Shingo**
*industrial engineer, and expert on the Toyota Production System*

Remember, the Three Spaces of *Trust, Change,* and *Continuous Improvement* are not phases in your journey; they are not items to check off one-by-one on a to-do list. Rather, they are spaces within your organization that you need to shape and develop, and then maintain, in order for your Lean journey to be successful. You need to start to develop the foundational *Space of Trust* first, but it will need continual reinforcement while you are building the other spaces. I believe that there can be substantial overlap in the development of each of the Three Spaces.

You must start to develop the *Space for Change* before you can begin your first kaizen event, but this amounts to setting up the fundamentals for Organizational Change Management and some key communication channels in the organization from top to bottom. Once this space is started, you can continue to develop it while commencing your first CI events.

When you start your first CI events, your goal is for every team to be successful. You need to be prepared to accept whatever they develop in each event, so plan the scope of each event carefully—you won't have the choice to back out later. Once you commit to the team that they have the authority to change a process, follow through. Make sure you show the team that you trust them, and that you believe in them. And tell them that. Be there to celebrate their accomplishments, and to show them your gratitude for trusting in the program, and in the Lean methodology.

Throughout the development and sustainment of the Three Spaces, there needs to be a solid working relationship between the Lean champion and the Lean practitioner. This partnership is crucial for the Lean journey to be successful. Each one must be able to be honest and forthright with the other, so that the approach can be adapted when challenges arise. When this partnership works, it will be obvious, and the Lean champion should be able to recognize it.

# 81

## Striving for Congruence

*"Never forget your effect on people."*

**Captain D. Michael Abrashoff[1]**
*former commander, U.S. Navy*

### CONGRUENCE OF BEHAVIOUR AND WORDS

In Chapter 31, Trust Principle #26: Be congruent, I discussed the importance of living the message as a leader, in order to be able to show that you are worthy of the trust of the people within your organization. I have discovered that modelling the way, every day, as a leader is one of the most challenging things to get right. Always being a walking, living, example always of the leadership values that you cherish is not only difficult but impossible. Of course, our people expect nothing less from us as their leaders. If we didn't agree with these obligations, we shouldn't have selected leadership as our chosen career path. But living up to the expectations of total congruence between our behaviours and our words, being in the spotlight of judgement by others all the time, isn't for the faint of heart.

Despite all the changes that I have been able to make in myself as a leader and as a person, I still find myself realizing that it isn't enough. Any gaps in my life between my values and my behaviour become clear areas for improvement for me. I have found recently that these cases of incongruence can create elements of stress in my life, and that resolving the incongruence can bring me peace.

## YOU SHOULD BE CHANGING...EVERYWHERE

Should you live one set of values at work and a different one at home? Many people think so, and perhaps I did for a time. But no longer. I see this dichotomy as another example of incongruence of my own leadership behaviour. Ask a new manager if he or she would give performance feedback to their own child the same way that they would their employees, and see if they try to tell you that "work is different than home." Really? Why should that be? Why would you have one approach for how you try to coach your employees and a different approach for how you try to guide your children?

How many parents would refrain from providing any feedback to their children for poor behaviour for months on end, and then once a year provide them with a written performance review and surprise them with a list of their faults, and then withhold increasing their allowance for the rest of the year? Likely, not many. In most cases, people recognize with their children that you need to take a child aside to discuss their behavioural challenges soon after the problem or incident, and then to carefully explain the expectations of correct behaviour going forward, while providing positive reinforcement of good behaviour. Yet, so many leaders think that their staff deserve a completely different approach to behaviour management, one that they would never dare use with their own family. We are leaders at work and we are leaders at home and in our communities. To live our leadership principles congruently means adhering to them in all of our leadership arenas. Although it is understood that we *love* our family members in a different way than we respect our employees, we need to consider treating our employees with a similar caring and compassionate approach that we would provide for members of our own family. It is only then that the leadership will begin to earn the trust of the people.

Once I really adopted the Lean mindset, and I recognized the detrimental effects of incongruence in myself, I started to see many things at home differently—even the small things. After my office 5S event, I couldn't stand looking at our linen closet the way it was. My wife thought it was crazy, but I made us 5S that closet—I volunteered to run up and down the stairs taking things to the different destinations, whether it be the pile for donations to the Salvation Army, or the pile to give to her younger sister, or for items that just needed to go in the garbage. And once the linen closet was done, we began to tackle the other parts of the house one-by-one. Given that I saw the benefit (and the reduced stress) of the Lean mantra "a place for everything, and everything in its place," I wanted the same benefits where we lived.

I just couldn't stand living one way at the office and a different way at home. The walk-in closet, the kitchen pantry, the basement storage areas, my workshop, one-by-one, they all got the treatment. Walmart received a lot of money from me given all the containers and bins that I bought in my quest for closet organization. Yes, I would agree with my wife, I might be crazy. But our house does look much better now, and not just when company is coming over.

I think that the biggest challenge for me in my quest for congruence between my work life and my home life was how I dealt with my children. I didn't see why I would not use on my own children the same approaches in which I believed at work—for instance, the philosophy of questioning myself after witnessing a behavioural issue if a lack of willingness was the problem before issuing a corrective consequence. At work, I came to realize that when I would apply this test before allowing myself to consider negative thoughts about a person's motives, I would usually arrive quickly at a more likely set of reasons as to why the problem occurred. Sadly, I sometimes find that it seems harder to be as rational at home as at work, due to the deeper emotional connection with family members. The small comfort for me is that, as a parent, I am confident I'm not alone in this internal struggle.

I think that in order to truly begin to transform yourself as a leader of the new culture, you need to remove any forms in your own life of incongruence with these leadership principles. Many of the principles can, and should, be adopted outside of your work life, with your children, or in community leadership roles. These principles include:

- Trust Principle #5: Believe that you can change (Chapter 10);
- Trust Principle #6: Free yourself from the need for external validation (Chapter 11);
- Trust Principle #8: Remember that authority matters (Chapter 13);
- Trust Principle #11: Always act with respect for people (Chapter 16);
- Trust Principle #13: Talk about problems openly, but focus on solutions (Chapter 18);
- Trust Principle #21: Listen effectively (Chapter 26);

- Trust Principle #22: Understand the true source of your value as a leader (Chapter 27);
- Trust Principle #23: Be a coach, not a judge (Chapter 28);
- Trust Principle #25: Eliminate competition in favour of teamwork (Chapter 30);
- Trust Principle #26: Be congruent (Chapter 31);
- Change Principle #10: Remember that we learn by doing (Chapter 43); and
- CI Principle #19: Reflect and improve (Chapter 52).

It seems ironic to me to find that some of these principles are harder to model at home than at work. You would think that you would be automatically prepared to invest much more of yourself in your own family than in your work life. Nonetheless, I think it is important, to make yourself more whole as a leader of this culture change, to adopt these key principles everywhere in your life. It is only then that you can truly feel congruent.

# 82

## Show Them It's Possible

*"If I had asked my customers what they wanted, they would have said 'a faster horse'."*

**Attributed to Henry Ford**
*founder of Ford Motor Company*

You are about to embark on a journey that will, if travelled correctly, fundamentally change the very culture of your people to that of a Lean management organization. As a result of the significant changes that will be necessary for both your team and your leadership, you will experience great challenges ahead. You will face the trials of change management within an organization. You might feel, at times, as though your authority and your leadership integrity are both being challenged, and it can be hurtful. So, how do you find the stamina to continue on in this type of challenging environment? I think it helps to remember why you are doing this.

In the preface, under the heading Why Would You Want to Bother?, I try to explain some of the benefits and the rationale for taking an organization down a transformational path of Lean management. In short, just remember at the very beginning of your transformation that you are initially doing it for your staff. That statement is somewhat heresy in the Lean world, as the philosophy that is taught is that all improvements are supposed to be focused around the "customer." But it's easier to focus on your team in the beginning, because you see them every day. By working to make Lean help your staff, I guarantee you that improvements will follow for the clients or customers your organization serves, once the staff really begin to engage.

You are trying to get the benefits of "switching on" your people through the culture change, and that is the prize that is awaiting you. You need to look forward to seeing the first few cautious early adopters sign up to test out a *kaizen* in their area, and then the next set of leaders and staff willing to give this Lean thing a try. If you put in the effort described in the *Space for Continuous Improvement* to make each CI event a success, the popularity of the Lean program will compound with each event. Just remember that, as the senior leader, you have a tremendously important role to play first in developing the *Space of Trust*.

You need to work on getting the staff, and the leadership, to really believe that things are different now in your organization. That it is a place where the ideas of the staff on how to improve how things get done are respected and heard and followed. That it is a place where the leadership trusts its people; as a result, the people will trust the leadership.

In a culture where leaders don't trust the staff, and the staff don't trust the leadership, someone has to break the cycle. Someone has to trust first, and that someone is the senior leader. You will have to show that you trust your people, perhaps despite a currently combative or suspicious culture of the organization. You will need to remain positive, despite a lack of validation from your people that the program is a good thing and that it is working. It will work, and if you remain true to the principles of engaging your team, they will recognize it and jump on board. And they will start to believe in you as well, even if they didn't believe in you before.

# 83

## It Feels Different in Here

*"Leadership is communicating to people their worth and potential so clearly that they come to see it in themselves."*

**Stephen R. Covey**[1]
*leadership author*

I think one of the most interesting things I have discovered at Manitoba Housing as we moved along our transformation into following Lean management principles, was this phrase that several people from outside the organization stated after spending a couple of hours in our head office: "It feels different in here." And each time, they would emphasize the word *feels*. Our new deputy minister said this a few weeks after he started his role in the fall of 2016. Outside visitors told us this on several occasions after touring and meeting with several people. New employees who came from other parts of government said the same thing. And I felt it too. It *was* different in Manitoba Housing in 2016, even compared to when I had started in 2012, and the corporation had already at that point made tremendous strides in organizational improvement. But what was it that made it feel different?

I think it was the *Space of Trust*. The trust relationships between the leadership and the people had greatly improved, and that changes the working environment in a very positive manner. A huge part of this change of *feel* also was no doubt due to the choice we made at the executive level to choose to view the team through the lens suggested by McGregor's Theory Y.[2] In other words, to consciously choose to believe that the staff were inherently motivated to do a great job every day, and that they wanted more responsibility, not less. This choice had a huge impact on how we viewed and treated our teams, and they felt it themselves. Our choice changed the environment, and because people become a product of their environment, it began to change the morale of the team in a fantastic manner.

We saw more smiles on the faces of staff in the hallways. People were happier. More people started to say that they liked coming to work and they admitted that it wasn't always that way at Manitoba Housing—but things were different now! Some of the seasoned employees who remembered the old days, with the previous generations of senior leaders, marvelled at the difference in approach between today and the old days. They said that this focus on "the people" was what was missing years ago, and that the change to where we had gone was fantastic.

I have to admit that although my career has progressed very differently than I would have predicted twenty years ago, I'm glad that I went down the path that I did. If I had not, I think that I would have missed what turned out to be the most pivotal transformation of myself as a leader and as a person. My only regret is that I wished that I had made the changes to myself earlier in my career.

If you are in the early stages of leading your organization down a path of transformation to following Lean Management principles, I wish you the best of luck. You have a tremendous opportunity in front of you, and if you are able to adopt the right leadership mindset yourself, you will have an excellent chance of success.

If there are only three things from this book that I could ask you to remember about the proper leadership mindset required to be successful in your Lean journey, it would be these:

1. As a leader, view yourself as a coach for your team, rather than the one with the answers;
2. Choose to look through the Theory Y lens when you view your people; and
3. Use self-reflection to strive for congruence everywhere for yourself as a leader, and as a person.

While I believe that I have been able to make the change completely for the first two items, I know that trying to achieve a consistent congruence of my behaviour and values and words will be something at which I will have to work for the rest of my life. However, I am confident that I'm not alone in that regard.

Although I arrived at Manitoba Housing thinking that my job was to teach them what I knew, I recognize the irony that I ended up learning and changing more than the people that I was entrusted to lead. I'm not the same leader that I was when I first joined the organization, and I'm not the same person either—and for that, I am eternally grateful.

At the beginning of the book, I referenced the story of The Angel in the Marble.[3] Look again at your team as that unfinished block of marble, but this time, know and believe that there is a beautiful sculpture inside, waiting to be revealed. All you have to do is remove what is holding back the true potential that has been contained within all this time. Free your mind from any self-constructed prisons that restrain you. I can only show you the door, but you will have to be the one to walk through it.

# Notes and References

1 Stephen R. Covey, *"The Seven Habits of Highly Effective People - Powerful Lessons in Personal Change, 25th Anniversary Edition,"* RosettaBooks LLC, 2013, Habit 2: Begin with the End in Mind, iBook format.

## PREFACE

1 Stephen R. Covey, *"The Eighth Habit - From Effectiveness to Greatness,"* Free Press, 2004, dedication, iBook format.
2 George F. Pentecost, *"The Angel in the Marble, and Other Papers,"* Hodder and Stoughton, London, 1883.
3 Joel Silver (Producer), The Wachowski Brothers (Directors), "The Matrix" [Motion Picture], 1999, United States: Warner Bros. Entertainment Inc.
4 W. Edwards Deming, *"Out of the Crisis,"* The MIT Press, 1982, page 53.
5 Manitoba Housing and Renewal Corporation, "Operations Values and Stakeholder Wheel," [diagram] 2015, used with permission.

## PART I UNDERSTANDING THE SPACES OF LEAN TRANSFORMATION

### Chapter 1

1 Elton Trueblood, *"The Life We Prize,"* Harper, University of Michigan, 1951, page 58.

### Chapter 2

1 Manitoba Housing and Renewal Corporation, "The Three Spaces of Lean Transformation," [presentation] delivered by Brent Timmerman and Steven Spry at the Government of Manitoba Lean Conference, October 2016, used with permission.
2 Manitoba Housing and Renewal Corporation, "The Three Spaces of Lean Transformation," [diagram] 2016, used with permission.
3 Stephen M. R. Covey, *"The Speed of Trust - The One Thing that Changes Everything,"* Free Press, 2006.

## Chapter 4

1  Sheryl Sandberg, *"Lean In: Women, Work, and the Will to Lead,"* LI Org, LLC, 2013.

# PART II UNDERSTANDING THE SPACE OF TRUST

## Chapter 5

1  Quoted by chief speechwriter, Samuel Rosenman, after the Quarantine of Aggressor Nations speech in Chicago, Doris Kearns Goodwin, *"No Ordinary Time: Franklin and Eleanor Roosevelt: The Home Front in World War II,"* Simon & Schuster, 1995, Chapter 1.

## Chapter 6

1  Simon Sinek, "Leaders Eat Last – Why Some Teams Pull Together and Others Don't (Deluxe Edition)," Portfolio Penguin, 2017, Chapter 21.
2  Dr. Jeffrey K. Liker, "Toyota Way: 14 Management Principles from the World's Greatest Manufacturer," The Heart of the Toyota Production System: Eliminating Waste, McGraw-Hill Professional, 2004.
3  Peter Drucker, as quoted by Andrew Cave, "Culture Eats Strategy for Breakfast. So What's for Lunch?" [online article], Forbes, November 9, 2017, https://www.forbes.com/sites/andrewcave/2017/11/09/culture-eats-strategy-for-breakfast-so-whats-for-lunch/#187c93a77e0f, Last visited March 16, 2019.

## Chapter 7

1  Will Yakowicz, "Simon Sinek on Great Leaders – What separates great leaders from the good ones? Listen up as the TED talker explains the difference," [online article], August 19, 2013, https://www.inc.com/will-yakowicz-simon-sinek-why-business-leaders-need-to-eat-last.html, last visited October 18, 2018.
2  Captain D. Michael Abrashoff, *"It's Your Ship – Management Techniques from the Best Damn Ship in the Navy,"* Grand Central Publishing, 2002, page 43.

## Chapter 8

1  Douglas McGregor, *"The Professional Manager,"* New York: McGraw-Hill, 1967, page 163.
2  Douglas McGregor, "The Human Side of Enterprise," First published in Adventure in Thought and Action, Proceedings of the Fifth Anniversary Convocation of the School of Industrial Management, Massachusetts Institute of Technology, Cambridge, April 9, 1957. Cambridge, MA: MIT School of Industrial Management, 1957; and reprinted in The Management Review, 1957, 46, No. 11, 22–28.

## Chapter 9

1 Malcolm Gladwell, *"The Tipping Point - How Little Things Can Make a Big Difference,"* Back Bay Books, New York, 2000, 2002, page 167.
2 Malcolm Gladwell, *"The Tipping Point - How Little Things Can Make a Big Difference,"* Back Bay Books, New York, 2000, 2000, pages 140–155.
3 George L. Kelling and James Q. Wilson, *"Broken Windows - The Police and Neighborhood Safety,"* The Atlantic Monthly, March 1982 Issue.
4 "Crime: Diary of a Vandalized Car," [Magazine article], Time, February 28, 1969, http://content.time.com/time/magazine/article/0,9171,900702,00.html.
5 Peter Senge, "The Fifth Discipline: The Art and Practice of the Learning Organization," Crown Business, New York, 1990, 2006, Chapter 5.

## Chapter 10

1 Stephen R. Covey, *"The Seven Habits of Highly Effective People - Powerful Lessons in Personal Change, 25th Anniversary Edition,"* RosettaBooks LLC, 2013.
2 Stephen M. R. Covey, *"The Speed of Trust - The One Thing that Changes Everything,"* Free Press, 2006.

## Chapter 11

1 Stephen R. Covey, *"The Seven Habits of Highly Effective People - Powerful Lessons in Personal Change, 25th Anniversary Edition,"* RosettaBooks LLC, 2013, iBooks format, Habit 2: Begin with the End in Mind, A Principle Center.
2 Kathleen Kennedy, Allison Shearmur, Simon Emanuel (Producers), Gareth Edwards (Director), "Rogue One - A Star Wars Story" [Motion Picture], 2016, United States: Lucasfilm Ltd.
3 Stephen R. Covey, *"The Seven Habits of Highly Effective People - Powerful Lessons in Personal Change, 25th Anniversary Edition,"* RosettaBooks LLC, 2013, pages 150–208, iBooks format, Habit 2: Begin with the End in Mind.
4 Simon Sinek, *"Leaders Eat Last - Why Some Teams Pull Together and Others Don't (Deluxe Edition),"* Portfolio Penguin, 2017, iBooks format, Chapters 6–7.

## Chapter 12

1 Simon Sinek, *"Starts With WHY - How Great Leaders Inspire Everyone to Take Action,"* Portfolio Penguin, 2009, page 70–74, 105–106.
2 Simon Sinek, *"Starts With WHY - How Great Leaders Inspire Everyone to Take Action,"* Portfolio Penguin, 2009, page 106.
3 Sam Walton and John Huey, *"Sam Walton, Made in America,"* New York: Bantam Books, 1992, page 128.

## Chapter 13

1  Aphorism for a friend (18 September 1930) [Einstein Archive 36-598]; as quoted in Albert Einstein: Creator and Rebel (1988) by Banesh Hoffman.

2  Linton Sellen, *"The Workplace Leader – Certificate in Leadership Development,"* [Training Seminar], QNET, Fall 2016.

## Chapter 14

1  General George S. Patton Jr., *"War as I Knew It,"* Houghton Mifflin Company, 1947, page 357.

2  Linton Sellen, *"The Workplace Leader – Certificate in Leadership Development,"* [Training Seminar], QNET, Fall 2016.

3  James P. Womack, Daniel T. Jones, and Daniel Roos, *"The Machine That Changed the World: The Story of Lean Production—Toyota's Secret Weapon in The Global Car Wars That is Revolutionizing World Industry,"* New York: Free Press, The Elements of Lean Production, Chapter 4: Running the Factory, Lean Organization at the Plant Level, iBooks format, 1990.

## Chapter 15

1  Simon Sinek, "The Difference Between Direction and Directions," [Blog post], http://blog.startwithwhy.com/refocus/2009/11/the-difference-between-direction-and-directions.html, 2009, last visited October 13, 2018.

2  Linton Sellen, *"The Workplace Leader – Certificate in Leadership Development,"* [Training Seminar], QNET, Fall 2016.

3  James P. Womack, Daniel T. Jones, Daniel Roos, *"The Machine That Changed the World: The Story of Lean Production—Toyota's Secret Weapon in The Global Car Wars That is Revolutionizing World Industry,"* Free Press, New York, The Elements of Lean Production, Chapter 4: Running the Factory, Diffusing Lean Production, iBooks format, 1990.

## Chapter 16

1  Jeffery K. Liker and Gary L. Convis, *"The Toyota Way to Lean Leadership – Achieving and Sustaining Excellence Through Leadership Development,"* McGraw-Hill Education, 2012, page 35–40.

2  Jeffery K. Liker and Gary L. Convis, *"The Toyota Way to Lean Leadership – Achieving and Sustaining Excellence Through Leadership Development,"* McGraw-Hill Education, 2012, pages 38–39.

3  Simon Sinek, *"Leaders Eat Last – Why Some Teams Pull Together and Others Don't (Deluxe Edition),"* Portfolio Penguin, 2017, iBooks format, Chapter 3: Belonging – From "Me" to "We".

## Chapter 17

1 Martin Luther King, Jr., in "Why I Am Opposed to the War in Vietnam," [Speech], at Ebenezer Baptist Church in Atlanta, Georgia, 30 April 1967.

## Chapter 19

1 Bill Gates, "Teachers Need Real Feedback," [TED Talks Education], May 2013, https://www.ted.com/talks/bill_gates_teachers_need_real_feedback#t-31969, last visited October 13, 2018.

## Chapter 21

1 Jack Welch, "*Jack: Straight From the Gut*," Warner Books, 2001, chapter 3.
2 Linton Sellen, "*The Workplace Leader – Certificate in Leadership Development*," [Training Seminar], QNET, Fall 2016.
3 Captain D. Michael Abrashoff, "*It's Your Ship – Management Techniques from the Best Damn Ship in the Navy*," Grand Central Publishing, 2002, pages 74–85.

## Chapter 22

1 Simon Sinek, "*Leaders Eat Last – Why Some Teams Pull Together and Others Don't (Deluxe Edition)*," Portfolio Penguin, 2017, iBooks format, Chapter 2: Employees are People Too.
2 Abraham H. Maslow, "A Theory of Human Motivation," *Psychological Review*, 1943, 50, 370–396.
3 Abraham H. Maslow, "*Motivation and Personality*," Harper, 1954.

## Chapter 23

1 Rear Admiral Grace Hopper, "The Captain is a Lady: CBS 60 Minutes Segment," [Video Broadcast], Morley Safer (interviewer), March 6, 1983.
2 Ian Bryce, Mark Gordon, Gary Levinsohn, Steven Spielberg (Producers), Steven Spielberg (Director), "Saving Private Ryan" [Motion Picture], 1998, United States: DreamWorks Pictures.

## Chapter 24

1 Taiichi Ohno, "MICHIKAZU TANAKA OF DAIHATSU ON "WHAT I LEARNED FROM TAIICHI OHNO" [Website article], John Shook, Lean Enterprise Institute, April 8, 2009, https://www.lean.org/shook/DisplayObject.cfm?o=910, last visited October 15, 2018.
2 Stanley Milgram, "Behavioral Study of Obedience," *Journal of Abnormal and Social Psychology*, 1963, 67, 371–378.

3 Simon Sinek, "*Leaders Eat Last – Why Some Teams Pull Together and Others Don't (Deluxe Edition),*" Portfolio Penguin, 2017, iBooks format, Chapter 13: Abstraction Kills.

4 Simon Sinek, "*Leaders Eat Last – Why Some Teams Pull Together and Others Don't (Deluxe Edition),*" Portfolio Penguin, 2017, iBooks format, Chapter 13: Abstraction Kills.

5 Jeffery K. Liker and Gary L. Convis, "*The Toyota Way to Lean Leadership – Achieving and Sustaining Excellence Through Leadership Development,*" McGraw-Hill Education, 2012, pages 37–38, 67–68.

6 Jeffery K. Liker and Gary L. Convis, "*The Toyota Way to Lean Leadership – Achieving and Sustaining Excellence Through Leadership Development,*" McGraw-Hill Education, 2012, page 25.

7 Mike Rother, "2018 Canadian LEAN Conference | Embracing Excellence," [Conference address], CME Manitoba (Conference organizers), June 4–June 7, 2018.

## Chapter 25

1 John C. Maxwell, "*The Power of Leadership,*" Honor Books, 2001, page 12.

2 Linton Sellen, "The Workplace Leader – Certificate in Leadership Development," [Training Seminar], QNET, Fall 2016.

## Chapter 26

1 Peter Drucker, "Peter Drucker: Father of Modern Management – A World of Ideas," [Transcript of Interview], Bill Moyers (Interviewer), November 17, 2017, https://billmoyers.com/content/peter-drucker/, last visited October 16, 2018.

2 Stephen R. Covey, "*The Seven Habits of Highly Effective People – Powerful Lessons in Personal Change, 25th Anniversary Edition,*" RosettaBooks LLC, 2013, Habit 5: Seek First to Understand, Then to be Understood, iBook format.

3 James M. Kouzes and Barry Z. Posner, "*The Leadership Challenge (5th Edition) – How to Make Extraordinary Things Happen in Organizations,*" Jossey-Bass, 2012, Practice 2: Inspire a Shared Vision, Chapter 4: Envision the Future, Find a Common Purpose, iBook format.

## Chapter 27

1 James M. Kouzes and Barry Z. Posner, "*The Leadership Challenge (5th Edition) – How to Make Extraordinary Things Happen in Organizations,*" Jossey-Bass, 2012, Practice 4: Enable Others to Act, Chapter 9: Strengthen Others, Enhance Self-Determination, iBook format.

2 Jeffery K. Liker and Gary L. Convis, "*The Toyota Way to Lean Leadership – Achieving and Sustaining Excellence Through Leadership Development,*" McGraw-Hill Education, 2012, pages 54–81.

# Chapter 28

1  W. Edwards Deming, The Deming Institute, [website]: http://quotes.deming.org/ authors/W._Edwards_Deming/quote/468, last visited October 20, 2018.

2  James M. Kouzes and Barry Z. Posner, *"The Leadership Challenge (5th Edition) – How to Make Extraordinary Things Happen in Organizations,"* Jossey-Bass, 2012, Practice 4: Enable Others to Act, Chapter 9: Strengthen Others, iBook format.

# Chapter 29

1  Liker and Convis, the Toyota Way to Lean Leadership, pages, 54–81.

# Chapter 30

1  John R. Wooden, [website], The Wooden Effect, https://www.thewoodeneffect.com/ motivational-quotes/, last visited, October 20, 2018.

2  Linton Sellen, "The Workplace Leader – Certificate in Leadership Development," [Training Seminar], QNET, Fall 2016.

# Chapter 31

1  John C. Maxwell, *"The 21 Most Powerful Minutes in a Leader's Day – Revitalize Your Spirit and Empower Your Leadership,"* Maxwell Motivation, Inc., 2000, Week 5, The Law of E.F. Hutton.

2  James M. Kouzes and Barry Z. Posner, *"The Leadership Challenge (5th Edition) – How to Make Extraordinary Things Happen in Organizations,"* Jossey-Bass, 2012, Practice 1: Model the Way, iBook format.

3  Stephen M. R. Covey, *"The Speed of Trust – The One Thing that Changes Everything,"* Free Press, 2006, pages 54–55.

4  Mohandas Gandhi, Response to a journalist's question about what his message to the world was. Mahatma: Life of Gandhi 1869-1948 (1968) Reel 13.

5  Stephen M. R. Covey, *"The Speed of Trust – The One Thing that Changes Everything,"* Free Press, 2006, page 62.

# Chapter 32

1  As quoted by Susan Fourtané, "Elon Musk: The Story of a Maverick," [online article], Interesting Engineering, September 30, 2018, https://interestingengineering. com/elon-musk-innovator-and-engineer, last visited October 20, 2018.

2  Paul Soubry, Jr., Presentation to the Housing Operations Committee of the Manitoba Housing and Renewal Corporation, January 29, 2015.

## PART III UNDERSTANDING THE SPACE FOR CHANGE

### Chapter 33

1  Dan Millman, "*Way of the Peaceful Warrior*," HJ Kramer, 1980, page 130.

### Chapter 34

1  James Humes, "The Art of Communication is the Language of Leadership," [online article], Fresh Business Thinking, March 27, 2008, https://www.freshbusinessthinking.com/the-art-of-communication-is-the-language-of-leadership/, last visited on October 20, 2018.

### Chapter 35

1  Rev. Theodore Hesburgh, "The Hesburgh-Yusko Scholarship Program," [website], University of Notre-Dame, https://hesburgh-yusko.nd.edu/assets/172346/28009_hysp_tri.pdf, last visited March 5, 2019.
2  Simon Sinek, "*Starts With WHY – How Great Leaders Inspire Everyone to Take Action*," Portfolio Penguin, 2009, pages 37–51.
3  Simon Sinek, "*Starts With WHY – How Great Leaders Inspire Everyone to Take Action*," Portfolio Penguin, 2009, page 66.

### Chapter 36

1  Glenn Nausley, "Working to Be Lean, Green, and Energy Wise," [online article], Manufacturing Engineering, March 16, 2016, http://www.sme.org/MEMagazine/Article.aspx?id=8589938628, last visited October 20, 2018.
2  Jeffery K. Liker and Gary L. Convis, "*The Toyota Way to Lean Leadership – Achieving and Sustaining Excellence Through Leadership Development*," McGraw-Hill Education, 2012, pages 240.

### Chapter 37

1  John C. Maxwell, "*Developing the Leader Within You*," Nashville: Thomas Nelson, 1993, Chapter 4, The Ultimate Test of Leadership: Creating Positive Change.
2  Jeff Hiatt, "The ADKAR Model," [Web-page], Prosci, https://www.prosci.com/adkar/adkar-model, last visited October 20, 2018.
3  W. Edwards Deming, often stated by Deming in 4-day Deming Seminars, The Deming Institute, website: http://quotes.deming.org/authors/W._Edwards_Deming/quote/10240, last visited October 13, 2018.

# Chapter 38

1 William Hollingsworth Whyte, "Is Anybody Listening?" [magazine article], Fortune, September issue, 1950, Start Page 77, Quote Page 174, New York: Time, Inc.

# Chapter 39

1 Stephen R. Covey, "*The 8th Habit – From Effectiveness to Greatness*," New York: Free Press, 2004, Chapter 1 – The Pain, Why Start an 8th Habit?, iBooks format.
2 James M. Kouzes and Barry Z. Posner, "*The Leadership Challenge (5th Edition) – How to Make Extraordinary Things Happen in Organizations*," Jossey-Bass, 2012, Practice 1: Model the Way, Find Your Voice, iBook format.
3 "Morehouse College Martin Luther King Jr. Collection," Robert J. Woodruff Library, Atlanta University Center, http://mcmlk.auctr.edu/notable-items.asp, last visited October 20, 2018.
4 Martin Luther King, Jr., "I Have a Dream Speech," March on Washington, 1963, National Archives, [web-page], https://www.archives.gov/files/press/exhibits/dream-speech.pdf, last visited October 20, 2018.
5 Gary Younge, "*Martin Luther King: the story behind his 'I have a dream' speech*," [online article], The Guardian, August 9, 2013, https://www.theguardian.com/world/2013/aug/09/martin-luther-king-dream-speech-history, last visited October 20, 2018.

# Chapter 40

1 John Shook, "Taiichi Ohno's Birthday, and 100 Years of Lean," [online article], Lean Enterprise Institute, February 29, 2012, https://www.lean.org/shook/DisplayObject.cfm?o=2010, last visited October 20, 2018.

# Chapter 41

1 Frances Hesselbein, "The Key to Cultural Transformation," [journal article], Leader to Leader, Francis Hesselbein Leadership Forum, Spring 1999.
2 Jeffrey K. Liker, "*The Toyota Way: 14 Management Principles from the World's Greatest Manufacturer*," McGraw-Hill Education, 2003.

# Chapter 42

1 Karen Martin, "Lean Leadership, Part 1 of 3," [presentation], The Karen Martin Group, August 9, 2016, page 15 of 47, https://www.slideshare.net/KarenMartinGroup/lean-leadership-part-1-of-3, last visited October 20, 2018.

## Chapter 43

1  Aristotle, Nichomachean Ethics, Book II, 350 BC.

## Chapter 44

1  Jeffery K. Liker and Gary L. Convis, *"The Toyota Way to Lean Leadership – Achieving and Sustaining Excellence Through Leadership Development*," McGraw-Hill Education, 2012, page 58.

## Chapter 45

1  As quoted by Barton Swaim, "'Trust, but verify': An untrustworthy political phrase," [online article], The Washington Post, March 11, 2016, https://www.washingtonpost.com/opinions/trust-but-verify-an-untrustworthy-political-phrase/2016/03/11/da32fb08-db3b-11e5-891a-4ed04f4213e8_story.html?utm_term=.6d35732798b6, last visited October 20, 2018.
2  Mike Rother, *"Toyota Kata: Managing People for Improvement, Adaptiveness, and Superior Results*," New York: McGraw-Hill, 2010, Chapter 6 – Problem Solving and Adapting: Moving Toward a Target Condition, This is PDCA (Plan-Do-Check-Act), iBooks format.

## Chapter 46

1  Although this quote is commonly attributed to Peter Drucker, Sir William Thomson, First Baron Kelvin of Largs, is credited with having stated in a lecture "I often say that when you can measure what you are speaking about, and express it in numbers, you know something about it; but when you cannot measure it, when you cannot express it in numbers, your knowledge is of a meagre and unsatisfactory kind; it may be the beginning of knowledge, but you have scarcely, in your thoughts, advanced to the stage of science, whatever the matter may be." "Electrical Units of Measurement," [lecture], May 3, 1883, Popular Lectures, Vol 1, Page 73, https://archive.org/stream/popularlecturesa01kelvuoft#page/72, last visited October 21, 2018.

## Chapter 47

1  Jon Katzenbach and Ashley Harshak, "Stop Blaming Your Culture: Start using it instead — to reinforce and build the new behaviors that will give you the high-performance company you want," [online article], strategy+business, January 19, 2011, Spring 2011/Issue 62, Organizations and People, https://www.strategy-business.com/article/11108?gko=f4e8d, last visited October 21, 2018.

# Chapter 48

1  Benjamin Franklin (although earlier versions of this quote exist, it is often attributed to Benjamin Franklin for making it famous), "Niles' Weekly Register – The Past, The Present, For the Future," H. Niles, February 5, 1820, page 386 (Public Lands).

# Chapter 49

1  Michael E. Porter, "What is Strategy?," *Harvard Business Review*, November-December 1996 Issue.

2  Michael Barber, "*How to Run a Government – So That Citizens Benefit and Taxpayers Don't Go Crazy*," UK: Penguin Random House, 2015.

3  Robert S. Kaplan and David P. Norton, "The Balanced Scorecard—Measures that Drive Performance," [online article], *Harvard Business Review*, January-February 1992 Issue, https://hbr.org/1992/01/the-balanced-scorecard-measures-that-drive-performance-2, last visited October 21, 2018.

4  Robert S. Kaplan and David P. Norton, "*The Balanced Scorecard – Translating Strategy Into Action*," Harvard Business School Press, Boston, 1996.

5  Paul R. Niven has written at least 6 books supporting the use of the Balanced Scorecard Methodology, but one book is primarily used by the author while employed within government service: "Balanced Scorecard Step-by-Step for Governments and Nonprofit Agencies, Second Edition," Hoboken, NJ: John Wiley & Sons, 2008.

# Chapter 50

1  Anthony C. L. Blair, "Hansard," United Kingdom House of Commons, 6th series, volume 439, column. 302, November 9, 2005, responding to Charles Kennedy in the House of Commons during Prime Minister's Questions. Blair was referring to the likely defeat in Parliament of additional powers to detain terror suspects without charge, which happened later that day.

2  Peter Drucker, "The Practice of Management," Harper & Row, New York, 1954.

3  Jeffery K. Liker and Gary L. Convis, "*The Toyota Way to Lean Leadership – Achieving and Sustaining Excellence Through Leadership Development*," McGraw-Hill Education, 2012, page 238.

4  Henry A. Landsberger, "*Hawthorne Revisited*," Ithaca, New York: The New York School of Industrial and Labor Relations, 1958.

# Chapter 51

1  As quoted by Mackubin Thomas Owens, "Marines Turned Soldiers," *National Review*, December 10, 2001.

2  Paul R. Niven, "Balanced Scorecard Step-by-Step for Governments and Nonprofit Agencies, Second Edition," Hoboken, NJ: John Wiley & Sons, 2008.

# Chapter 52

1 Paul R. Niven, "*Balanced Scorecard Step-by-Step for Governments and Nonprofit Agencies, Second Edition,*" Hoboken, NJ: John Wiley & Sons, 2008, Chapter 8 – Performance Measures, Targets, and Initiatives, (Section) Targets, iBooks format.

2 Jim Collins and Jerry I. Porras, "*Built to Last – Successful Habits of Visionary Companies,*" New York: HarperBusiness, 2002.

3 John F. Kennedy, "Special Message to the Congress on Urgent National Needs," [speech], Delivered in person before a joint session of Congress, May 25, 1961, Section IX: Space, https://www.nasa.gov/vision/space/features/jfk_speech_text. html, last visited October 22, 2018.

4 Paul R. Niven, "*Balanced Scorecard Step-by-Step for Governments and Nonprofit Agencies, Second Edition,*" Hoboken, NJ: John Wiley & Sons, 2008, Chapter 8 – Performance Measures, Targets, and Initiatives, (Section) Targets, Setting Performance Targets, iBooks format.

# Chapter 53

1 Warren G. Bennis, [speech], University of Maryland Symposium, January 21, 1988.

# Chapter 55

1 W. Edwards Deming, as quoted by Peter Senge, "*The Fifth Discipline – The Art & Practice of The Learning Organization,*" New York: Currency Doubleday, 2006, Introduction.

2 Dan Pink, "The Puzzle of Motivation," [video], TED Talk, July 2009, https://www. ted.com/talks/dan_pink_on_motivation?language=en, last visited October 29, 2018.

3 Sam Glucksberg, "The Influence of Strength of Drive on Functional Fixedness and Perceptual Recognition," *Journal of Experimental Psychology*, Vol 63(1), 36–41, January 1962.

4 Karl Duncker and Lynne Lees, "On Problem Solving," *American Psychological Association, Series: Psychological Monographs*, 58(5) Whole No. 270, Washington D.C., 1945.

5 Dan Pink, "Drive: The Surprising Truth About What Motivates Us," New York: Riverhead Books, 2009, Chapter 2, iBooks format.

6 Dan Ariely, Uri Gneezy, George Loewenstein, and Nina Mazar, "Large Stakes and Big Mistakes," *The Review of Economic Studies*, Vol. 76, 451–469.

7 Dr. Bernd Irlenbusch, "When Performance-Related Pay Backfires," 2009, The London School of Economics, announcement of workshop on June 30, 2009, http:// www.lse.ac.uk/website-archive/newsAndMedia/news/archives/2009/06/perfor-mancepay.aspx, last visited October 29, 2018.

8 Dan Pink, "*Drive: The Surprising Truth About What Motivates Us,*" New York: Riverhead Books, 2009, Introduction, iBooks format.

## Chapter 56

1 Ridley Scott, "Sir Ridley Scott's Kingdom of Heaven," [website], Fox News, Partial transcript of "Hannity & Colmes," May 5, 2005, Published May 6, 2005, Updated January 13, 2015, https://www.foxnews.com/story/sir-ridley-scotts-kingdom-of-heaven, last visited October 29, 2018.

## Chapter 57

1 Simon Sinek, "*Leaders Eat Last – Why Some Teams Pull Together and Others Don't (Deluxe Edition),*" Portfolio Penguin, 2017, Chapter 18: Leadership Lesson 2: So Goes the Leader, So Goes the Culture, iBooks format.

## Chapter 58

1 Heraclitus, as quoted by Plato, "Cratylus" [dialogue], approximately 400BC.

# PART IV UNDERSTANDING THE SPACE FOR CONTINUOUS IMPROVEMENT

## Chapter 59

1 Mike Rother, "Toyota Kata: Managing People for Improvement, Adaptiveness, and Superior Results," McGraw-Hill, New York, 2010, Parts III and IV.

## Chapter 60

1 Although this quote has been recently attributed to Henry Ford, the earliest verifiable source is from Jessie Potter, Director of the National Institute for Human Relationships, Oak Lawn, Illinois, in her opening remarks at the seventh annual Woman to Woman conference in Milwaukee, Wisconsin on October 23, 1981: Tom Ahern, "Search for Quality Called Key to Life," [newspaper article], The Milwaukee Sentinel, Page 5, Part 1, October 24, 1981, Google News Search.

2 Stephen R. Covey, "*The Seven Habits of Highly Effective People – Powerful Lessons in Personal Change, 25th Anniversary Edition,*" RosettaBooks LLC, 2013, Habit 7: Sharpen the Saw – Principles of Balanced Self-Renewal, iBook format.

## Chapter 61

1 Stephen R. Covey, "*The Seven Habits of Highly Effective People – Powerful Lessons in Personal Change, 25th Anniversary Edition,*" RosettaBooks LLC, 2013, Habit 3: Put First Things First, The Quadrant II Tool, iBook format.

2 Stephen R. Covey, "*The Seven Habits of Highly Effective People – Powerful Lessons in Personal Change, 25th Anniversary Edition*," RosettaBooks LLC, 2013, Habit 3: Put First Things First, iBook format.

3 Cyril Northcote Parkinson, "Parkinson's Law," [Magazine article], *The Economist*, November, 1955.

## Chapter 62

1 Sam Walton, as quoted: Don Soderquist, "*The WAL-MART Way: The Inside Story of the Success of World's Largest Company*," Nashville, Tennessee: Nelson Business, 2005, page 60.

## Chapter 63

1 Reverend H. K. Williams, "The Group Plan" in the "Young People's Service," *The Biblical World*, Volume 53, Number 1, Chicago, Illinois: University of Chicago Press, January 1919, page 81.

## Chapter 64

1 Max De Pree, "*Leadership is an Art*," New York: Currency Doubleday, 2004, page xxii.

## Chapter 65

1 Irving Janis, "Groupthink," [Journal article], *Psychology Today*, 5 (6): 43–46, 74–76, November 1971.

## Chapter 66

1 Mark Wager, [web-site], https://i.pinimg.com/originals/c0/e5/35/c0e535e1ed-363ba7820ece488c7d3fad.jpg, last visited November 3, 2018.

## Chapter 68

1 Walter Elliot, "*The Spiritual Life: Doctrine and Practice of Christian Perfection*," New York: The Paulist Press, 1918, page 364, https://archive.org/details/thespiritu-allife00ellliuoft/page/n377, last visited November 3, 2018.

# Chapter 70

1 Mike Rother and John Shook, *"Learning to See: Value-Stream Mapping to Create Value and Eliminated Muda,"* Cambridge, MA: Lean Enterprise Institute, Version 1.4, October 2009.
2 Taiichi Ohno, *"Toyota Production System: Beyond Large Scale Production,"* Portland, Oregon: Productivity Press, 1988.

# Chapter 71

1 Charles F. Kettering, as quoted by W. Clements Zinck, "Dynamic Work Simplification," Krieger, 1971, Page 122.
2 Thomas Wedell-Wedellsborg, "Are You Solving the Right Problems?" *Harvard Business Review,* January-February, 2017.
3 Taiichi Ohno, "Toyota Production System: Beyond Large-Scale Production," Productivity Press, Portland, 1978, Page 123.
4 Mike Rother, *"Toyota Kata: Managing People for Improvement, Adaptiveness, and Superior Results,"* New York: McGraw-Hill, 2010, Chapter 6 – Problem Solving and Adapting: Moving Toward a Target Condition, Figure 6–7, iBooks format.
5 The American Society for Quality, "The Define Measure Analyze Improve Control (DMAIC) Process," [website], ASQ, http://asq.org/learn-about-quality/six-sigma/overview/dmaic.html, last visited December 10, 2018.
6 Mike Rother, *"The Toyota Kata Practice Guide,"* McGraw-Hill, New York, 2018, page 64–65.

# Chapter 72

1 Mike Rother, *"The Toyota Kata Practice Guide,"* McGraw-Hill, New York, 2018, page 176.
2 Mike Rother, *"Toyota Kata: Managing People for Improvement, Adaptiveness, and Superior Results,"* New York: McGraw-Hill, 2010.
3 Mike Rother, *"The Toyota Kata Practice Guide,"* McGraw-Hill, New York, 2018.

# Chapter 73

1 As quoted by Charles Stewart, "Haud Immemor: Reminiscences of Legal and Social Life in Edinburgh and London 1850–1900," William Blackwood & Sons, Edinburgh and London, 1901, page 33.

# Chapter 74

1 Thomas W. Faranda, "Uncommon Sense: Leadership Principles to Grow Your Business Profitably," Knowledge Press, 1991, Page 41.
2 Jeffery K. Liker and Gary L. Convis, *"The Toyota Way to Lean Leadership – Achieving and Sustaining Excellence Through Leadership Development,"* McGraw-Hill Education, 2012, pages 126–146.

## Chapter 75

1  John Shook, "Innovation in the Work," [website article], Lean Enterprise Institute, John Shook's eLetters, September 22, 2016, https://www.lean.org/shook/DisplayObject.cfm?o=3301, last visited November 3, 2018.

## Chapter 76

1  Fujio Cho, as quoted by Jeffrey K. Liker and James M. Morgan, "The Toyota Way in Services: The Case of Lean Product Development," Academy of Management Perspectives, 20.10.5465/AMP.2006.20591002, 2006.
2  Tim Dietrich, "Climbing Mount Everest – Next Steps in Lean," [Conference presentation], Lean Process Improvement for the Public Sector conference, The Canadian Institute, Marriott Bloor Yorkville Hotel, Toronto, Ontario, Canada, December 6–7, 2017.
3  Mike Rother, "*Toyota Kata: Managing People for Improvement, Adaptiveness, and Superior Results*," New York: McGraw-Hill, 2010.
4  Mike Rother, "*The Toyota Kata Practice Guide*," New York: McGraw-Hill, 2018, page 64–65.

## Chapter 78

1  Baltasar Gracián y Morales, "The Art of Worldly Wisdom," translated from the Spanish by Joseph Jacobs, Macmillan and Co., New York, 1892, Page 40.

## Chapter 79

1  Shigeo Shingo, "Kaizen and the Art of Creative Thinking: The Scientific Thinking Mechanism," Enna Products Corporation, Pennsylvania State University, 2007, page 170.
2  Stephen R. Covey, "*The Seven Habits of Highly Effective People – Powerful Lessons in Personal Change, 25th Anniversary Edition*," RosettaBooks LLC, 2013, Habit 2: Begin with the End in Mind, iBook format.

# PART V UNDERSTANDING THE NEW WAY

## Chapter 81

1  Captain D. Michael Abrashoff, "*It's Your Ship – Management Techniques from the Best Damn Ship in the Navy*," Grand Central Publishing, 2002, page 46.

# Chapter 83

1 Stephen R. Covey, *"The Eighth Habit - From Effectiveness to Greatness,"* Free Press, 2004, Chapter 6: Inspiring Others to Find Their Voice—The Leadership Challenge, Leadership Defined, iBook format.

2 Douglas McGregor, "The Human Side of Enterprise," First published in Adventure in Thought and Action, Proceedings of the Fifth Anniversary Convocation of the School of Industrial Management, Massachusetts Institute of Technology, Cambridge, April 9, 1957. Cambridge, MA: MIT School of Industrial Management, 1957; and reprinted in The Management Review, 1957, 46, No. 11, 22–28.

3 George F. Pentecost, *"The Angel in the Marble, and Other Papers,"* Hodder and Stoughton, 1883.

# Index